SECRET
MILAN

Massimo Polidoro

JonGlez

Massimo Polidoro, journalist and writer, taught anomalistic psychology at the University of Milano-Bicocca. He is the author of over thirty books, including "Final Séance: The Strange Friendship between Houdini and Conan Doyle", and "Secrets of the Psychics: Investigating Paranormal Claims", both published in the United States by Prometheus Books. www.massimopolidoro.com

We have taken great pleasure in drawing up
Secret Milan and hope that through its guidance
you will, like us, continue to discover unusual,
hidden or little-known aspects of the city.
Descriptions of certain places are accompanied
by thematic sections highlighting historical details
or anecdotes as an aid to understanding the city in
all its complexity.
Secret Milan also draws attention to the multitude
of details found in places that we may pass every
day without noticing. These are an invitation to
look more closely at the urban landscape and,
more generally, a means of seeing our own city
with the curiosity and attention that we often
display while travelling elsewhere …

Comments on this guidebook and its contents,
as well as information on places we may not have
mentioned, are more than welcome and will enrich
future editions.

Don't hesitate to contact us:
• Éditions Jonglez, 17, boulevard du Roi,
  78000 Versailles, France
• E-mail: info@jonglezpublishing.com

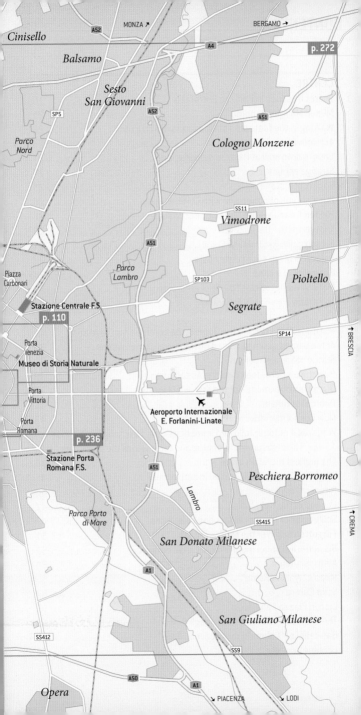

Cinisello
Balsamo

Sesto
San Giovanni

MONZA ↗
BERGAMO →

p. 272

A52
A4

SP5

A52

A51

Parco
Nord

Cologno Monzene

SS11

Vimodrone

A51

Parco
Lambro

SP103

Pioltello

Segrate

Piazza
Carbonari

Stazione Centrale F.S.
p. 110

SP14

BRESCIA ↑

Porta
Venezia

Museo di Storia Naturale

Porta
Vittoria

Aeroporto Internazionale
E. Forlanini-Linate

Porta
Romana

p. 236

Stazione Porta
Romana F.S.

A51

Peschiera Borromeo

Lambro

CREMA ↑

SS415

Parco Porto
di Mare

San Donato Milanese

A1

San Giuliano Milanese

SS412

SS9

A50
A1

Opera

↘ PIACENZA   ↘ LODI

CONTENTS

NORTH-WEST

CONTENTS

SOUTH-WEST

CONTENTS

CONTENTS

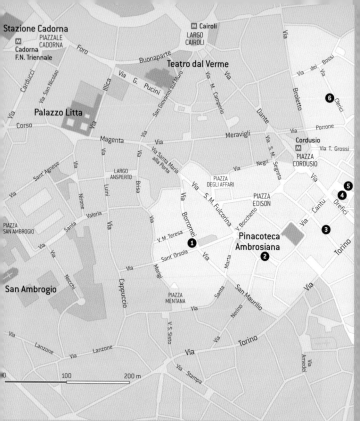

CENTRE

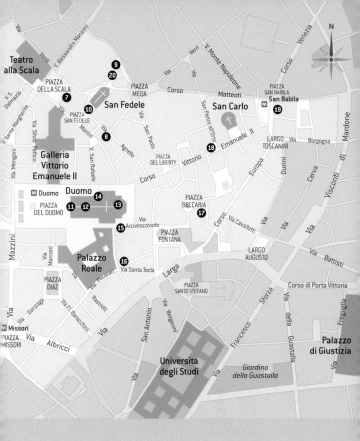

SECRET FRESCOES IN PALAZZO BORROMEO ❶

7, Piazza Borromeo
• Access only on special open days – for example, the Cortili Aperti (Open Courtyard) days or those organised by the FAI (Fondo per l'Ambiente Italiano, an Italian environmental agency). Sometimes a polite request for admission may let you take a quick look.
• Public transport: MM1 Cordusio; MM1-2 Cadorna

> *The frescoes by the "Master of the Borromeo Games"*

In the main courtyard of Palazzo Borromeo there is a small wooden door right in the centre of the frescoed façade. Nowadays used as offices by a private firm of architects, the space beyond contains one of the best-hidden gems in the city: a series of wall frescoes depicting games that were part of courtly life in fifteenth-century Milan. Unfortunately, the public can only gain access to these on special occasions – for example, "Open Courtyard" (*Cortili Aperti*) days or the open days organised by the FAI (Fondo per l'Ambiente Italiano, an Italian environmental agency); sometimes, however, a polite request for admission may let you take a quick look. You can also glimpse these masterpieces through the ground-floor window in the courtyard, if the lights are on inside.

The space itself has a very high ceiling and the frescoes begin about 1 metre above floor level, atop wainscoting painted to look like marble. Nowadays, however, only those on three of the walls remain.

The fresco on each wall shows a different game or amusement: tarot cards, *palla* (ball) and *palmata* – the last two both ancestors of real tennis. Throughout the pictures, the blue of sky, sea and clothing has faded as the original azurite pigment has dissolved; now, a sort of uniform red prevails in the background of each image. In the tarot fresco, five elegantly-robed figures are shown seated at a table playing cards; in the central fresco, the four players of *palmata* are shown with raised hands trying to touch the palm of their opponent; and in the third fresco the figures are all women, one of whom is about to strike a ball with what looks like a modern baseball bat.

The humidity that has slowly seeped up the walls has gradually eroded the colour in the frescoes; so, for example, in the tarot scene what remains is mainly the preparatory sketch for the work. The frescoes themselves have been dated to 1445–1450, but the artist has not been identified and is therefore generally referred to as the *Maestro dei Giochi Borromeo* (Master of the Borromeo Games). The influence here of Pisanello and Masolino da Panicale is clear. Still, these secular frescoes – which predate Andrea Mantegna's *Camera degli Sposi* in Mantua's Palazzo Ducale or the frescoes of *The Months of the Year* in Ferrara's Palazzo Schifanoja – were themselves the model for a series of comparable cycles in a number of patrician residences in Lombardy (for example, Angera, Cassine, Masnago and Oreno).

MUSEO MANGINI BONOMI

❷

20, Via dell'Ambrosiana
• Open Monday to Thursday, 3pm–7pm; Wednesday, 3pm–5pm (guided tours on Monday and Thursday, lasting from 3pm to 4pm).
• Tel: 02 86451455
• Public transport: MM2 Duomo, Cordusio, MM3 Duomo; tram 1, 2, 12, 14, 16, 27
• www.museomanginibonomi.it

> *A curious museum dedicated to the daily life of our ancestors*

O pposite the Pinacoteca Ambrosiana is one of the best-hidden museums in the city. The former home of the collector Emilio Carlo Mangini, this is packed with his rich array of objects and curios dating back over the last 150 years, each one of which illustrates some aspect of the professional and private life of our ancestors. The collection is divided into forty-one very different sections: wooden horses, toys, mason's tools, clocks and timepieces, signs and notices, mirrors, scientific instruments, safes and strongboxes, irons, chests, optical instruments, and a whole range of work tools. The basement of the building, which itself dates from the fifteenth/sixteenth centuries, has recently been restored and now houses an important collection of weaponry and armour, complete with arquebuses, helmets, swords, shields and even instruments of torture. There is also an ancient double well of the sixth–eighth centuries AD, part of which even dates back to Roman times. Among the more curious

objects in the collection are a lock of Madame de Pompadour's hair, rings-cum-pistols dating from 1820, musical chamber pots, a clockwork monkey smoking a cigarette, an eighteenth-century vacuum cleaner, playing cards dating from 1620 and even a small puppet theatre.

The Milan-born Mangini collected most of the objects in this remarkable home-museum during his travels throughout Italy and Europe. Having put together this unique collection, he then bequeathed it to his heirs as a foundation, so that the objects would not be dispersed.

WALKING IN THE FOOTSTEPS
OF ALESSANDRO MAZZUCOTELLI

Casa Ferraro – 3-5, Via Spadari
Casa Galimberti – 3, Via Malpighi
Casa Guazzoni – 12, Via MalpighiCasa Campanini – 11, Via BelliniCasa
Moneta – 3, Via Ausonio
• Public transport: MM1, MM3 Duomo, Cordusio; tram 2, 3, 14

> *Wrought ironwork by an Art Nouveau artist*

The wrought ironwork designed by Alessandro Mazzucotelli in the early decades of the twentieth century often goes unnoticed, either hidden inside palatial interiors or because you have to look up to see it. Nevertheless it is one of the most beautiful examples of Milanese Art Nouveau.

A tour around the masterpieces left to the city by this great artist – sought out by the finest architects for his creativity and his ability to give iron the lithe and "flowery" look so typical of Art Nouveau – has to begin at Casa Ferraro in the city centre. On this building, which has one of Milan's most popular fine food shops on the ground floor, the complex floral motifs of the balustrades climb upwards to link the various balconies.

On the front of the imposing Palazzo Castiglioni (47 Corso Venezia), the first real example of Art Nouveau in Milan, Mazzucotelli's twisted ironwork is perfectly integrated with the circular openings hollowed into the rough stone for the small ground-floor windows. Inside, the same artist's "dragonfly lamp" can be admired in the entrance hall, as well as the balustrade of the main double staircase.

Mazzucotelli also designed the wrought-iron terraces of Casa Galimberti, with brightly coloured ceramics covering the façade, and those of the adjacent Casa Guazzoni; as well as the gate and large woven leaves of the balconies of Casa Campanini and the naturalistic elements of Casa Moneta. At Casa Moneta, in addition to leaves, flowers and animal silhouettes outlined in a clever use of form, look out for the butterflies on the entrance gate – outstanding examples of Art Nouveau decoration.

ART NOUVEAU IN MILAN

Although the ornamental style known in Italy as "Stile Liberty" was most highly developed in Turin, Milan also has several fine examples. The most beautiful spot is at the junction of Malpighi, Melzo and Frisi streets, site of the former Dumont cinema (now the local library). Nearby is the building that used to be the Bagni di Diana (now a hotel, see p. 167), Casa Centenara (66 Corso Buenos Aires) and the building at numbers 11–13 Viale Piave, both by Giovan Battista Bossi, who also designed Palazzo Castiglioni and Casa Galimberti.

LONG-HAIRED SOW
AT PALAZZO DELLA RAGIONE

❹

Piazza dei Mercanti
• Public transport: MM1 Duomo, Cordusio; MM3 Duomo

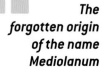

The forgotten origin of the name Mediolanum

On the façade opposite the Palazzo della Ragione, the capital of a column in the second arch bears a little noticed Roman bas-relief depicting a *scrofa semilanuta* (long-haired sow).

Legend has it that the founder of Milan was the Celt Bellovesus, who crossed the Alps and then came down into the Po valley. Having reached a post that had been indicated to him in a dream by a goddess, Bellovesus is said to have seen a wild sow with one very distinctive characteristic: its pelt was long and woolly at the front of its body, hence *scrofa semilanuta* (literally, "half-wooled"). Having built his city in that spot, he named it Mediolanum.

However, another version says it was the Romans who gave the city its name, probably rendering their version of the Celtic toponym meaning "in the middle of the plain (*planum*; but in Celtic languages the initial "p" is dropped). Just like the origin of the name of Rome itself, the etymology of *mediolanum* is still a matter of debate – there are a further twenty or so theories.

While there may not be any conclusive archaeological evidence, the linguist Christian Guyonvarc'h argues that the term *mediolanum* actually meant "central sanctuary"; the translation "central plain" is wrong, he says, because some of the places with the same name are actually located in upland areas. So to make sense of the term its religious significance has to be taken into account.

All in all, there are about 60 or so toponyms similar to Mediolanum in the Celtic area of mainland Europe, most of them to be found in the region once known as Gaul.

Intended to house tribunals, the Palazzo della Ragione was built in 1233 by the *podestà* Oldrado da Tresseno. It was also known as the *Broletto Nuovo*, the diminutive deriving from the term *brolo* for an open-air space where justice was administered.

STRANGE ECHOES

The Palazzo della Ragione has a wide-arched portico on all four sides, which has its own very strange echo effect. If you speak with your face close to one of the stone columns, you can be heard by someone diagonally opposite.

BANKRUPTS' STONE

In the small square outside, lawyers in search of clients would offer cheap legal advice, while notaries had small portable desks at which they wrote out documents. This was also the place where insolvent merchants were submitted to the humiliation of the "bankrupts' stone": having lowered their trousers, they had to beat down with their bare buttocks on a large block of black marble, performing that ritual act three times before being taken off to the debtors' prison of La Malastalla. While this was going on, all the bankrupt's worldly possessions were auctioned off by a judge in the *parlera* of the Loggia degli Osii, a small balcony decorated with an eagle in the middle of the Gothic structure built at the behest of Mattero Visconti in 1316. Today the bankrupts' stone has gone, its place taken by a sixteenth-century well surmounted by a post and beam construction.

A similar stone still exists in Florence (see *Secret Florence* and *Secret Tuscany* in this series of guides).

POSSIBLE LINK OF *PANETTONE* WITH CELTIC WORSHIP

Traditional fare at Christmas time in Lombardy and throughout Italy, the famous *panettone* is a vanilla-flavoured sugarloaf baked with raisins and other dried fruits (apricots, oranges, lemons, figs and apples). Although various legends have tried unconvincingly to explain its origin, *panettone* unquestionably originated in Milan.

Founded by the Insubri Celts around 600 BC, *Mediolano,* as it was then known, was a place that observed the Celtic celebrations of the rebirth of the Sun at the winter solstice (around the period of what would become the Christian Christmas), a feast intended to promote a rich harvest from the crops that were generally sown from January and early February onwards. Called Yule, this was the first seasonal festivity celebrated by the Neolithic tribes of northern Europe. And on that occasion the Druids, Celtic priests, offered to each other and then to the assembled people a type of sugarloaf made with barley and filled with apples and raisins. This, the main sacred food of the Yule festivity, was eaten together with a drink of barley fermented with honey. This drink, the ancestor of beer which is itself brewed using barley, is not however to be confused – as some have done – with hydromel, which was made up of honey and cider. Milan, conquered by the Romans in 222 BC, became part of the Empire and was henceforth known as *Mediolanum*. However, Celtic customs and practices were absorbed by Latin traditions; at this time, for example, the winter solstice became the time for the celebration of the birth of the Sun god Mithras, a date which would subsequently become that of the birth of Christ. The Romans also celebrated *Saturnalia*, which marked the triumph of Saturn (associated with winter when the Sun was "underground") over Jupiter (associated with the celestial Sun and therefore summer). For them, Saturn represented the Golden Age, the original Sun from which Jupiter himself descended. During the Saturnalia no one worked and candles and bonfires illuminated the night. Copious feasting played a large part in the festivities, with participants being served a ritual cake after the celebrations. Baked with wheat or barley flour, this was sweetened with honey and stuffed with the fruits in season. This baked wheaten mix was the origin of the host in Christian celebrations, while Roman historians of the second and third centuries AD already spoke of the Milanese origin of the *panettone*, a "large sugarloaf" made from a dough that had been set aside to rise, then placed in a mould and baked in an oven.

Its reputation and fame established *panettone* as a regular part of Christmas from the eighteenth century onwards. For example, the philosopher and historian Pietro Verri (1728–1797) referred to it as a *pane di tono* (luxury bread) to be eaten on special occasions only. Even before that, the Flemish artist Pieter Brueghel the Elder (1525–1569) painted a picture in which a large *panettone* on a table is identified as "Cake with Seasonal Fruit". The image was probably inspired by the recipe book written by the Lombard Bartolomeo Scappi (1500–1577), head cook to popes Pius IV and Pius V. The Dutch painter Jan Albert Rootins (1615–1674) also included a magnificent *panettone* right at the centre of his *Still Life with Fruit*. The expression *pane di tono* having lost its original meaning, people opted for a more immediate and down-to-earth explanation. Thus the legend of the *pane di Toni* came about, attributing the creation of *panettone* to a baker called Toni who had worked in the Della Grazie bakery in Milan at the time of Ludovico il Moro (1452–1508). This young man, in love with the boss's daughter, was said to have invented the sugarloaf in order to impress the father of his beloved. Customers then began to ask for the *pane di Toni* by name, the expression developing into the Milanese *panatón* and finally the Italian *panettone*.

Another legend has it that *panettone* was invented at the very court of Ludovico il Moro on Christmas Eve some time in the years 1494–1500. On one of those Christmases, the planned dessert was burned while being cooked, so one of the kitchen hands – again called Toni – who had mixed up leftovers into sugarloaf for himself, served his creation to the court. It is said that the dessert was such a success that Ludovico himself asked what it was called. When the young Toni was called to answer this question, he said it had no name. There and then, Ludovico decided it would be called *pane di Toni*, later transformed into *panettone*.

HIDDEN TREASURES OF PALAZZO GIURECONSULTI ❺

Chamber of Commerce – Palazzo Giureconsulti
2, Piazza Mercanti
• Visits by appointment: 02 85155814
• Public transport: MM1 Duomo, Cordusio; MM3 Duomo; tram 2, 3, 12, 14, 16, 19, 27

> *A clock, an ancient road and some frescoes ...*

Still surviving within the sixteenth-century Palazzo Giureconsulti, the Napo Torriani tower takes its name from a man who was a member of the Council of Elders of the People of Milan. The tower itself dates from the thirteenth century, and the remains which are incorporated within the later structure can now be visited on request. Through a skylight you can even see the interior structure and mechanism of the clock that graces the façade of the old city-hall tower and was installed to sound both the daily curfew and fire alarms. Palazzo Giureconsulti also contains a number of other curiosities. The basement level still has some Roman remains, including a water cistern and part of the old *decumanus*, the main road that ran through the centre of the ancient Mediolanum.

On the ground floor is the Hall of Columns. This occupies the room where the Assembly of Jurisconsults – one of the most important patrician institutions of old Milan – used to meet; with its pairs of twinned columns, this place looks just as it did in the Renaissance. On the first floor do not miss the Sala Parlamentino ("Small Parliament") which has kept its original

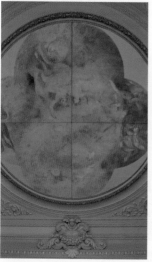

furnishings intact, including the solid wooden benches that formed the seats of the chamber. The ceiling fresco by Bossi was painted in 1700. The Sala Donzelli also has a ceiling fresco, painted in 1948 by Rivetta, which depicts a model of Palazzo Giureconsulti being presented to Pope Pius IV. Other frescoes dating from the sixteenth and seventeenth centuries – by such artists as Besozzi, Busca and Panza – have been removed from old vaulted ceilings which were subsequently destroyed and now embellish various rooms within the palazzo. On the top floor is the building's ultimate surprise: a roof terrace that offers a fine view of Piazza del Duomo, Piazza Mercanti and the entire city.

TRIPTYCH OF THE DAY

The most significant of the art treasures housed within the Chamber of Commerce is Gaetano Previati's *Trittico del Giorno* (1907). These three allegorical paintings comprise a central image of *Apollo Driving the Chariot of the Sun* flanked by two other pictures entitled *Day: Dawn* and *Night: The Lovers*. Unfortunately, like the other works by Previati belonging to the Chamber of Commerce (including the series *Trade Routes*), these are not on regular display, although they are sometimes lent for exhibitions. To learn more, visit www.mi.camcom.it.

FRESCO GALLERY IN PALAZZO CLERICI ❻

5, Via Clerici
• Visits by appointment only
• Tel: 02 863 313271
• Public transport: MM1 Corduisio; tram 1, 2, 12, 14

> **A spectacular Tiepolo fresco in a magnificent gallery**

Palazzo Clerici is one of the most opulent residences of eighteenth-century Milan. Booking is required to visit its spectacular Antechamber of Mirrors (also known as the Great Gallery or Tapestry Gallery), but it is more than worth taking the trouble.

The decoration of this gallery space of some 22 metres by 5 metres would alone consume a large part of the wealth of the Clerici family. It contains various features of remarkable quality: wooden wainscoting by the master cabinet-maker Giuseppe Cavanna, a collection of precious tapestries and, most importantly, a spectacular ceiling fresco by Giovanni Battista Tiepolo.

The Tiepolo fresco, painted in 1741, rejoices in the title *The Journey of the Sun through the Free Heavens Inhabited by the Gods of Olympus and Surrounded by the Earthly Creatures and Animals that Symbolise the Continents*. As this suggests, the centre of the composition is the Chariot of the Sun, preceded through the heavens by the figure of Hermes. If you begin to examine this work at the top of the long wall on the left as you enter the room, the first scene depicts the myth of Proserpina, who was kidnapped by Pluto, king of Hades. To the side is a group around Dionysus; in an atmosphere of post-revelry exhaustion rather than ease, the god is left to his own devices. Then come the allegories of the continents: Asia is dominated by the silhouette of two camels laden with oriental merchandise; America is depicted by two figures (a Native American and a young female settler). An allegory of The Sea follows, with a corner occupied by an allegory of the arts: a *putto* holding an artist's palette and an old man with a mandolin. Alongside the *putto* is a figure which is a self-portrait, a feature that Tiepolo often included in his paintings.

The ceiling on the opposite side of the gallery contains the allegories of Africa (a huge trunk and two tusks herald the arrival of an elephant) and Europe, where can be seen a warrior in gleaming helmet and cuirass (perhaps Perseus) and Poseidon in the background. After this last continent, Tiepolo paints a very famous myth: *The Rape of Venus*. The figures in the last allegory depict various rivers: one may be the Arno and another the Tiber, but the others cannot be identified.

The magnificence of this single fresco ruined Count Antonio Giorgio Clerici, no expense being spared to make the gallery and the entire house into a setting worthy of such a masterpiece.

PALAZZO MARINO'S *SALA DELLE FESTE* ❼

Palazzo Marino
Piazza della Scala
• Public transport: MM1-3 Duomo; tram 1
• Visits: Monday to Friday, 9.30am–12.30pm and 2.30pm–4.30pm
• Booking required: tel. 02 88456617 or e-mail:
presidenzacc@comune.milano.it

> **Yes,
> Palazzo Marino
> is open
> to the public**

Since 1861 the sixteenth-century Palazzo Marino has housed Milan City Council. Many take this to mean it is not open to the public, but it can be visited (only by appointment, however). Built for the Genoese count Tomaso Marino, a rich and powerful tax-farmer, the building is associated with a number of legends. It was originally designed so that Marino could woo the beautiful Arabella Cornaro, daughter of a Venetian nobleman. The architect Galeazzo Alessi was commissioned to create "the finest palazzo in all of Christendom". The building proved fit for purpose, and Arabella did marry Marino. However, after his death and that of Alessi, the palazzo was gradually neglected. In a ruined state, it was later bought by the city and then by Maria Teresa of Austria, only becoming the City Council headquarters at the end of Austrian rule.

Beyond the entrance, the visit begins in the main courtyard, which miraculously escaped the damage that the 1943 bombing raids caused to the rest of the building. With porticoes of paired Tuscan-order columns, this striking setting preserves all the original 1560 decorations. These were inspired by two themes: in the lower order is a celebration of heroic endeavour, with scenes from the Labours of Hercules; in the upper order is a celebration of the power of love, with scenes from Ovid's *Metamorphoses*.

From the courtyard you pass into the Feast Room (now Sala Alessi), which was destroyed during the war but restored to its ancient splendour by a project completed in 2002. The original frescoes dated from 1568 and depicted mythological allegories; over the two main doorways are busts of Mars and Minerva, while the sky of the ceiling is borne up by caryatids. To one side of the room is the city's official standard, depicting St Ambrose with the *scrofa semilanuta* at his feet. The visit also takes in other rooms, including the Sala della Giunta, where the frescoes are said to be by Tiepolo; these were originally in Palazzo Casati (now Palazzo Dugnani) but were removed in wartime to protect them from damage.

One last curiosity: three years after the death of Tomaso Marino, the palazzo saw the birth of his granddaughter, who would become famous in her own right. Mariana de Leyva was raised at the Convent of the Humble Sisters of Monza, taking her late mother's name, Virginia Maria, when she herself became a nun at the age of 16. She was later immortalised as the "Nun of Monza" in Manzoni's *I Promessi Sposi* (*The Betrothed*).

BAS-RELIEF OF A LAMB ⑧

19, Via Agnello
• Public transport: MM1 Duomo, San Babila

> ***A reminder of the existence of the Contrada del Agnello***

Above the house door at 19 Via Agnello is a small bas-relief of a lamb (*agnello* in Italian), which gives the street its name. Even if the lamb is one of the most widespread symbols of Christian iconography (corresponding to the paschal or Easter lamb which was an allegory of Christ), this bas-relief is a reference

to the name of one of the old *contrade* (neighbourhoods) of Milan. Elsewhere, for example, is the *Scrofa semilanuta* (this is to be found in Via Mercanti and indicates the *contrada dei Rostri* in the Porta Nuova district) and the smaller head of a female wolf on the palazzo at the corner of Via Torino and Via Lupetta (the Contrada della Lupa in Porta Ticinese district). In each case, the animals were the symbols of the respective *contrada*.

NEARBY

MARIE-ANTOINETTE'S LAST PIECE OF EMBROIDERY ⑨

The museum within the former home of Alessandro Manzoni (1 Via Morone; open Tuesday to Friday, 9am–12 noon and 2pm–4pm) contains the last surviving piece of embroidery by the French Queen Marie-Antoinette, made in 1793 while she was imprisoned in the Conciergerie awaiting execution. The work was given by a prison warder to Sophie de Condorcet, who then gave it to Guilia Beccaria, Manzoni's mother.

THE STAIRS ON WHICH MANZONI FELL ⑩

On 6 January 1873 Alessandro Manzoni fell and hit his head against one of the steps in the Church of San Fedele (in the piazza of the same name). Just a few months later, on 22 May, he died of meningitis at the age of 88. A bronze plaque to the left of the high altar marks the place where Manzoni used to come to pray; a statue of the writer also stands in the square in front of the church.

THE *CONTRADE* OF MILAN

Based on an earlier – now lost – medieval map which used to be in the State Archives of Castello Sforzesco, a map drawn up by the topographer Giovanni Francesco Krauss in 1763 provides precious information on Milan during the era of the Communes and the centuries immediately afterwards. Using that source, in 1935 Professor Alessandro Colombo was able to reconstruct the administrative districts into which the city was divided at the time. This was a period when Milan was still concentrated within the ancient moat dug in 1157 by Guglielmo da Guintellino, in a vain attempt to resist the advance of Frederick Barbarossa. That moat was subsequently widened and deepened to create the Inner Moat, which then became a navigable waterway used to transport marble from Candoglia on Lago Santo Stefano for the construction of the Duomo.

Within that perimeter, the city was divided into six *sestieri* (sixths) corresponding to six city gateways: Porta Nuova, Porta Orientale, Porta Romana, Porta Ticinese, Porta Vercellina and Porta Comacina. These *sestieri* were in turn divided into five *contrade* each. Professor Colombo tried to establish the names of all thirty, traces of some having been entirely lost. His work can be consulted at www.acquafallata.it.

MATTHÄUS RÖRICZER AND THE DUOMO: THE CONTROVERSIAL REVELATION OF THE SACRED GEOMETRY USED BY MEDIEVAL STONEMASONS

The church with the fourth-largest floor area in Europe – after St Peter's in Rome, St Paul's in London and Seville Cathedral – Milan Cathedral took more than four centuries to complete: from 1386 to 1813. During that time it was often the subject of disputes between the master architects of the various guilds of *muratori* (stonemasons) who worked on it.

The initial floor plan was *ad quadratum* – that is, based upon a square and double square, with central nave and side aisles of the same height. However, this plan was later abandoned during the raising of the building for an elevation *ad triangulum*. This was when the controversy arose, due to apparently insoluble problems: the height of the equilateral triangle which was the basis of an *ad triangulum* elevation clearly was not the same as the length of one of its sides, and the superimposition of this upon the *ad quadratum* floor plan would mean undermining the planned proportions and sacred geometry of the building.

When called upon to re-establish that sacred geometry, the Piacenza mathematician Gabriele Stornaloco suggested rounding up the height of the naves from 83.138 *braccia* (ells) to 84, which could then be easily subdivided into six units of fourteen. Although acceptable, Stornaloco's proposal was itself subsequently changed, with the height of the cathedral being lowered to bring it more into line with classical proportions. This compromise in the measurements of the structure made the German master mason Heinrich Parler furious, with his protestations leading in 1392 to his resignation from the post of project consultant. His place was taken in 1394 by another German – Ulrich von Ensignen from Ulm – but he too only stayed six months. The Lombard *muratori* continued to argue among themselves, each supporting their own ideas, and thus the French master architect Jean Mignot was called to oversee the work. But he didn't last long either. Criticising the *muratori,* who were determined to give the cathedral its own particular style even if that meant flouting the principles of Gothic architecture, he made the still famous comment *ars sine scientia nihil est* (art without knowledge is nothing), to which the *muratori* promptly responded *scientia sine ars nihil est* (knowledge without art is nothing) and by 1401 Mignot was back in Paris, having failed to make any progress with the intransigent *muratori*. Following their own empirical methods, they did however complete the choir and transepts by around 1450.

A few years later a huge scandal was caused by another German, Matthäus Röriczer, the third generation of a family of master builders who had worked on the cathedral of Regensburg: though bound by an oath to protect the craft secrets of the *muratori* from the non-initiated, Röriczer published numerous details which until then had been concealed within notebooks for the exclusive use of master masons. Amounting to little more than a small pamphlet, this – the only work Röriczer ever published – is of fundamental importance, being the only known contemporary discussion of the sacred geometry employed by medieval stonemasons. Entitled *On the Ordination of Pinnacles*, it describes the method to be followed in order to raise a pinnacle of the correct proportions upon a given ground area. Adopting such schema, the *liberi muratori* could, with ruler and compass, take a given measurement and apply geometry to achieve a life-size plan. This was then drawn on a "tracing surface" of plaster and life-size models or moulds in wood were created (depending upon whether the stones were to be rough-cut or dressed). Röriczer's publication demonstrated the simplicity of the method. Instead of constant reference to scale measurements on a plan such as found in contemporary architecture – a procedure which, in the absence of finely calibrated instruments, tends to lead to error – the pinnacle (or any other component of the architectural structure) was "developed" upwards from a square base; thus, whatever the original size of that square, all the parts of the pinnacle would be in proportion to it. And as the size of that square could be derived from the overall geometry of the cathedral, the size of the pinnacle would thus be harmonised with the structure as a whole.

Matthäus Röriczer dedicated his pamphlet to Prince Wilhelm, Bishop of Eichstad, a patron of early stonemasons and a man who was deeply interested in the exact methods applied in the geometry of religious buildings.

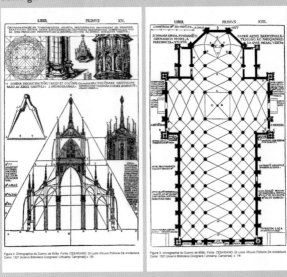

Figure 4: Orthographia do Duomo de Milão. Fonte: CESARIANO, Di Lucio Vitruvio Pollione De Architectura. Como: 1521 (Acervo Biblioteca Cicoginara / Unicamp, Campinas) c. 15r

Figure 3: Ichnographia do Duomo de Milão. Fonte: CESARIANO, Di Lucio Vitruvio Pollione De Architectura. Como: 1521 (Acervo Biblioteca Cicoginara / Unicamp, Campinas) c. 14r

Later, in 1521, Vitruvius drew upon that work when presenting a diagram of the cathedral based on a rhombus. The triangular transversal elevation of the structure is, in this design, shown superimposed on concentric circles within which are traced a square and a hexagon, the drawing thus showing the relation that existed between the elevation and the *ad quadratum* floor plan.

STATUE OF SAINT NAPOLEON

Duomo di Milano
Piazza del Duomo
• Public transport: MM1, MM3 Duomo; tram 2, 3, 12, 14 16, 24, 27

The invention of a new saint in homage to Napoleon

One statue stands out among the many that grace Milan Cathedral – opposite Palazzo Reale, on the third buttress along the main façade, it can easily be seen from the street. The boy in old-fashioned dress, with his feet in chains but his arms folded defiantly, is none other than "San Napoleone", an imaginary modern saint who appeared in the short time that Milan was ruled by Napoleon Bonaparte. In 1805 the diminutive Corsican dared to have himself crowned with the Iron Crown of Lombardy in front of the Duomo as "Emperor of the French and King of Italy", uttering the famous phrase *Dieu me la donne, gare à qui la touche* (God gives it to me, woe betide any who touches it). Legend has it that the story was deliberately fabricated to pay tribute to the emperor in Milan Cathedral, where all the Church's saints were already represented in marble under the protective sign of the "Madonnina".

As a consequence, Cardinal Caprara, who was present at Napoleon's coronation, tracked down a mysterious San Neapolis, a fourth-century Christian martyr who was associated with the emperor because of their similar names, and rechristened San Napoleone. Inspired by the lives of other saints, the story of the young man who was tortured and died in prison was remade.

HOW THE EMPEROR TOOK OVER THE ASSUMPTION

Napoleon did not have a feast day, so, as an ultimate tribute, the saint was added to the calendar on 15 August, the emperor's birthday, displacing the Feast of the Assumption of the Blessed Virgin Mary, to whom the Duomo is dedicated. The Assumption was not celebrated again until after the fall of the French in 1814.

DUOMO STATUE: MODEL FOR THE STATUE OF LIBERTY?

Among the statues of Milan Cathedral, on the balcony above the central entrance, stands *La Legge Nuova* (The New Law), designed in 1810 by Camillo Pacetti.

According to legend, the female figure with arm raised, torch in hand and spiked crown on her head, served as a model for the Statue of Liberty designed by Bartholdi in 1885 for New York. Whether this is true no one can say with certainty, but the cathedral holds many mysteries, such as the burnished calf of one of Christ's torturers depicted on the main portal. All tourists touch it, as it is said to ward off bad luck, but not many know that a shell fragment was embedded at this very spot in the 1943 bombing.

DUOMO MERIDIAN

Piazza del Duomo
• Open daily from 7am to 7pm
• Public transport: MM1, MM3 Duomo

> **A meridian
> line across
> the floor
> of the Duomo**

Entering the Duomo by the main doorway, you'll notice a copper line set into the floor; running from south (on the right) to north (on the left), this then continues 3 metres up a wall, to end at a painting depicting the astrological sign of Capricorn.

This metal strip forms an old meridian installed at the behest of Joseph II, which was to be used to measure the precise moment at which the Sun reached its zenith and, above all, to establish the correct date of Easter (a moveable religious feast). It was installed and calibrated in 1776 by two astronomers from the Brera: Giovanni Angelo De Cesaris and Guido Francesco Reggio.

The instrument is still one of great precision. Set into the vault of the first side chapel on the far right (above one of the lateral windows) is the window through which passes the ray of light that functions as the gnomon. Some 24 metres above ground level, this opening can also be seen from outside when you go up to the roof (see photo below). At midday, a ray of light passing through this window strikes the copper strip, alongside which signs of the zodiac are engraved in the marble. The sign that corresponds to that point of impact depends upon the time of year.

When it was first installed – the ecclesiastical authorities had insisted on this location near the doorway so that the work would not interfere with religious services – an official was responsible for going out onto the cathedral forecourt and waving a small flag as soon as he saw the disk of light hit the meridian strip. Another official, stationed at the top of Milan's clock tower on the Palace of Jurisconsults, would then wave his flag so that it could be seen at Castello Sforzesco, where a third gave the signal to fire the cannon that indicated midday.

For more information on the meridians, see p. 42 - 45.

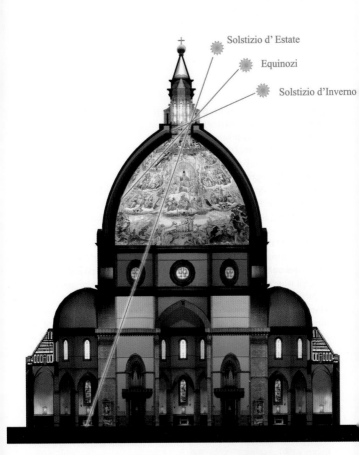

Solstizio d' Estate

Equinozi

Solstizio d'Inverno

HOW DOES A MERIDIAN WORK?

Instead of using the shadow of a gnomon, these use a small hole placed at a certain height, through which the sun's light falls onto a meridian line (i.e. one aligned exactly north-south). The fact that the sun's rays perform the function of the shadow in a traditional sundial means that the opening is sometimes referred to as a "gnomonic opening." The higher the opening, the more efficient the meridian, hence the interest in using cathedrals (see the following section "Why are meridians installed in cathedrals?"); the circumference of the hole had to be no more than one thousandth of the height above the ground. Obviously, the opening had to be installed on the south side of the building in order to let in the rays of the sun, which lies to the south in the northern hemisphere.

The meridian line should run from the point which stands perpendicularly below the axis of the opening, not always easy to determine using the instruments available to scientists in the past. The length of the line depends on the height of the opening; in some cases, where the building was not long enough to trace the entire meridian line across the floor (as was the case at Saint-Sulpice in Paris), an obelisk was added at its end, so that the movement of the sun's ray could then be measured up the vertical. In summer, when the sun is highest in the sky, the sun's ray falls onto the meridian line closer to the south wall (where that line begins) than it does in winter, when the sun is lower over the horizon and the rays tend to strike towards the far end of the meridian line.

The main principle behind the working of the meridian is that at noon, solar time, the sun is at its apex and, by definition, its rays fall straight along a line running exactly north-south. So, the exact moment when those rays strike the meridian line, which does run north-south, indicates the solar noon. Furthermore, the exact place on the meridian line where that ray falls makes it possible to determine the day of the year: the point right at the beginning of the line is reached solely on the day of the summer solstice, whilst the exact end of the line is reached on the day of the winter solstice. Experience and observation meant that the meridian line could be calibrated to identify different days of the year.

Once this was done, one could use the line to establish the date of various moveable feasts, such as Easter – one of the great scientific and religious uses of meridians. Similarly, one could establish the different periods corresponding with the signs of the Zodiac, which explains where one finds such signs indicated along the length of a number of meridian lines.

WHY WAS 4 OCTOBER FOLLOWED IMMEDIATELY BY 15 OCTOBER IN THE YEAR 1582?

THE MEASUREMENT OF TIME AND THE ORIGIN OF THE MERIDIANS

The entire problem of the measurement of time and the establishment of calendars arises from the fact that the Earth does not take an exact number of days to orbit the sun: one orbit in fact takes neither 365 nor 366 days but rather 365 days, 5 hours, 48 minutes and 45 seconds.

At the time of Julius Caesar, Sosigenes of Alexandria calculated this orbit as 365 days and 6 hours. In order to make up for this difference of an extra 6 hours, he came up with the idea of an extra day every four years: thus the Julian calendar – and the leap year – came into being.

In 325 AD, the Council of Nicaea established the temporal power of the Church (it had been called by Constantine, the first Roman emperor to embrace Christianity). The Church's liturgical year contained fixed feasts such as Christmas, but also moveable feasts such as Easter. This latter was of essential importance as it commemorated the death and resurrection of Christ, and so the Church decided that it should fall on the first Sunday following the full moon after the spring equinox. That year, the equinox fell on 21 March, which was thus established as its permanent date.

However, over the years, observation of the heavens showed that the equinox (which corresponds with a certain known position of the stars) no longer fell on 21 March...The 11 minutes and 15 seconds difference between the real and assumed time of the Earth's orbit around the Sun was resulting in an increasing gap between the actual equinox and 21 March. By the 16th century, that gap had increased to ten full days and so pope Gregory XIII decided to intervene. Quite simply, ten days would be removed from the calendar in 1582, and one would pass directly from 4 October to 15 October... It was also decided, on the basis of complex calculations (carried out most notably by the Calabrian astronomer Luigi Giglio), that the first year of each century (ending in 00) would not actually be a leap year, even though divisible by four. The exceptions would fall every four hundred years, which would mean that in 400 years there would be a total of just 97 (rather than 100) leap years. This came closest to making up the shortfall resulting from difference between the real and assumed time of orbit. Thus 1700, 1800 and 1900 would not be leap years, but 2000 would... In order to establish the full credibility of this new calendar – and convince the various Protestant nations that continued to use the Julian calendar – Rome initiated the installation of large meridians within its churches. A wonderful scientific epic had begun...

The technical name for a leap year is a bissextile year. The term comes from the fact that the additional day was once placed between 24 and 25 February. In Latin, 24 February was the sixth (sextus) day before the calends of March, hence the name bis sextus, to indicate a supplementary sixth day. The calends were the first day of each month in the Roman calendar.

THE HIGHEST MERIDIAN IN THE WORLD

From the 15th to the 18th century almost 70 meridians were installed in churches in France and Italy. Only ten, however, have a gnomonic opening that is more than 10 metres above floor level – that height being crucial to the accuracy of the instrument:

S. Maria del Fiore (Florence)	90.11 m
S. Petronio (Bologna)	27.07 m
St-Sulpice (Paris)	26.00 m
Monastery of San Nicolo l'Arena (Catania, Sicily)	23.92 m
Cathedral (Milan)	23.82 m
S. Maria degli Angeli (Rome)	20.34 m
Collège de l'Oratoire (Marseille)	17.00 m
S. Giorgio (Modica, Sicily)	14.18 m
Museo Nazionale (Naples)	14.00 m
Cathedral (Palermo)	11.78 m

WHY WERE MERIDIANS INSTALLED IN CATHEDRALS?

To make their measurements more precise, astronomers required enclosed spaces where the point admitting light was as high as possible from the ground: the longer the beam of light, the more accurately they could establish that it was meeting the floor along an exactly perpendicular plane. Cathedrals were soon recognised as the ideal location for such scientific instruments as meridians. Furthermore, the Church had a vested interest as well, because meridians could be used to establish the exact date of Easter.

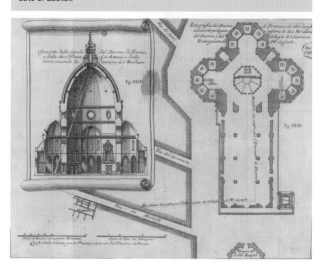

RITUAL OF *LA NIVOLA* ⓭

Duomo
Piazza del Duomo
• Takes place on the Saturday prior to 14 September
• Public transport: MM1, MM3 Duomo

> *The ancient ceremony of the Holy Nail*

Every year, on the Saturday before 14 September (feast day of the Veneration of the Holy Cross), an ancient ceremony is celebrated within the Duomo. This dates from over four hundred years ago and is related to the veneration of the cathedral's precious relic of the Holy Nail. Conserved within a display case of rock crystal and silver decorated with precious stones, this relic has three parts: an iron rod whose ends are bent into a circle (in appearance rather like a horse's bit); a second rod which is twisted around the first (perhaps to serve as a handle); and a third component which is the nail itself. A large piece of hand-forged iron, this has a tip which has been bent into the form of a hook within one of the rings of the "bit"; the other end is enlarged slightly, so that it forms a sort of large nail head. According to legend, it was the Emperor Constantine who inherited this from his mother, Helena (see opposite) and then lost it. For some inexplicable reason, the nail, in the meantime bent into the form of a horse's bit, then reappeared in the forge of a Milan blacksmith. It was St Ambrose who recognised this piece of iron to be one of the Holy Nails from Christ's Cross and thus had it taken to the Church of Santa Tecla. When that church was demolished, the Holy Nail was transferred to the Duomo. The first documentary reference to its existence dates from

1575, when – during the plague – St Carlo Borromeo had it carried in procession from the Duomo to the Church of San Celso, pleading for divine intercession to put an end to the epidemic. Nowadays, the Holy Nail is suspended above the high altar in the Duomo, attached to the keystone of the vault and lit by a red lamp. During the ceremony, the nail is lowered from its case using *La Nivola*, a sort of seventeenth-century elevator which is now fully mechanised. Made of sheet metal, this "pod" measures around 3 metres in length and is covered with canvas and painted with images of angels and cherubs within vaporous clouds. The paintings were made by Landriani in 1612.

LEGEND OF THE HOLY NAILS

The traditional accounts vary, some saying that three nails were used for the Crucifixion, some four: two for Christ's hands, one for his feet and one to fix the *titulus crucis* to the top of the Cross (the *titulus* being the plaque with the initials INRI, short for the Latin expression *Iesus Nazarenus Rex Iudaeorum*: Jesus of Nazareth, King of the Jews). The first reference to these instruments of Christ's Passion is to be found in St Ambrose's funeral oration for his friend the Emperor Theodosius, delivered on 25 February 395 (*De obitu Teodosii, 47*). On that occasion, Ambrose referred to the great care that the Empress Helena had lavished upon her son, Constantine, claiming that during a visit to the Holy Land in 327–328 the future saint had taken part in the search for the Cross and the nails used in crucifying Christ. The Cross itself she left in Jerusalem, but the "nails with which Our Lord was crucified, she [also] found. She had a horse's bit made from one of them, and another was made into a diadem; she used one for decoration, and one for devotion. To her son Constantine, she sent a diadem studded with precious stones, which were held in place upon the most precious gem of all: the nail from the Cross of our divine redemption. She also sent him the bit. Constantine used both objects and handed on the faith to his successors. Helena acted with great wisdom in placing the cross upon the head of kings, because thus Christ's Cross was adored through the figure of kings."

It is not known what subsequently became of the Holy Nails, which were however among the most precious relics of the Christian world. St Gregory of Tours says that one of them was thrown into the sea to calm a tempest. It is possible that those which have survived were handed down by the emperor's descendants. Sixth-century documents in Constantinople speak of the veneration of various Holy Nails, which were undoubtedly those found by St Helena, or were part of the original relics kept in the Basilica of Hagia Sophia. After the city was looted by the Crusaders in 1204, the nails disappeared.

Various places of worship today boast the presence of one of the nails: apart from the nail in the Milan Duomo, there is said to be a fragment of Constantine's horse's bit in Rome and in Jerusalem (in the Basilica of the Holy Cross). Another fragment has, since 1260, been recorded in Carpentras (France), which has adopted it as a symbol. The Cathedral of Colle Val d'Elsa (Tuscany) contains a twisted nail that is said to have been that which held the *titulus*. Finally, until very recently it was believed that another nail was fixed within the iron Crown of Monza, which some held to be the actual crown of Emperor Constantine. Analysis, however, has now revealed that the structure of the crown is actually silver and not iron.

SCULPTURES OF BOXERS, ACTORS AND CELEBRITIES

⑭

Cathedral roof terraces
- Open daily, 9am–5.45pm (2 November to 2 February, 9am–4.45pm)
- Admission: €8 (by lift) or €5 (on foot)
- Public transport: MM1, MM3 Duomo; tram 12, 13, 16, 23, 24, 27; bus 54

Mussolini on the Duomo

On the roof terraces of the cathedral, small sculptures of celebrities from the time of the 1920s restoration are to be seen along the *falconatura*, typical Gothic decorations with figures of different subjects. To see them, turn your back on the *Madunina* and look towards the two exit doorways.

Curiously, none of the relief sculptures has anything to do with religion. On the left are four pairs of fighting boxers. Perhaps they were celebrities at the time, but the only ones whose names have not sunk into oblivion are Primo Carnera (the first Italian to win the world heavyweight championship) and Erminio Spalla (the first Italian to become European boxing champion, and later a well-known actor).

On the right are a series of faces: some curly-haired male figures whom it is difficult to identify; Mussolini, his jutting jawline unmistakable in

spite of the mop of curls added later in an attempt to disguise the figure; the orchestra conductor Arturo Toscanini; and a "doublet" combining the faces of Il Duce and King Vittorio Emanuele II just as they appeared, side by side, on the postage stamps of the day.

There are also depictions of a rather random collection of objects: a Roman helmet, the fasces of a Roman lictor (the fascist emblem), a pair of tennis rackets and tennis balls, a rugby ball and some mountain-climbing equipment. These images were just one way of proclaiming that the cathedral represented the universe of humanity and thus brought together all the things and people that might be encountered in the world.

The Duomo roof terraces are used in summer for concerts and evening events. Programme available at www.vividuomo.it.

FORGOTTEN ORIGIN OF THE MILAN SERPENT ⓲

Palazzo Arcivescovile
Via dell'Arcivescovado-Piazza del Duomo
• Public transport: MM1, MM3, Duomo

> *Why did the serpent become the symbol of the Visconti family?*

Very often in Milan you come across the strange symbol of a snake devouring a man. This serpent – guivre in the language of heraldry – is known to the Milanese as *el bissun* and was the famous symbol of the Visconti family. Even though it is one of the best-known symbols of the City of Milan itself, the origin of this figure is unclear. Some historians argue that it became part of the Visconti armorial bearings thanks to Otton Visconti, known as Ottorino (1207–1295), the powerful son of the feudal lord Ubaldo Visconti. Born in Milan, Otton was elected archbishop of the city after a tough contest against the other candidate, Martino della Torre. To thank Pope Gregory X (Tedaldo Visconti) for his support, Otton included within his armorial bearings "the Moor vomited forth by the serpent", a reference to the fact that, immediately prior to becoming pope (1271–1276), Tedaldo had – with the future Edward I of England – taken part in the Ninth Crusade (1271–1272) to Acre in the Holy Land. Another legend has it that it was Azzone Visconti who took the serpent as an emblem in 1323 after a lucky escape. While he was with his troops camped alongside Pisa, he did not notice that a viper had slid into his helmet; however, when he put on the headgear the serpent simply slithered away without biting him. There are even older legends as well. One tells of Desiderius, the last Lombard king, who fell asleep under a tree and dreamed that a viper had twisted itself around his head like a crown. Again, according to the king, it was miraculous that the snake had not bitten him, hence the royal decision to adopt it as a symbol.

It is also said that the serpent became the symbol of the Visconti family after Umberto, the founder of the dynasty, had rid Milan of a terrible dragon. A number of popular legends say that an enormous serpent with a dragon's head lived in Lake Gerundo, an expanse of water then located to the east of the city (now dried up). The creature would devour all those who approached the banks of the lake, particularly children (another heraldic name for this symbol is a "serpent vorant a child"). One day a courageous unknown knight, who happened to be on the Calvenzano side of the lake, encountered the serpent and killed it, thus saving the child it had just seized. The lake then immediately dried up, providing the local people with good fertile land. The knight turned out to be Umberto Visconti, who founded the dynasty and thus took as its symbol the "serpent vorant a child". In Calvenzano the main street is still called Via della Biscia (Serpent Street).

If, as all these stories suggest, the origin of the *bissun* is unclear, its importance certainly is not: the symbol has been adopted by Milan City Council, by Inter Milan F.C., by Canale 5 and by Alfa Romeo.

BISCIONE: A SYMBOL MORE ESOTERIC THAN HERALDIC?

For all its association with the Viscontis, the crowned *biscione* is in fact an esoteric symbol that dates from long before Ottone Visconti chose it as part of his family crest. More than a simple viper, the serpent here is a *basilisk*, a mythological creature which Pliny the Elder described as a serpent wearing a golden crown.

In alchemy, the basilisk was referred to as the "philosophers' child". It symbolised man's base nature, which might then be transmuted or "spewed forth" into his higher nature. Thus it represented the true alchemist, who aimed for inner transformation in order to achieve spiritual awakening.

The tantric yoga treatises of early Hinduism referred to an electromagnetic force that circulated within man and within nature. They called this force *Kundalini* and described it as a crowned serpent that rose up in order to illuminate the human spirit. This is very probably why the ancient Egyptians (and then the Greeks and Romans) depicted their god Serapis with a serpent's body and a human head, in an image that is very similar

to the *biscione* (see illustration). Serapis was the deity of subterranean mysteries, celebrated in sacred crypts and grottoes. He also represented the vital power that circulated within the Earth itself, moving like a serpent along the telluric lines of force within the globe.

The Insubres, the Celtic people who founded the original Milan (*Mediolanum*) in the seventh century BC, also venerated the serpent, believing that it was a sea serpent that had peopled the Earth when it emerged from the original waters of Creation. In fact, numerous primitive belief systems see the serpent as the vassal of the Almighty, often depicting it wearing a crown.

Such notions also appear in Early Christian iconography: the biblical story of Jonah swallowed and then spewed forth by the whale uses these two actions as symbols of earthly death and resurrection to enlightenment. This biblical story reappears in the legend of Theodoric the Great, Ostrogoth king of Italy, who claimed to have been swallowed and then regurgitated by a monstrous serpent. This was said to have taken place in the city of Arona, which significantly belonged to the Visconti family.

AMBROSIANEUM 🄰

3, Via delle Ore
• The rooms can be visited during public conferences and events
(www.ambrosianeum.org)
• Public transport: MM1, MM3, Duomo; tram 12, 15, 23, 27; bus 54

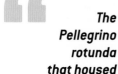

The Pellegrino rotunda that housed the archbishop's stables

The curious decagonal building behind the Archiepiscopal Palace once housed the archbishop's stables; it was designed in 1573 by the architect Pellegrino Pellegrini de' Tibaldi, who was simply known as "Il Pellegrino" (The Pilgrim), for Archbishop Carlo Borromeo. The choice of a ten-sided ground plan was due to the particular characteristics of the site Borromeo selected for his stables: given that the ground area was not very large, the architect decided to build upwards and downwards, creating a stable on three levels, with each forming a ring around an open central space. At the top level was the barn, the central opening making it possible to distribute the hay to the lower levels. At ground level, approached by a slight slope paved with cobblestones, were the stables for the more thoroughbred horses (with space for a maximum of eighteen), while at the lower ground level were stables for the draught animals.

The twentieth century obviously soon saw these stables fall into disuse; then, after the Second World War, the building became home to the

Ambrosianeum, a cultural foundation responsible for promoting the study of theology in a secular world. The premises can nowadays be visited during the numerous public events that the institution holds. However, the openings at the centre of each floor have been covered over, and the stables themselves have become conference rooms. From the lower ground level a spiral staircase leads up to the ground floor, and if you leave at the back of the building on the first floor you'll find a curious Greek temple façade, complete with columns and architrave, which faces towards the Archiepiscopal Palace.

MILAN'S "WALK OF FAME"

21, Largo Corsia dei Servi
• Public transport: MM1 San Babila

A forgotten "Walk of Fame"

Although located in the very centre of the city, this "Walk of Fame" – whose collection of foot and hand prints was inspired by the one outside Grauman's Chinese Theater in Hollywood – is in a dark and overlooked passageway.

The idea for an Italian version was first promoted in 1984 by the magazine *TV Sorrisi & Canzoni* and linked with the Gran Premio Internazionale dello Spettacolo (the Italian version of the Oscars, popularly known as the *Telegatti* because the statuette was in the form of a cat). It was intended that the "Walk" would have the handprints of the more famous guests at the ceremony and of the award winners. Having made hand and, sometimes, footprints within a slab of plaster, the stars then gouged out their signature and the plaster was used to cast a concrete paving-stone to be inserted alongside the others.

Over the years, various actors, directors, comedians, singers and TV presenters left their handprints here: some great stars, others figures that are now practically forgotten. Among the more renowned in this Gallery of Fame are Francis Ford Coppola, Michael Douglas, Ben Kingsley, Christopher Lambert, Sophie Marceau, Robert Mitchum, Philippe Noiret, Nick Nolte, Sylvester Stallone, Sharon Stone, Ed Wallach, Robert Wagner, Rachel Welch, plus such Italians as Renzo Arbore, Sandra Mondaini, Raimondo Vianello and rock band I Pooh.

The entrance to the passageway is at 21 Largo Corsia dei Servi, opposite

the post office on the corner; it was originally chosen because the offices of the magazine *Sorrisi e Canzoni* used to be in this building (now moved to the Mondadori premises in Segrate). However, the Milan *Telegatti* awards ceremony came to an end in 2004, the occasion then being revived in Rome in 2006 before being finally abandoned in 2008. The handprints in the pavement – dating up to 2004 – are still there.

CARERE·DEBET·OMNI·VITIO·QVI
IN·ALTERVM·DICERE·PARATVS·EST

STATVA·VIRILE·ROMANA·DETTA
'OMM·DE·PREJA·O·SCIOR·CARERA,
VN·TEMPO·IN·VIA·S·PIETRO·ALL'ORTO
DVRANTE·IL·DOMINIO·AVSTRIACO
FV·PER·MILANO·O·BELLO·CHE·PER

SCIUR CARERA

13, Corso Vittorio Emanuele
• Public transport: MM1 Duomo, San Babila

In Milanese dialect *sciur* means *signor*, but "Sciur Carera" is a statue not a real person; also known as *Omm de Preja* (Man of Stone), this work stands under the porticos at 13 Corso Vittorio Emanuele. A Roman work dating from the third century, the marble relief depicts a now armless male figure in a densely-folded toga. The head is not original and dates from the tenth century: the fashioning of the hair is typical of medieval clerics and the head is, in fact, a portrait of Archbishop Adelmanno Menclozzi.

> **He who is ready to criticise his neighbour must be without fault**

The name "Carera" comes from the Latin inscription on the work, which is taken from Cicero and reads: *Carere debet omni vitio qui in alterum dicere paratus est* (He who is ready to criticise his neighbour must be without fault).

The figure has been moved various times over the centuries. During the period of Austrian rule it was in Via San Pietro all'Orto, and served the same purpose for the Milanese as the statue of Pasquino did for the Romans – it was a place where they could surreptitiously attach notes and posters that satirised or criticised their Habsburg rulers. In fact, it was here that, on News Day 1848, the famous "Cigar Strike" was announced, a minor gesture of rebellion which ultimately led to the outbreak of open revolt in Milan.

The strike was called because the Austrians had introduced yet another tax – this time on cigarettes and cigars. In protest, the people of the city decided to stop smoking altogether, and in response the Austrian military governor – General Radetzky – ordered his soldiers to smoke ostentatiously as they walked around the city. In 18 March 1848, a working-class man was so infuriated when an Austrian blew smoke in his face that, his anger probably heightened by his own withdrawal symptoms, he snatched the cigar from the soldier and threw it on the ground. He was then immediately defended by the other Milanese present, and both the offending soldier and those who had come to his assistance were put to flight. Open revolt quickly erupted throughout the city, resulting in the so-called *Cinque Giornate* (Five Days) that ended in the liberation of the city.

The habit of attaching political slogans and satire to the statue continued until quite recently – that is until, in the mid-twentieth century, the work was transferred to its present position on the outside wall of a modern building.

LION IN PIAZZA SAN BABILA

Piazza San Babila
Public transport: MM1 San Babila

War booty that isn't

In the courtyard of the Basilica of San Babila is a column topped by the stone statue of a lion, which some might think was more suited to St Mark's Square in Venice.

Legend has it that this is a trophy of war. Five centuries ago, Venetian forces intent on adding Milan to their list of conquests failed to reckon with the tough resistance of the Milanese themselves. Warned by a baker who heard the Venetian soldiers approaching in the dead of night, the Milanese forces counterattacked, putting the enemy to flight and seizing their standards and ensigns. Among the ruins of the battlefield was found a large stone lion, which it was decided should be raised on a plinth in Piazza San Babila.

However, all this is only an imaginary association based upon the statue's similarity to the Venetian lion. In fact, the lion was part of the old Porta Orientale or Porta Renza (also known as the Porta Argentea because through it led the road to *Argentiolum*, the modern-day town of Gorgonzola). Facing east, the gateway was obviously the starting-point of the road to Venice (indeed, the road that starts in Piazza San Babila is still known as Corso Venezia) and it served to identify one of the six districts into which the city was divided. It was just coincidence that the symbol of this particular district was a lion.

The city gateway was demolished in 1818 and the material "recycled" for use in a new bell-tower for the church, the previous one having collapsed some 200 years earlier, in 1575. The lion – which together with various mythological creatures had graced the base of the gateway – was then set up in the basilica courtyard as the emblem of the district.

In 1650, it was Count Carlo Francesco Serbelloni, a *magistrato delle strade* (responsible for the maintenance of roads and bridges), who paid for the erection of a Doric column on which to raise the lion. The inscriptions on the four sides of the base are badly eroded and very difficult to read. However, two names are legible: those of Serbelloni himself (a member of a very ancient Lombard family, his name is given in the old version: *Sorbelloni*) and of a certain Antonio Pirovano, whose identity cannot be established with any certainty.

At one time a number of Italian cities were divided into *sestieri* (sixths), just as Venice is today. In Milan, this division into six districts coincided with the six main gateways into the city: Porta Nuova, Porta Orientale, Porta Romana, Porta Ticinese, Porta Vercellina and Porta Comacina. Each *sestiere* was in turn divided into five *contrade* (neighbourhoods).

THE AUSTRIAN NUMBER ON CASA DEGLI OMENONI

⓴

Casa degli Omenoni
3, Via degli Omenoni
• Public transport: MM1, MM3 Duomo

> **The old method of numbering houses**

1722, the number above the doorway to the famous Casa degli Omenoni, does not refer to the year of the building's construction, which dates from 1562 to 1566; it is a surviving relic of the old system of street numbering as introduced by the Austrians.

Under orders from Emperor Joseph II, the Austrian minister Johann Wilczeck ordered the Marquis Ferdinando Cusani, appointed to oversee the city's highways and roads, to indicate the name of each street with a corner inscription. For the first time houses were also numbered; these numbers, known as *teresiani* because first used during the reign of Archduchess Maria Teresa, Joseph II's mother, followed a system that started from the Palazzo Reale (number 1) and then progressed in a spiral movement unfurling from the city centre towards its more outlying areas (marked by the Spanish ramparts). At the time the highest house number was 5314.

As the population grew within Milan, it was decided in 1830 to create new

house numbers by adding letters to the old (for example, 320 became 320A and 320B, etc.). Only in 1866 did the increasing problems posed by such a system of house-numbering lead to the introduction of the current system of numbering in streets, with even numbers on the right and odd numbers on the left, the lowest numbers being at the end of the street nearest the city centre.

The Austrian system still exists in Venice (see *Secret Venice* in this series of guides).

You can see other traces of the old system nearby: in Via Morone (number 1166) and at 8 and 19 Via Sant'Andrea (828 and 808). Other similar street numbers are also legible in Via Durini, Piazza Mercanti, Via Meravigli, Via Bagutta and Corso Venezia, as well as at Porta Vigentina.

BAS-RELIEF OF "CALUMNY TORN APART BY LIONS"

This strange sculpture is located below the cornice of the Casa degli Omenoni. The two lions are a reference to the owner of the house, the sculptor Leone Leoni, who had his studio here; the satyr symbolises the envy and calumny of which he was sometimes the victim.

Apart from the addition of wrought-iron balconies, the façade of the original building has survived intact, the only part to do so. It is decorated with eight large telamones (male figures as supporting pillars) designed by Leoni himself but carved by the sculptor Antonio Abbondio. These sculptures were also referred to as "The Prisoners", like the six famous statues that Michelangelo created for the tomb of Pope Julius II. Leoni was a friend of Michelangelo's and owned a "picture of giants" by him, as well as paintings by Titan and Correggio and even Leonardo da Vinci's *Atlantic Codex* (now in the Ambrosiana). It is also possible that the telamones were inspired by Vitruvius's description of the "Persian Gateway" built by the Spartans, in which statues of prisoners of war served to hold up the roof. Leoni was so pleased with the sculptures that he gave each one an individual name, inscribed behind their heads: Svevus, Quadus, Adiabenus, Parthus, Sarmata and Marcomanus (the names of the two central figures are missing). Each refers to six different peoples of the ancient world who were conquered by the Romans; perhaps this serves to support the claim that the figures were inspired by Vitruvius. Whatever the origin of the idea, the Milanese were soon referring to the statues as *Gli Omenoni* (The Big Fellows) and that was the name by which this street became known in the nineteenth century. With an interior entirely restructured in 1929 by Piero Portaluppi (see p. 72), the building now houses a private association, Il Clubino, which is not open to the public.

LEONINE SCULPTOR

Aretino relates that Leone Leoni led a very eventful life; in some ways he was a precursor of the impulsive and violent artist later exemplified by Caravaggio. Just like that painter, Leoni was imprisoned. In Rome he was implicated in a plot against the pope's jewel-smith and was arrested. Later, in Genoa, he was sentenced to have a hand severed after becoming involved in a brawl in which he had scarred a German; he only escaped the punishment thanks to the intervention of Admiral Andrea Doria. In Milan, Leoni became an engraver at the Imperial Mint and it was in his studio that were cast the twelve statues that make up the large "Escorial Retable", the work of Leoni's son Pompeo, together with the large bronzes for the tombs of Emperor Charles V and his son Philip II, King of Spain (also in the Escorial outside Madrid). Leoni's other monumental works include the tombs of Gian Giacomo Medici, Marchese di Marignano (in Milan Cathedral) and Vespasiano Gonzaga (in Sabbioneta), as well as the statue of "Ferrante I Gonzaga Defeating Envy" (in Guastalla).

NORTH-WEST

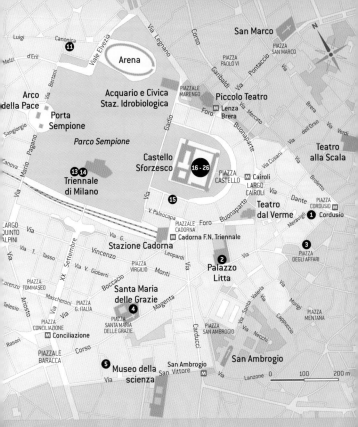

LARGE WINDOW
IN THE CHAMBER OF COMMERCE

0

Palazzo Turati
9B, Via Meravigli
• Visits by appointment; phone 02 85155224 / 5288
• Public transport: MM1 Cordusio; tram 16, 19

A stained-glass window by one of the masters of Chiarismo

On the first floor of the building housing the Chamber of Commerce is a splendid stained-glass window by one of the most important figures of the *Chiarismo* movement: Cristoforo De Amicis. Recent restoration by Ernesto Brivio has revived the full luminosity of the colours – *Chiarismo* was primarily concerned with vivid chromatic effects – and the window can now be seen by the public (on request). Made in 1957 by the best glass-master in Milan, it depicts various aspects of the establishment's work: commerce, industry, craft trades and agriculture.

It was in 1956 that the Chamber of Commerce launched the competition for designs for a large new window that was to adorn their new Via Meravigli premises. De Amicis' work was selected because it best depicted the rebirth of Milan's economy after the crisis following the Second World War.

At the centre of the composition is Mercury, the Roman god of commerce and promoter of all that human activity can achieve. The god is shown in a rather relaxed, non-academic pose against a field of colour in which blue triumphs (blue, turquoise, cobalt and ultramarine), highlighted here and there with touches of purple and violet. With an imperious gesture, he seems to point to the admirable conquests of the past and promise new ones for the future. At his feet are five figures of wise men wearing capes; these seem to symbolise the multifaceted genius of the artisans, merchants and bankers who formed the core of the medieval burgher class. In the background is a depiction that might be taken as symbolic of their achievements: the building site of the "grand fabric" of Milan Cathedral. The panel on the right is dedicated to Agriculture, with the beautiful and buxom form of Ceres (or Pomona), the Roman goddess of harvests; she rests within the womb of the Earth, seeming to owe her fecundity to the hard work of the men active upon the surface of the land. To the left is the figure of Industry, which stands out against a background dominated by a tall chimney beneath which stand various low-rise industrial units, typical of factory architecture here. Thanks to the continuity in the depiction of sky and land, and the flowing lines of force that run throughout the composition, the three different scenes form a single narrative whole. The winged figure of Mercury embodies the dynamism that animates and encourages men as they undertake their wide variety of tasks; the Sun rotating in the sky above provides the energy required for such work.

TRACE OF A TEAR IN PALAZZO ARESE LITTA ❷

24, Corso Magenta
• Open during special events; see www.lombardia.beniculturali.it
• Public transport: MM1, 2 Cadorna

A tear shed for Napoleon

The story goes that *duchessa* Barbara Litta was so moved when Napoleon Bonaparte paid a personal visit to her salon that she could not hold back a tear. Where that tear fell to the floor in the so-called *Salone Rosso* (Red Salon) is marked to this day by a pearl set into the centre of a mosaic flower.

The splendid Palazzo Arese Litta, designed by Francesco Maria Richini for Conte Bartolomeo Arese, who became President of the Milan Senate in 1660, was built in the years from 1642 onwards. It now houses the Cultural Department of the Regional Government of Lombardy.

The superb monumental staircase rises through a double turn in three flights of stairs. These stairs, together with the impressive glazed bays adorned with family crests, survived the wartime bombing of Milan thanks to the diligence of an official who had them dismantled and placed in safe-keeping. Unfortunately the same could not be done for the cupola over the main hall. Apart from the *Salone Rosso*, the most magnificent rooms in the palazzo are the *Sala degli Specchi* (Gallery of Mirrors) and the *Salone della Duchessa*, which has kept its original tapestries, gilded stuccowork and paintings by Martin Knoller and Giuseppe and Agostino Gerli. The small *Salone della Duchessa* also has a concealed door within the wood panelling; this was normally used by servants but could also allow visitors to leave the palazzo unobserved. A further feature is a hidden opening at floor level: linked to a secret passage, this made it possible for the *duchessa* to eavesdrop on what her guests were saying when she was not present.

CERAMIC DECORATION
OF THE TAVERNA FERRARIO

③

Palazzo Mezzanotte
Piazza Affari
• Visits possible during the "open days" organised by the Italian
environmental agency FAI, or other public events
• Public transport: MM1–2 Cadorna, MM1 Cordusio; tram 1, 16

> **When
> Giò Ponti
> was the artistic
> director
> of a porcelain
> company**

bove the old *Sala delle Grida* (Bid
Room) in Palazzo Mezzanotte, where
business was still settled by shouted
bids right up until the 1990s, is a vast room
which was built in 1931 as a public restaurant.
This is the Taverna Ferrario, so named after
the first proprietor. A large square space
around a central opening, the design recalls
an ancient amphitheatre, with some Roman remains visible here (there
are even more substantial ones in the Roman theatre nearby). The wall

decorations were commissioned
from Giò Ponti, at the time
artistic director of the Richard
Ginori porcelain company.
To delimit this concave space,
Ponti opted for a schema of
ceramic panels, which on the
main support pillars depict
six large female figures (each
2.5 metres high) intended as
allegorical representations of
the natural produce bought
and sold within the old market:
there is, therefore, a cherry girl,
a florist, a market gardener,
a fruit seller, a water-carrier
and a fishwife. For the walls of
the raised gallery that still runs
round the space at the centre,
the artist designed delightful
arabesque compositions with
symbols of old and new games
and sports: tennis, golf, tarot
cards, dominoes, chess, snakes
and ladders, cars and children's
toys.

OLD SACRISTY
OF SANTA MARIA DELLE GRAZIE

❹

Piazza Santa Maria delle Grazie
• Open Tuesday to Sunday, 8.30am–7pm (only during exhibitions)
• Public transport: MM1–2 Cadorna; tram 16

A hidden sacristy with a secret underground passage

Usually closed to the public, the Old Sacristy – also known as the Monumental Sacristy – is a little gem that you only get the chance to visit when it is used for exhibitions.

From the outside all you see is a parallelepiped in brick, broken only by the frames of the rectangular windows and the oculus that gives onto the cloister. However, inside, this is an extraordinary space, made all the more atmospheric by skilful use of artificial lighting. The rectangular room is covered by a barrel vault complete with lunettes, all painted as a star-strewn sky, and at the end of the room is a small frescoed apse. The inner faces of the pilasters around this apse bear half-length relief portraits of Ludovico il Moro and his son Massimiliano. It is said that the ceiling fresco was actually by Leonardo da Vinci, but there is no proof of this. The side walls are lined with two levels of beautiful inlaid cabinets, above which are a series of paintings depicting scenes from the Old and New Testaments. Made by Father Vincenzo Spadotto in 1489, these cabinets were intended to house the church furnishings and vestments that had been donated by Ludovico himself. When he was taken prisoner by the French, these were sent as part of the ransom and never returned to the church.

Behind the cabinets is the entrance to a secret underground passage – nowadays probably closed off. This allowed Il Moro to ride here on horseback from his apartments in Castello Sforzesco.

MIRACLE OF THE REFECTORY

Painted by Leonardo da Vinci in 1495–1497, the fresco on the wall between the convent refectory and kitchens depicts *The Last Supper* and was probably intended to remind the monks of Christ's sacrifice even as they sat at their meals. It is a miracle that the work survived wartime bombing. After that damage to the building, *The Last Supper* was protected using oilcloths and sandbags.

SECRETS OF LEONARDO DA VINCI'S *THE LAST SUPPER*

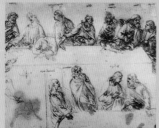

Leonardo used live models for the figures of the twelve Apostles and Christ in his famous *Last Supper*. For Jesus himself he desperately sought a suitable model, not finding anyone whose face adequately rendered the idea of purity, of a personality unaffected by sin. A legend that has now partially become accepted as historical fact says that he finally found the right model in a piazza in Rome, a beautiful 19-year-old youth with innocent, clean-shaven features. Having left his portrayal of Judas until last, it was more than two years later that da Vinci had to search out a suitable model. He found one in a local tavern, a hard-faced young man whose features reflected the vice and physical and moral depravation that the artist had imagined as key traits of the Apostle who betrayed Jesus Christ. Having sketched the young man, Leonardo was about to leave the inn when the sitter spoke to him: "Don't you recognise me? I'm the one who was a model for you a few years back, for Christ's face."

The story reflects an ideal truth: that Good and Evil can be part of the same person; that each and every man can either evolve or regress, be pure and beautiful or become depraved and coarsened. Each of us has the free will to choose our future, which is decided by the decisions we make and the actions we perform.

The figure of the young St John in *The Last Supper* shows a beautiful young man with almost feminine features – a fact which has led some to come up with the crazy notion that he can be identified with Mary Magdalene. The fact is that John was simply the youngest of Christ's twelve apostles; according to the Gospels, he was around 24 when Christ summoned him. The male and female qualities of his beauty symbolise the androgynous state of the Perfect Man, who inwardly realises a full synthesis of the qualities and potential of both male and female. John's own writings in the New Testament would thus become a favourite with the more heterodox of Christian thinkers (gnostics, hermeticists, alchemists, etc.).

In his sketch of the composition of *The Last Supper* (see illustration), Leonardo clearly identifies the figures in the fresco. The Apostles form four groups of three, leaving Christ relatively isolated at the centre of the composition. From left to right for someone looking at the fresco, the first group consists of Bartholomew, James the Lesser and Andrew, the second group of Judas (white-haired and leaning towards St John), Simon Peter and John, who is clean-shaven. The third group comprises Thomas, James the Greater and Philip, who is also clean-shaven, and the fourth group has Matthew (apparently shaven), Judas Thaddeus (also known as Lebbaeus) and Simon the Canaanite (also known as Simon the Zealot).

LEONARDO DA VINCI AND CHRISTIAN ASTROLOGY

Leonardo da Vinci probably drew upon his knowledge of astrology when creating *The Last Supper*, associating each Apostle with a sign of the zodiac, as was customary at the time. According to this tradition, Christ was to be identified with the Sun and the twelve Apostles with the signs of the zodiac (or, more precisely, with the qualities they were said to represent).

The composition thus aimed to express the entire universe of Christianity, using a symbolism similar to that found in the stained-glass windows through which sunlight enters cathedrals. This Christian astrology can trace its roots back to the Three Kings, who followed the star that led them to the newly born Christ in Bethlehem (see p. 211). It was subsequently developed by Pseudo-Dionysius the Areopagite and St Thomas Aquinas, and later by such Renaissance figures as Cornelius Agrippa, Giordano Bruno and Leonardo da Vinci himself. As can be seen from certain of his writings, Leonardo believed that man was made up of four fundamental elements (Air, Fire, Earth and Water), whose composition had a decisive effect upon his dominant temperament (nervous, sanguine, lymphatic or bilious; see illustration). This is why he divided the twelve Apostles into four groups, reflecting the division of the twelve signs of the zodiac.

First group (from left to right)

Bartholomew – Libra (level-headedness and balance)

James the Lesser – Pisces (lower fish in the astrological pair, which symbolises devotion and the giving of oneself)

Andrew – Sagittarius (animal part of the astrological symbol, representing discipline and self-control).

Second group

Judas Iscariot – Cancer (bias and withdrawal into self)

Simon Peter – Aries (impetuosity and lack of restraint)

John – Aquarius (courtesy and fraternity)

Third group

Thomas – Gemini (first figure in the astrological pair – reason and logic)

James the Greater – Pisces (upper figure in the astrological pair, representing sacrifice and faith)

Philip – Sagittarius (human part of the astrological figure, representing creativity and superiority of spirit)

Fourth group

Matthew – Scorpio (organisation)

Judas Thaddeus – Gemini (second figure in the astrological pair, representing apostleship and clarification)

Simon the Canaanite – Virgo (modesty and diplomacy). The evangelists Mark (Lion, representing impartiality, an attribute of Christ) and Luke (Taurus, representing maternity and filial relationship) do not appear in the fresco; they were not amongst Jesus' original twelve Apostles. The same is also true of the later Apostle Matthias, who after Christ's Ascension was chosen to take the place of Judas Iscariot, who had hanged himself after betraying Jesus.

FONDAZIONE PORTALUPPI ❺

5, Via Morozzo della Rocca
• Open during exhibitions or conferences, and the "open days" organised in spring by the FAI (around late March)
• Public transport: MM1 Conciliazione, MM2 Sant'Ambrogio; tram 15

Studio of the architect who modernised Milan

The building that houses what used to be Piero Portaluppi's studio was designed by the architect himself in the late 1930s and his heirs have today transformed it into a Foundation named after him. The elegant façade is typical of Portaluppi's style, the unusual basement strip faced with metal giving the building a rather "naval" appearance in keeping with the concerns of that particular decade.

The Foundation occupies two vast rooms, together with a library and the curator's office. The large windows overlook an interior courtyard which contains Roman ruins. In the meeting-room itself there is an exhibition of some project designs and scale models, some of which perfectly exemplify this architect's ironic stance with regard to modernism and urban design. Thus you find the gigantic skyscraper designed for the S.K.N.E. company in New York (Portaluppi himself read the initials as *sk[appa]ne*, which in Italian means, "Get out of here!"); the residential blocks for the Allabanuel district (which he read backwards, to form the Milanese expression *L'è una balla*: "It's a hoax"); and his design for an infernal utopia called "Hellytown". Note the remarkable floor in this room, which is a composition of samples of all sorts of Italian marbles: as good as a catalogue which allowed clients to choose the marbles they wanted in comfort.

Portaluppi also designed remarkable furniture and decorations, including the "*Omnibus*" desk, a cupboard-wardrobe, a desk with a thousand drawers and a wall chiffonier which was actually a cocktail cabinet.

PIERO PORTALUPPI: ARCHITECT

Portaluppi, born in Milan in 1888, worked as an architect from 1911 to 1967, the year of his death. Between 1912 and 1930 he designed numerous power stations for sites across the entire arc of the Alps while pursuing an academic career, ultimately becoming dean of the Milan Architecture Faculty in 1963. He is particularly remembered in Milan for certain of his designs, including: the Hoepli Planetarium; the Arenagario (which now houses the Museum of the Twentieth Century); the Necchi-Campiglio Villa; the arched building in Via Salvini; and the offices of the RAS insurance company in Via Torino. He was also responsible for the restoration of the church of Santa Maria della Grazie, the Casa degli Atellani (where he once lived), the Brera Picture Gallery and the Museum of Science and Technology. Alongside his various passions – Portaluppi was a noted film buff and satirical cartoonist – he also designed and collected sundials, his collection now being on display at the Museo Poldi Pezzoli.

VERDI MUSEUM AND CRYPT   ❻

Rest Home for Aged Musicians – Fondazione Giuseppe Verdi
29, Piazza Buonarroti
• Crypt open daily, 8.30am–6pm
• For the house and the museum rooms, visits by appointment; call
02 4996009 or access www.casaverdi.org

Mortal remains of Giuseppe Verdi

The inner courtyard of the Rest Home for Aged Musicians contains the crypt where lie the mortal remains of Giuseppe Verdi and his wife Giuseppina Strepponi. Officially opened on 19 March 1903, the crypt is decorated with mosaics based on cartoons inspired by the work of *Deus Loci* and created by Lodovico Pogliaghi, who also did the central doorway to the cathedral. This rich decoration is due to the generosity of Teresa Stolz, a close friend of the composer and a soprano who was one of the greatest interpreters of his work.

A wall plaque – whose presence was suggested by Queen Margherita – also commemorates Verdi's first wife, Margherita Barezzi, and on the floor is a bronze palm frond placed there by the Carrara Verdi family. Two crowns on the walls bear dedicatory inscriptions by King Vittorio Emanuele III and the then Minister of Education, who visited the tomb in 1901.

It was Verdi himself who, in 1889 at the age of 76, had acquired 3,000 square metres of land here as a real-estate investment. It was only later that he decided that the plot should be used to build a rest home for aged musicians who had been less fortunate than himself.

He commissioned the designs from the architect Camillo Boito, the brother of his friend and librettist, Arrigo. The rest home was ready to open its doors in 1898, but only admitted its first guests after Verdi's death. The composer had wanted this arrangement so as to dispense with the need for official thanks, etc. Thus the first musicians took up residence in 1902, on 10 October (Verdi's birthday).

In 1999, the centenary of the Fondazione Verdi, a museum was created here as well. This has various pieces of furniture that had belonged to the composer, including the spinet on which he practised when young and two pieces presented to Verdi by the Khedive of Egypt, Ismail Pasha, when *Aida* was premiered at the Cairo Opera House in 1871. There is also the Erard piano on which Arturo Toscanini played in 1898, when he was just over 20 years old. The paintings include Giovanni Boldini's *Portrait of Giuseppe Verdi,* as well as the clothing that the composer had in his apartment at the Grand Hotel Et De Milan when he died.

NEARBY

PORTRAITS OF VERDI AND MICHELANGELO

Piazza Buonarotti – the site of the rest home – contains a *Monument to Giuseppe Verdi* by Enrico Butti (1913). A few metres away, at 20 Via Buonarroti, is a fine house that dates from around the same time as Casa Verdi and bears another affectionate mark of homage to the *maestro*: a graffito reproduction of one of his most famous portraits. This goes together with a copy of a portrait of Michelangelo, after whom the street is named. Both of them are enclosed within *trompe l'œil* wooden frames, as if they were hanging in some interior.

NUDE STATUES OF CÀ DI CIAPP ⑧

Villa Romeo
48, Via Buonarroti
• Public transport: MM1 Buonarroti

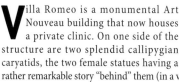

Villa Romeo is a monumental Art Nouveau building that now houses a private clinic. On one side of the structure are two splendid callipygian caryatids, the two female statues having a rather remarkable story "behind" them (in a very literal sense).

> *Two scandalous statues that were moved*

That a work of domestic architecture could prove scandalous may now be difficult to believe. However, when – in 1904 – the architect Giuseppe Sommaruga unveiled the house at 47 Corso Venezia that had been commissioned by the rich engineer Ermenegildo Castiglioni, he found himself the object of vituperative criticism.

His attempt to introduce within Milan the Art Nouveau style that was all the rage throughout Europe was – in the eyes of traditionalists – a shameless affront. Those porthole-shaped windows were too daring, and the bare rocks set as the foundation of the house too modern. Who cared that the sharp contrast between the smooth finished walls and the raw rustication was deliberate, the artist striving to generate visual tension between the materials themselves and the wealth of decorative motifs and forms framing windows and doorways?

Still, the greatest scandal was caused by another feature of his designs: the two large marble statues of female figures sculpted by Ernesto Bazzaro. Standing over the main doorway, these seemed to present their perfectly formed backsides to passers-by below; hence, the Milanese nickname of the building, *Cà di Ciapp* (Buttock House). Here he had gone too far, and Sommaruga was forced to remove the statues, replacing them with innocuous floral motifs that had none of the vivid modelling of the statues.

However, the architect did not destroy the nudes: a few years later he used them on another building he was designing, this Villa Romeo-Faccanoni. The statues are still there, far from the city centre, and now no one bats an eyelid.

ORIGIN OF THE WORD *CARYATID*

The term comes from the Greek *Karuatides*, that is, "women of Caria", which referred to the decorative female statues that served as columns, supporting balconies or cornices on the top or back of their heads.

Legend has it that the woman of Caria — reduced to slavery after the destruction of their city — served as the models for some such statues.

VILLA FOSSATI

17–19, Via Paolo Uccello
• Public transport: MM1 Lotto-Fiera

A grim heritage

All that distinguishes Villa Fossati from similar squat structures in this neighbourhood is a plaque on the outer wall recalling a terrible period in the building's history.

Built in the seventeenth century for the Pecchio family, in the nineteenth century the villa became a meeting-place for such Risorgimento patriots as Federico Confalonieri. However, in 1944, it earned itself the name *Villa Triste* when it became the headquarters of the infamous fascist police squad headed by Pietro Koch. Enclosed by barbed wire and protected by an alarm system, the villa had some five torture chambers set up in its basement. It was here that antifascists and members of the Resistance were brought for brutal interrogation. This cruel violence swiftly became an end in itself, with the villa attracting those who were part of the entourage of such famous figures as the actors Osvaldo Valenti and Valeria Ferida or the aristocrat Count Guido Stampa. These came here to acquire cocaine and also to enjoy the screams of the prisoners which shattered the silence of the neighbourhood day and night. Finally, following protests from both the local population and Cardinal Schuster, it was the fascists themselves who decided to close down the villa's interrogation centre.

For obvious reasons not wanting to move back into the building at the end of the war, the Fossati family donated it to the Pontifical Institution for Foreign Missions, which in its turn ceded it to the Congregation of the Missionary Sisters of the Immaculate Virgin. They made the place their general headquarters and

also set up a nursery school, which closed down just a few years ago. The villa is not open to visitors, but on Sunday morning – when the doors are opened for those attending mass at the small church of San Siro alla Vepra alongside – you can go into the garden. With its entrance at 20 Via Masaccio, this church is famous for the frescoes painted here in 1468 by various Lombard artists, and for its large holy-water stoup (made from the upturned lid of a Early Christian sarcophagus). It owes its name to the old name for the Olona River, as does the neighbourhood of San Siro itself.

NAZIS IN MILAN

Following the armistice which the Kingdom of Italy signed with the Anglo-American forces on 8 September 1943, Adolf Hitler supported the establishment of a puppet Repubblica Sociale Italiana (RSI). In theory, this was led by Benito Mussolini, whom German paratroopers had freed from captivity, but there was no doubt that it was the German themselves who really commanded this fake state, with the SS entering Milan in September 1943. Set up at the Hotel Regina in the very centre of the city (on the corner of Via Santa Margherita and Via Silvio Pellico), the municipal and interregional headquarters of the military authorities were under the command of the SS colonel Walter Rauff, inventor of the *Gaswagen* (mobile gas chambers). Although that building no longer exists, a plaque recalls that right up to the Liberation it was used to detain, torture and kill those whom the Nazis and fascists considered their enemies (Jews, anti-fascists, members of the Resistance and other "suspect" characters). Those who did not die at the Hotel Regina were incarcerated in San Vittore prison, where a plaque (at 2 Piazza dei Filangieri) commemorates the humiliation, punishment and torture suffered by those who worked and fought for the freedom and honour of their country.

Various fascist groups helped the Germans in rounding up such "suspects" – for example, the Legione Muti, the X Mas, the Brigate Nere and the Kock gang. Number 2 Via Rovello, now the site of the Teatro Piccolo but formerly the Cinema Fossati, bears a plaque which reminds passers-by that this used to be the barracks of the infamous Legione Muti. And in Via Tivoli was the Salinasi barracks commanded by Pasquale Cardella, who personally headed the firing-squad which, on 10 August 1944, shot fifteen patriots in Viale Loreto. There was also another Nazi-fascist barracks at 10 Corso Littorio (now Corso Matteotti), while the propaganda office of X Mas was located in Piazza Fiume (now Piazza della Repubblica).

One of the most terrifying of all places in Milan at the time was the Central Station itself. There, carefully concealed from the eyes of other travellers, the basement areas under platform 21 were used – from December 1943 onwards – to load cattle trucks with the Jews and political opponents being sent to the death camps; once filled, the trucks were raised

to track level using goods elevators and then hitched to a locomotive. The Nazis and the so-called *repubblichini* (those serving the RSI) crammed more than 1,500 people into these cattle trucks, of whom very few survived the camps. Amid the mosaic decoration of the station's Sala Regia (see p. 325) you can still see a swastika dating from this period.

CASCINA BOLLA

9, Via Paris Bordone
• Public transport: MM2 Amendola Fiera, Lotto Fiera 2; bus 90, 91

Leonardo da Vinci lived here

Today very little remains of Cascina Bolla, a fifteenth-century building which has now been incorporated into a modern villa. However, through the foliage of the poplar trees beyond the gate, you can still glimpse something of the silhouette of this hunting-lodge in Late Gothic style, its brick window surrounds so typical of the Renaissance.

This *cascina* ("farmhouse" in Tuscan), listed in the fifteenth century as an *osteria* (inn), was originally surrounded by a moat edged by a tall wall, the only access being by drawbridge. The watchtower built on the eastern side of the property still stands, complete with a fresco of flying birds.

Owned by the Caimi family, the *cascina* became the property of the De Bolli in 1478. Some claim it then passed into the hands of the jurisconsult Giuseppe Bolla in 1496. Whatever the truth, new research in 1983 established that Leonardo da Vinci was very probably living in Cascina Bolla at the time he painted *The Last Supper* within the Convent of Santa Maria delle Grazie. The Ministry of Culture has now listed the *cascina* as a historic building.

Legend has it that there was once an underground tunnel linking the *cascina* with Castello Sforzesco.

LEONARDO DA VINCI'S VINEYARD

Opposite Santa Maria delle Grazie – in whose refectory Leonardo painted *The Last Supper* – stands Casa degli Atellani, where the artist owned a vineyard to which he was particularly attached.

The building dates from the end of the fifteenth century. Constructed at the behest of Ludovico il Moro, it was part of a residential area for his faithful courtiers and was intended to house the Atellani family. Nowadays it is divided into two parts: the older part still maintains most of its original appearance, while the newer part was reconstructed after being badly damaged in the bombing raids of August 1943.

Leonardo's vineyard covered 8,320 square metres within the space now occupied by the palazzo's enclosed garden; as a document dated 26 April 1499 reveals, it was a gift from Il Moro himself in recognition of the artist's services. Leonardo was very attached to this property – in part because he hoped ownership would guarantee him the status of a citizen of Milan. In spite of his peregrinations, he kept himself regularly informed about the property and even made some sketches of it. He is known to have visited the property in 1508, when it was returned to him after initial confiscation by the King of France following the fall of Ludovico. Finally, in the will he drew up on 23 April 1519, Leonardo mentions not only his famous works of art but also the vineyard, leaving half each to his faithful servants Giovan Batista de' Vilanis and Salaj; the latter built himself a home there.

In spite of numerous changes to the surrounding urban fabric, the vineyard remained miraculously intact for centuries. Art historian Luca Beltrami was amazed when he visited it in 1920, managing to take a few snapshots just before it was bulldozed to make way for new housing. The architect Portaluppi, who oversaw the restoration of the Casa degli Atellani in the 1920s, wanted to preserve in the garden "a tree-filled rectangle of ground where, defying the passage of time, there is still a pergola of vines, the remnants of Leonardo's vineyard". However, a fire in a painter's studio reduced those remnants to ashes.

The garden in which the last traces of Leonardo's vineyards survived until so recently is now private. However, from the street you can glance through into the fine porticoed courtyard and see some of what remains of the old house.

Garden of Casa degli Atellana. 65, Corso Magenta. Public transport: MM1 Cadorna; tram 16.
Private garden not open to the public.

BELL-TOWER
OF SANTISSIMA TRINITÀ CHURCH

⓫

9, Via Giannone
• Public transport: MM2 Moscova; tram 3, 4, 7, 12, 14; bus 43, 57

A medieval bell-tower in a modern courtyard

Within the courtyard of a building giving onto Via Giannone can be seen a free-standing bell-tower that dates from 1230 – all that is left of the old church of Santissima Trinità, which was bulldozed in 1968.

This bell-tower, bought by a private individual after it had been spared demolition, now belongs to a company whose offices are located within the building (the owner was one of the founders of the FAI*). Together with the church, it once stood in the heart of what was called the Borgo degli Scigolatt (Market Garden District) and is nowadays better known as "Chinatown".

It was in this church administered by the Order of Humble Friars, who also had their monastery here, that Brother Bonvesin de la Riva was appointed provost in

1291. Author of a famous treatise on Milan – *De Magnibus Urbis Mediolani* – he was also the first to introduce within the Roman Catholic world the practice of ringing the Angelus bell in the evening. In 1608 Cardinal Federico Borromeo ordered that the monastery foundation become a parish church; then, just eight years later, a fire destroyed that building, leaving only the bell-tower intact. However, the church was subsequently rebuilt, with the tower heightened in order to house an additional bell. In 1968 the administrators of the building agreed to a property development project that involved the demolition of the church and the construction of apartment blocks. The city's Superintendent of Architectural Heritage found out only just in time to save the bell-tower, but was too late to save the monastery buildings.

*Fondo per l'Ambiente Italiano (Italian National Trust).

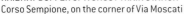

RAILWAY BUFFER OF A GHOST TRAIN STATION
Corso Sempione, on the corner of Via Moscati
• Public transport: tram 1

In the middle of the dividing strip that runs along the centre of Corso Sempione there is a long-abandoned railway buffer. This "shock absorber" is a genuine piece of industrial archaeology because it bears witness to the presence here of a long-gone railway station on the line from Milan to Gallarate. In 1877 Piazza Sempione was also home to the terminus on the famous horse-drawn tramway linking Milan and Saronno.

GIORGIO DE CHIRICO FOUNTAIN

Parco Sempione (Triennale Gardens)
Piazza Castello-Piazza Sempione
• Public transport: MM1 Cadorna, Cairoli; MM2 Lanza, Cadorna; bus 43, 50, 57, 58, 61; tram 1, 2, 4, 12, 14 19, 29/30 • Open November to February 6.30am–8pm; March to April 6.30am–9pm; May 6.30am–10pm; June to September 6.30am–11.30pm; October 6.30am–9pm

The Mysterious Baths of de Chirico

The enigmatic fountain that Giorgio de Chirico designed for Parco Sempione in 1973 was long abandoned to neglect and the action of the elements. However, in 2008 it was restored and can now be seen it all its original splendour in the Triennale Gardens.

Created for the *Contatto Arte/Città* exhibition that was a part of the 15th Milan Triennale, these *Bagni Misteriosi* were donated to the city by the artist himself. De Chirico, born at Volos (Greece), was 85 at the time and in this work offered a surrealist view of the sea he loved so much. Within the sinuous enclosure of a low wall are two bathers, a fish, a large brightly coloured swan, a coloured hemisphere, a source of water and a cabin raised on piles. The curved interior is painted to simulate the flow of water.

The entire structure was made in Vicenza stone, a limestone rich in shell fossils, with the company Marmi Vicentini di Chiampo taking only thirty-five days to complete the work. However, the figures of the fish and the two bathers were carved by de Chirico himself.

Nowadays, the fish – comparable to the one in the 1934 painting *Nuotatore misterioso* – is to be seen at the Fondazione Giorgio e Isa de Chirico. The *Two Bathers* – now considered among de Chirico's finest work – have been moved to the new Museo del Novecento at Arengario. Both pieces will be replaced here by copies.

At present, the bizarre fountain is outdoors, as the original design intended. However, it is likely that it will be enclosed within a clear display case to protect it from the weather, Vicenza limestone being particularly friable.

NEARBY

OPEN-AIR MUSEUM

The gardens which how house the *Bagni Misteriosi* were designed in 1933 by Giovanni Muzio and were intended as the entrance to the Triennale building. They are now home to a number of works of art, forming a sort of Open Air Museum. These pieces include Pinuccio Sciola's *Pietra Sonora*; Gaetano Pesce's *Le Signore*, rounded forms in bronze where you can also sit down; the Mendini brothers' *Ebdomero*, which resembles a dinosaur head; Ettore Sottsass's *Sassi nel parco*; and various other installations in which architects and designers reinterpret the notion of "furnishing open space".

STUDIO-MUSEO ACHILLE CASTIGLIONI

27, Piazza Castello
• Open for guided tours by appointment only, Tuesday to Friday, 10am, 11am, 12 noon
• Appointments: Tel. 02 8053606 or info@achillecastiglioni.it
• Public transport: MM1 Cairoli, Cadorna; bus 61

In the workshop of a creative mind

This studio has not changed since Achille Castiglioni (1918–2002) worked here on his famous design projects, which included lamps (*Arco, Taccia, Parentesi* and *Lampadina*), chairs (*T 12 Palini*), stools (*Mezzadro*), armchairs (*Sanluca*), coffee pots (*Pitagora*), hospital beds (*Omsa*) and sets of cutlery (*Dry*). However, the design of which he himself was most proud was the simple *VLM* electric switch, which is now to be found in all Italian homes. A good fourteen of Castiglioni's creations are on display at the New York MoMA, and others are to be found in museums throughout the world.

When the designer died, his heirs signed an agreement with the Milan Triennale to transform his working studio into a public museum, which would also serve as an archive. Guided by Castiglioni's wife or perhaps one of his daughters, you can now stroll for an hour around the workshop of this creative mind, inspecting sketches and original studies and discovering how some of his best ideas took shape. The material on display includes the series of improbable objects which Castiglioni collected throughout his life, using them to illustrating the wonderful courses on aspects of design which he taught first at Turin Polytechnic, then at Milan Polytechnic. The visit takes in all four rooms of the studio: one containing prototypes and scale models, one reserved for drawing equipment and various curiosities, one with collections from various sources, and finally the meeting-room which now houses an array of objects illustrating a long period in the history of design.

GIFT ROLL OF TOILET PAPER

At the end of the tour you can sign the visitors' book or leave a comment. Sometimes you might even be presented with a gift: a roll of toilet paper. It isn't a joke: this original gift contains a rolled-up "parchment" illustrating all Achille Castiglioni's creations. In itself this is a remarkable example of the philosophy that the designer championed throughout his career: whatever object he created, "function" always took precedence over "form".

"COLUMN OF INFAMY" PLAQUE

Castello Sforzesco
Piazza Sempione
• Public transport: MM1 Cairoli
• Open 6.30am–8pm (longer opening hours in summer)

A terrible story

In the Portico dell'Elefante within the castle's ceremonial courtyard is the seventeenth-century plaque that stood at the base of the so-called "Column of Infamy". This is associated with a terrible story that reveals how fear and fanaticism can transform civilised people into killers impervious to reason. The incident was also recounted by Manzoni in 1849.

When the Black Death swept through in Milan in 1630, rumours spread that it was the work of so-called *untori*. Supposedly paid by foreign powers determined to bring down the Duchy of Milan, these figures were said to spread an oily substance upon walls and doors that served to transmit the disease (*untori* comes from the Italian verb *ungere* meaning "to spread", "to anoint"). Hysteria reached such a point that someone simply seen leaning against a wall could be taken for an *untore* and then roughed up or even killed. This happened to the Commissioner for Health himself, Guglielmo Piazza, who was accused by two women of wiping his hands across a wall and then admitted – under torture – to being an *untore*, naming his barber, Gian Giacomo Mora, as his accomplice. At the time, barbers were often barber-surgeons, and Mora's shop in Corso di Porta Ticinese proved to be full of creams and unguents he used in his work, all of which were taken for means of spreading the disease. Arrested and subjected to the most blood-curdling torture, Mora too hoped to save his life by confessing; but in doing so, he signed his own death warrant. Both he and Piazza were taken to Piazza Vetra, where they were broken on the wheel, left on public display for six hours (as a warning to other *untori*) and then burnt alive; their ashes were cast into the River Vetra, which flowed nearby. The barber's house was demolished and in its place the granite "Column of Infamy" was set as a perpetual reminder of the evil of those who had engineered the plague. On a wall alongside was a plaque recalling each of

the tortures to which the two men had been subjected. However, over time, the column came to symbolise not the infamy of the two unfortunate victims but rather the savagery of those who had tortured and killed them. In 1778, the column itself was removed and destroyed, whilst the plaque remained in place until 1803. Now Mora is commemorated by a plaque and sculpture at the site of his barber's shop (see p. 215).

BAS-RELIEF OF AN INDECOROUS YOUNG GIRL ⓱

Civiche Raccolte d'Arte (City Art Collections)
Castello Sforzesco
Piazza Castello
• Public transport: MM 1 Cairoli, Cadorna; tram 1, 4, 19; bus 50, 58, 61
• Open Tuesday to Sunday, 9.30am–5.30pm

A girl shaving her pudenda

A depiction of a young girl shaving her pudenda is not often found among works of ancient art. However, there is no doubt about what is depicted in the twelfth-century bas-relief that was once clearly visible on the outer façade of the old Porta Vittoria city gateway, now to be seen in Room VI of the Museo d'Arte Antica within Castello Sforzesco.

Originally, Porta Vittoria was known as Porta Tosa (*tosa* = young girl in Milanese dialect) or Porta Tonsa (*tonsa* = shaven), both nicknames clearly due to this bas-relief; the names in fact even persisting after, in the sixteenth century, St Carlo Borromeo had insisted that the offending image be removed. The gateway only became Porta Vittoria much later, to commemorate the victory over the Austrians after they had been driven out of the city.

Shown within a classical arcade, the young girl is dressed in a long robe raised to expose herself. Her hair is gathered in a chignon by a crown, which led the Milanese to identify her as the wife of Frederick I Barbarossa, delighted to have any excuse to mock the emperor. However, the girl may simply have been a prostitute, given that the City Council of the day encouraged prostitutes to shave their pubic hair for hygienic reasons.

Some have argued that the image served an apotropaic function, intended to ward off evil spirits. According to this reading, the girl is the goddess Flora, exposing her pregnant belly as a symbol of fertility.

One further theory associates this bas-relief with the legend of *la sconcia fanciulla* (the brazen girl) who, when the forces of Frederick I Barbarossa were besieging Milan in 1162, went up onto the fortifications, stripped naked in front of the Germans and then began to trim her pubic hair with a pair of scissors, oblivious to the arrows that whizzed by her ears. This humiliating taunt was as courageous as it was futile: Frederick's forces captured the city soon afterwards and razed substantial parts of it to the ground.

BELL OF THE HOUSE OF SAVOY

Castello Sforzesco
Piazza Castello
• Public transport: MM1 Cairoli-Cadorna; tram 1, 4, 19; bus 50, 58, 61
• Open Tuesday to Sunday, 9.30am–5.30pm

> *The only monument recalling the brief rule of the House of Savoy in Lombardy*

The sole monument that recalls the brief rule of the House of Savoy in Lombardy is a bell.

After the death of Charles II of Spain in 1706, Milan would for ninety years pass under Austrian rule, which ended with the arrival of Napoleon. There was, however, a brief interruption to that period of Habsburg supremacy: for three short years, from 1733 to 1736, the city was governed by the Kingdom of Sardinia.

The bell, originally located in Torre di Bona (Bona Tower), was used by the castle's defenders to sound the alarm in times of danger, but was damaged by a cannonball when the forces of Carlo Emanuele III of Savoy were besieging Milan. Then, after the city was taken, the interim governor of the castle, Marchese Vittore-Amadeo de Seyssel, decided to have the damaged bell recast, entrusting the famous Milan bell caster, Bartolomeo Bozzo, with the task.

The new bell is decorated with garlands, sacred figures and the armorial bearings of the Marchese d'Aix and the family of his bride, Princess Pozzo della Cisterna. The Latin inscription recounts the history of the bell and its restoration in 1734, together with the signature of the master caster. The first two lines, at the top of the bell, might be translated as follows: "The French castle having been taken in assault by the Sardinian troops and then rebuilt on its own ruins, this [bell], which had been damaged by a missile, is now dedicated to Carlo Emanuele." Beneath, the text continues: "In the name of the King of Sardinia, the superintendent of the castle ordered that it be remade on 30 October 1734", which is followed by "The Work of Bartolomeo Bozzo".

MASTER BELL CASTER IN GREAT DEMAND

Bartolomeo Bozzo was one of the most highly-respected bell casters in Milan. He worked for most of the eighteenth century, from 1723 to 1795, establishing his reputation thanks to the sonority of his bells. He made some of the most famous in Milan, some of which bear his name (in the old spelling of "Bartollomeo Bozzo"). These include the bells of the old public clock of the Brera; the bells of the clock on the Palazzo dei Giurisconsulti in Piazza Mercanti, one was which was made by his son Luigi and is signed "Bozzi"; and a bell in the basilica of Sant'Ambrogio, which bears the Latin signature "Bozzius". Other Bozzo bells are to be found in Monza, in Villa Reale cathedral, in the monastery of Morimondo, in the *Torrazzo* (Big Bell Tower) of Cremona cathedral and at the sanctuary of Madonna della Fontana in Sannazzaro de' Burgondi.

PENTIMENTI IN THE RONDANINI *PIETÀ* ⑲

Castello Sforzesco
Museo d'Arte Antica
Piazza Castello
• Public transport: MM1 Cairoli-Cadorna; tram 1, 4, 19; bus 50, 58, 61
• Open Tuesday to Sunday, 9.00am–5.30pm

> *An incomplete Pietà: Michelangelo's pentimenti*

Most people are not even aware of its existence, and even those who do know it sometimes do not see the *pentimenti* in this unfinished work. The Rondanini *Pietà* is the last known work by Michelangelo, carved when the artist was 90 years old and approaching death. In a space designed by the BBPR architectural studio, it now stands in the last room of the castle's Museo d'Arte Antica, the final masterpiece of the collection.

First mention of the work comes in two letters of 1564, the year of Michelangelo's death, written by Daniele da Volterra, the master's pupil, to Giorgio Vasari and Leonardo Buonarroti respectively. These give an inventory of goods taken at the artist's death and mention "the half-begun work of Christ with another figure above, attached together, sketched in but not finished".

The marble sculpture depicts the Deposition from the Cross, with Christ unusually shown borne up by Mary herself in a vertical position. But one of the most interesting and less evident aspects of this work is that, given it was left unfinished, you can still see the *pentimenti* very clearly. For example, on the left, Christ's right arm is entirely detached from his body – the result of a *pentimento* that has yet to be concealed. On the left, opposite the Virgin's veil, you can see the eye, eyebrow and hint of a nose that form the sketched-in beginnings of a face turning sideways.

Although still working on the piece, Michelangelo – who felt death approaching – in 1561 gave the sculpture to his servant, Antonio del Francese. All trace of the work was then lost for two centuries, until – in 1807 – it turned up in a list of goods belonging to Marchese Rondanini of Rome. It was valued at only 30 *scudi*, revealing how little understanding there then was of what is now considered Michelangelo's most dramatic and moving masterpiece. Palazzo Rondanini and the collections it housed were then sold to the Counts Sanseverino-Vimercati, with Milan City Council acquiring the *Pietà* for Castello Sforzesco in 1952, thanks to funds raised through a public appeal. The restoration to remove the yellowish-brown patina left by dust and chemical residues was completed in 2004, thus bringing out the full complexity of the work on the piece. One last curiosity: the marble sculpture stands on a funeral stele dating from the first century AD.

LEONARDO DA VINCI AT CASTELLO SFORZESCO

It was Lorenzo il Magnifico, lord of Florence, who convinced Leonardo to go to Milan as a sort of artistic ambassador of the Tuscan city. The 40-year-old artist probably agreed to go because he had not been included in the group of Florentines whom the pope had summoned to Rome in 1480 to fresco the walls of the Sistine Chapel (an omission perhaps due to the charge of sodomy, subsequently dropped, made against Leonardo a few years earlier). In a letter to Ludovico il Moro — effective ruler of Milan thanks to his position as his nephew's guardian — Leonardo offered his services as a military engineer, architect, musician and — only last — as a painter and sculptor. Il Moro welcomed the offer and in 1482 Leonardo moved to Castello Sforzesco, where he remained for the next eighteen years, until French forces drove Ludovico from the city. Leonardo was in little demand in Milan as a military engineer, but as an artist he was called upon to create the luxury items and entertainments which Ludovico wanted as a means of glorifying his power. For Il Moro and his family, Leonardo decorated feasts and banquets, designed marvellous animated "sets" for theatrical performances, invented games, composed witty mottoes, improvised verse while accompanying himself on the lyre and devised all sorts of *mirabilia* to amaze the court and its guests. One of these creations was actually a water-powered alarm clock, with the sleeper being pulled by the feet until he awoke. Then there was a chemical concoction that was said to transform water into wine, and a special device for the duchess's bathroom ...

Little or nothing of all this work remains. Fortunately for us what has survived are some of the most amazing masterpieces Leonardo ever painted. *The Virgin of the Rocks* (now in the Louvre, Paris, with a later version in the National Gallery, London) was the fruit of the first commission the artist received in the city, which did not actually come from the court itself: the painting was created to be the altarpiece of the Chapel of the Conception in the (later demolished) church of San Francesco Grande at Porta Vercellina. There are also a number of "court" portraits: *The Lady with Ermine*, a portrait of Cecilia Gallerani, Il Moro's mistress (now in Cracow); *Portrait of a Musician* (Pinacoteca Ambrosiana), which may depict Franchino Gaffurio, chapel master at the cathedral and the most famous of the court musicians; *Portrait of a Lady*, whose subject was another woman dear to Il Moro's heart (perhaps Luria Crivelli, another of his mistresses). But the high point of Leonardo's artistic achievements in Milan is undoubtedly *The Last Supper*, which may have been painted outside the castle but was actually commissioned by Ludovico il Moro. Fervently devout, he had a particular devotion to the church of Santa Maria delle Grazie, which he intended to be his own mausoleum. Leonardo was also involved in various restructuring projects within the castle, including the decoration of the Sala delle Asse and of the small rooms of the Ponticella (see p. 101). He was also commissioned to create a large equestrian monument to Francesco Sforza, to be placed upon the ravelin at the entrance to the castle. Shortly after beginning this, Leonardo, finding himself in difficulty with his work on the horse and on the Ponticella, applied for payment of the two years' arrears owed to him and his assistants. Short of cash himself, Il Moro settled the account by giving the artist the vineyard at the Casa degli Atellani. Having completed the clay model of the horse, Leonardo then had to interrupt work on the equestrian monument: the bronze required to cast the statue was being used to make cannons to fight the advancing French army. When those troops arrived in the city, they used the clay model for target practice – and it then took another 500 years before Leonardo's horse was realised.

Leonardo himself was not disturbed by the arrival of the French, for whom he later worked. However, he did reflect painfully upon the end of the reign of a man who seemed destined to conquer Europe and ultimately lost "his state, his goods and his freedom, and nothing went as he wanted". Among the work Leonardo left unfinished here was the project for the complete rebuilding of Santa Maria delle Grazie.

THE MYSTERIOUS DRAGON FOUNTAIN

Cortile della Fontana
Castello Sforzesco
Museo d'Arte Antica
Piazza Castello
• Public transport: MM1 Cairoli-Cadorna; tram 1, 4, 19; bus 50, 58, 61
• Open from Tuesday to Sunday, 9am–5.30pm

> *One of three copies of the original fountain*

The emerald-green moss that grows undisturbed in the castle's small Fountain Courtyard makes this a very atmospheric place – which, unfortunately, can only be visited by those who pay for admission to the Museo d'Arte Antica. The courtyard owes its name to a fountain surmounted by the Visconti dragon (see Visconti Crest, p. 109). There is a curious and little-known story behind this piece.

Given that Piazza Martiri della Libertà in Seregno has an identical terracotta statue (minus dragon, which was removed recently), the issue as to which was the original and which the copy has been debated at length.

In fact, both are copies. The original – in white marble – was commissioned by the Sforza for the Castle of Vigevano and then transferred to Bellinzona, a Milanese stronghold up to the year 1500. Subsequently, the fountain was used as a holy water stoup in the Collegiate Church of Saints Peter and Stephen in that town, where it still stands. During work on the restructuring of the castle, Luca Beltrami had casts of that original fountain taken and then used them to produce at least three terracotta copies: the one in the castle, the one in Seregno and a third in the courtyard of Villa Mirabello (see p. 319), a Visconti country residence.

Beltrami originally set up the castle fountain within the Main Courtyard; but then, in 1953, it was dismantled and moved to its present site. The dragon was not part of the original. As can be seen from drawings which once belonged to him, it was created for the copies by Beltrami himself.

NEARBY

THE ONE ORIGINAL WINDOW IN CASTELLO SFORZESCO
In the Cortile della Fontana you can see a large terracotta-framed window. This is the one original window in the entire castle, having survived war, rebuilding work and alterations. When architect Luca Beltrami undertook the restoration of the castle in the late nineteenth century, he used this window as a model on which to base the reconstruction of others.

BRAMANTE'S BRIDGE

Castello Sforzesco
Piazza Castello
• Public transport: MM1 Cairoli-Cadorna; tram 1, 4, 19; bus 50, 58, 61
• Open occasionally on prior booking (Ad Artem 02 6596937); the interior
rooms (if open) are included in the museum visit

> *Discovering*
> *the castle's*
> *"Black Rooms"*

O nly rarely open to the public, the *Ponticella* (Small Bridge) is a covered way to the right of the castle; its twin-arch span across the moat serves to link the duke's private apartments with the *Ghirlanda*. The body of the structure already existed at the time of Francesco Sforza, but it was Ludovico il Moro – declared duke in 1494 – who had it extended and refurbished. The commission for the work went to Bramante, the famous architect from Urbino who, together with Leonardo, was one of the Court's most esteemed artists.

The first attribution of the bridge to Bramante was made by his pupil, Cesare Cesariano, in 1521, but doubt was later cast on the claim. It is now believed that even if Bramante did not carry out the work, the actual design ideas were his.

Largely rebuilt in the nineteenth century by Beltrami, the *Ponticella* has a sequence of three small rooms that give onto a small architraved portico whose slim columns are surmounted by capitals that are vaguely Corinthian in style. The inside wall of the portico – which can be seen from outside – has reproductions of ancient graffiti work.

The three rooms (at the moment closed to the public) are part of the castle's Museo d'Arte Antica (Rooms IX and X), with access directly from Leonardo's *Sala delle Asse*. In documents relating to the Sforza family, they are referred to as the *Salette Negre* (Black Rooms), because Il Moro spent fifteen days of mourning here after his beloved wife, Beatrice d'Este, died giving birth to their third child at the age of only 22.

In 1495, the three rooms were decorated under the supervision of Ambrogio Ferrari. Extant documents suggest that the decoration was in part designed by Leonardo. The rooms now contain fourteen lunettes with portraits of members of the Sforza family by an unknown artist. These were painted in the years 1525 to 1530 and originally come from the Casa degli Atellani. Experts argue that most of these portraits bear little or no resemblance to their subjects; the only exceptions, to some extent, are the portraits of Ludovico il Moro (whose white hair indicates the precocious ageing he suffered after the death of his wife) and of his sons Francesco II and Massimiliano. The rooms also contain works of sixteenth-century Lombard sculpture.

DEVIL IN THE SETTALA COLLECTION

Civiche Raccolte d'Arte
Castello Sforzesco
Piazza Castello
• Public transport: MM1 Cairoli, Cadorna; tram 1, 4, 19; bus 50, 58, 61
• Open Tuesday to Sunday, 9.30am–5.30pm

A seventeenth-century mechanical devil

" **A** cabinet from which suddenly erupts the terrifying face of a devil, which starts to leer, to stick out its tongue and to spit in the faces of passers-by, all accompanied by the fearful din of iron chains and wheels, perfectly suited to instil terror."

This is how, in a letter of 17 July 1739, the French traveller Charles de Brosses describes one of the star items in the Settala Collection, part of which now features in the Civiche Raccolte d'Arte at Castello Sforzesco.

This contraption, a clockwork automaton with the face of a demon, combines a sixteenth-century torso – perhaps originally from a "Christ at the Column" – with a wind-up mechanism that powers the movement of the turning head, rolling eyes and lolling tongue, as well as emitting some sort of inarticulate noise. The seventeenth-century description also mentions a collar and horns, but these are now lost.

Pietro Scarabelli's catalogue of the Museo Settala, published in Tortona

in 1666, contains an etching by Cesare Fiori depicting a "View of the Museum". Here you can see one large room divided into three galleries laid out as theatrical sets with thousands of objects, stuffed animals, pictures, boxes, vases, etc. On the right side of the image, this "mechanical devil" is clearly visible in a niche.

The *Wunderkammer* (cabinet of curiosities) owned by Manfredo Settala, a priest from San Nazzaro in Brolo, was one of the most famous in Italy. After Napoleonic looting and bomb damage, most of what remains is now in the Pinacoteca Ambrosiana.

AUSONIUS STONE

Castello Sforzesco
• Public transport: MM1 Cairoli-Cadorna; tram 1, 4, 19; bus 50, 58, 61
• Open daily 7am–6pm (summer 7am–7pm)

A Roman "welcome"

HEUS VIATOR! (Hail, O Traveller!). These words of welcome have a long history. They feature on what is known as the "Ausonius Stone", a wall plaque half-hidden within the interior of the castle, in a narrow passageway that runs from opposite the entrance to the museums towards the Rocchetta. The greeting is important because the poet with whom it is associated – Decimus Magnus Ausonius – is the author of the sole surviving description of fourth-century Mediolanum, which was then capital of the Roman Empire in the West.

In his *Ordo urbium nobilium* (Order of Noble Cities), which dates from around AD 388, Ausonius praises Milan in the terms reproduced on this plaque, which might be translated as follows: "Everything is wonderful in Milan: the abundance of all things; the number and elegance of the houses; the affable nature of the inhabitants; the joyful life which is led there; the beauty of

the site, which extends within a double ring of walls; the passion of the people; the circus, together with the majestic theatre and arcades; the temples; the Palatine castle and the rich Mint; the walls ringed with Baths dedicated to Hercules; the peristyles decorated with marble friezes; the palisaded ramparts enclosed with a moat. All of these things excel in beauty and magnificence, so that they bear comparison with Rome itself."

This stone plaque dates not from the time of Ausonius but from the sixteenth century. It used to be set within the façade of the Scuole Palatine that once stood on the site of the present-day Piazza Mercanti, but was destroyed by fire in 1664. When those school buildings were rebuilt, a statue was erected there dedicated to Ausonius (now missing an index finger) and a copy of his paean to Mediolanum.

ARGUS FRESCO

The Treasury (or Sala Luca Beltrami)
Castello Sforzesco
Piazza Castello
• Public transport: MM1 Cairoli-Cadorna; tram 1, 4, 19; bus 50, 58, 61
• Open during temporary exhibitions
(information at www.milanocastello.it/ita/mostre.html)

*A gem
hidden away
for 500 years*

Walking west from the courtyard of La Rocchetta, you come to Torre Castellana, on the ground floor of which is a superb fresco of Argus that has survived unseen for 500 years. Nowadays it is only open to the public on certain occasions. Commissioned by Ludovico il Moro – undoubtedly some time before 1493 – this fresco is located above the door that links the two small rooms of the Treasury. During the restoration of the vault here, the face in the fresco was damaged and that is why the masterpiece was covered up five years later. However, it was thanks to this cover that the rest of the fresco could emerge in perfect condition during the restoration work in 1893.

The figure with the damaged face has been identified as Argus, the mythological Titan said to have had one hundred eyes, fifty of which remained open while he slept. The two medallions in fake bas-relief depict two episodes from the Argus myth (*Mercury lulling Argus to sleep* and *Mercury with the body of the murdered Argus*). The peacocks to either side of the fresco are also a clear reference to the myth: the goddess Hera was said to have scattered the eyes of Argus across the bird's tail after the Titan's death. On the frame beneath the medallions there is a legend, now illegible, which has been reconstructed as follows: "I restored to Argus all the eyes which the gods took from him/That he might be a vigilant guardian and come to reinforce this anguine castle" (*anguine* – "serpent-like" – was a reference to the serpent

that figured in the armorial bearings of the Sforza family). However, it is difficult to understand why a figure who met such a tragic fate should have been chosen as the guardian of the castle's treasures. Thus it has been suggested that the figure is actually Janus, the mythical founder of Milan who was supplied to watch over the city's fate. Another mystery concerns the artist who painted the fresco. On its discovery the work was attributed to Leonardo da Vinci, then to Donato Bramante. Today the latter is simply credited with the design, and the actual fresco is said to be the work of his disciple Bramantino.

SYMBOLS ON THE DRINKING FOUNTAIN IN THE DUCAL COURTYARD

Castello Sforzesco
• Public transport: MM1 Cairoli-Cadorna; tram 1, 4, 19; bus 50, 58, 61
• Open daily, 7am–6pm (7am–7pm in summer)

> **Emblems of the Visconti-Sforza on a drinking fountain in the castle**

On the stone slab of an attractive drinking fountain fixed to the wall in the Ducal Courtyard of Castello Sforzesco are engraved five different symbols. Comprising three interlinked rings, a sun, a dog, a dove and a horse's bit, these apparently unrelated images are in fact the blazons (*imprese*) of individual members of the illustrious Visconti-Sforza family. The three rings adorned with a diamond, the emblem of Cabrino Fondulo, Lord of Cremona, are undoubtedly an allusion to his meeting with Sigismund of Hungary and the antipope John XXIII, which took place in Milan in 1414 when those two eminent figures were on their way to the Council of Constance via Mantua. Perhaps this symbol of a triple alliance was intended to suggest official recognition of his, as yet unconsolidated, dynasty by the highest authorities of the day. The radiant sun was the emblem of Gian Galeazzo Visconti and signified that, like the day star, the Duke of Milan was a source of life; casting light upon darkness (that is, evil), the sun was also a symbol of justice. Confirmation that the duke had achieved such an elevated status is also to be seen in the apse window of the cathedral, where the image of the radiant sun reappears. The emblem stressed that Gian Galeazzo was not to be considered an ordinary mortal: like a true monarch, he was divinely appointed and thus identified with characteristics associated with the deity.The dog (actually a greyhound or *veltro*, a medieval term for a hunting dog) is shown resting under a pine tree, its leash held by the hand of God. The motto reads QUIETUM NEMO IMPUNE LACESSET (Woe betide he who disturbs such hard-won peace). This is one of the emblems of Francesco Sforza, who married Bianca Maria, the only daughter of Filippo Maria Visconti, and thus perpetuated the family line. The peace referred to is undoubtedly the Peace of Lodi, which was signed on 9 April 1454 and brought to an end war between Milan, Florence and Venice. The small dove (sometimes superimposed upon a radiant sun) holds in its beak a cartouche bearing the motto À BON DROIT. This emblem expresses a vow for the peaceful and righteous exercise of power (*à bon droit*); the phrase itself reflects that used by Petrarch when addressing the young Gian Galeazzo. It was Bonna di Savoia, wife of Galeazzo Maria Visconti, who chose this symbol to adorn her chamber (Room XIII in the castle, as known as the "Dove Room"). The motto with the horse's bit reads ICH VERGIES NICHT (I forget nothing). This, too, was a symbol of Gian Galeazzo and reflected the fact that he had often to "take the bit" from his tyrannical uncle, Barnaba Visconti, whom he eventually overcame and imprisoned after suffering endless affronts. At the top of the fountain are two quinces (*cotogne* in Italian) which are a reference to the city of Cotignola, the birthplace of the Sforza dynasty.

WHAT IS AN *IMPRESA*?

Whereas heraldic blazons were symbols of an entire family – for example, the man-eating serpent that was the symbol of first the Visconti, then the Sforza – an *impresa* was the emblem of an individual member of that family, perhaps referring to a specific exploit (*impresa*) that was associated with him.

Such personal emblems first appeared in the twelfth century, so that the knights at tournament could be clearly identified.

They comprise two parts, a "body" (which could be the image of an animal, a plant, an object or one of the four elements) and a "soul", the legend or motto, which was usually written in a foreign language so that only the cognoscenti could read it.

Perhaps referring to a victory in the field of battle, an amorous conquest or certain personal qualities and traits, the emblem was intended to exalt the standing of the figure with whom it was associated.

EMBLEMS OF THE VISCONTI AND SFORZA FAMILIES

The various *imprese* associated with members of the Visconti and Sforza families refer to individuals who may have lived as much as two centuries apart, but were often depicted together in order to underline the continuity of the ducal family. In the courtyard of La Rocchetta, various such symbols embellish the capitals of the colonnade. Among others there is the *lion galé* (helmeted lion; *galea* being Latin for "helmet") which was the emblem of Galeazzo II Visconti but was later appropriated by Galeazzo Maria Visconti for himself. It is intended as a reference to someone who depends on the will of another and thus must restrain and conceal his fury – just like a helmeted lion. The motto with this emblem reads *Ich Off* (I hope), the implied continuation being "to return to my homeland": Galeazzo II spent ten years in exile. The same motto can also be seen on a modern blazon (on the Filarete Tower) which brings together the helmet and the Visconti serpent.

Another emblem – this time symbolising "temperance" – comprises three red-hot brands with buckets hanging from them. This was intended to indicate that a cold mind (the water in the buckets) could restrain excessive ardour. Galeazzo obtained this emblem after a duel with the French Connétable de Bourbon; thereafter, he also added a glowing brand and two buckets to the blazon of the helmeted lion.

Two heavenly hands hold a single heart in the image that represents the arranged marriage of Galeazzo Maria Sforza and the rich Bonna di Savoia, sister-in-law to the King of France. In another emblem two similar hands are holding a sieve of the type used to separate flour and bran; the motto reads *Tale a ti Quale a mi* (This for you, That for me). It is said that Bonna herself requested this so that it would be clear to her serially unfaithful husband that she might repay him in the same coin.

An emblem adopted by Ludovico il Moro comprises two lighthouses or "beacons" raised upon two rocks separated by a stormy sea (perhaps the port of Genoa). The motto reads *Tal trabalio mes places por tal thesaurus non perder* (I am happy to make such efforts in order not to lose such a treasure) – as if the duke were making it clear that he enjoyed going into battle in order to maintain his hard-won power.

NORTH-EAST

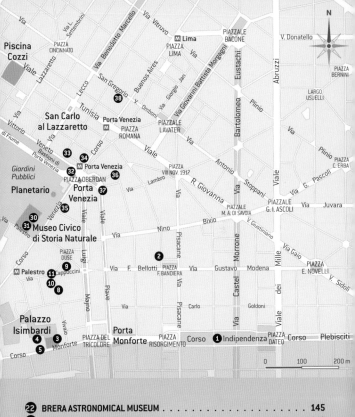

STATUE OF PINOCCHIO   ❶

Gardens in Corso Indipendenza (junction with Via Ciro Menotti)
• Public transport: bus 54, 61

> *A forgotten Pinocchio as a little boy*

Overlooked by one and all, a small fountain in Corso Indipendenza is decorated with a very touching statue of Pinocchio transformed into a little boy.

Unveiled on 19 May 1956, this stands alongside the playground of the Corso Indipendenza gardens and used to be an intriguing delight for children playing there. The statue was donated to the city by the Milanese arts association *Famiglia Artisica* and is the work of Attilio Fagioli, a sculptor who came from the birthplace of Pinocchio's creator, Carlo Collodi. The work shows Pinocchio the little boy looking on with satisfaction at his past, the puppet lying on the ground. The man behind the project for the fountain was the

poet Antonio Negri, who supplied an inscription that spells out the educational aims of the work: "How funny I was when I was a puppet. And you reading this, are you sure you have overcome the puppet that lives in you?"

In fact the statue was meant as a symbolic depiction of the transition from childhood to maturity. Regardless of what you might think of that intention today, it's true that very few children now wonder about the sculpture or the significance of the inscription: not only has someone removed the cat from the group and broken off part of Pinocchio's nose, but the fountain, corroded by the elements, is now empty of water.

PINOCCHIO: THE FIRST MASONIC PUPPET

Though not officially recognised, Carlo Collodi's membership in the Freemasons is widely believed to be confirmed by a range of evidence: he started a satirical newspaper entitled *Il Lampione* (The Lamp Post) in 1848, with the express aim of "illuminating all those held in thrall by the shadows"; his participation in the campaigns of Giuseppe Garibaldi, a famous *carbonaro* advocating liberal ideas and undoubtedly a Mason; his close relationship with Mazzini, who was a well-known Mason and of whom Collodi declared himself to be a "passionate disciple". Furthermore, the guiding principles of the Freemasons – *Liberty*, *Equality* and *Fraternity* – are embodied in *The Adventures of Pinocchio*: Liberty, because Pinocchio is a free being, who loves liberty; Equality, because Pinocchio's sole aspiration is to be equal to everyone else, accepting that all are born equal to each other; Fraternity, because this is the feeling that seems to motivate the characters at various points in the story. *Pinocchio* was also immortalised in a film by the American Walt Disney, himself a high-ranking Mason, and embodies the three founding principles of universal freemasonry: freedom of thought and will; psychological and social equality; fraternity between individuals, who can thus achieve universal understanding. More than a simple children's story, *Pinocchio* is an initiatory tale, as is Goethe's *Faust* and Mozart's *The Magic Flute*. It can be read at various levels as a Masonic parable, with the multiple meanings reflecting themes and formulas associated with the stages of initiation. Indeed, it is due to these veiled allusions to an initiatory path that Pinocchio owes its extraordinary success (its sales in twentieth-century Italy were second only to those of *La divina commedia*), for the various stages in the plot offer subliminal echoes of cognitive archetypes. A formidable didactic instrument, *Pinocchio* takes its place alongside the official educational literature of its day. A moral tale deeply imbued with the message of political emancipation, it is one of Tuscan culture's greatest contributions to Freemasonry. Pinocchio is subject to a long course of development. Initially nothing more than a "rough" piece of wood (just like the "rough" stone that all the uninitiated have cut and shape), he must become "polished" (a term which in the Masonic vocabulary means "enlightened"). The very name of Pinocchio derives from *pinolo*, the Italian word for "pine nut", thus there is a connection with pine trees, traditionally associated with Christmas – and Christmas itself is a symbol of the spiritual rebirth that the neophyte will experience when he receives the light of initiation.

Furthermore, it is no coincidence that the central character of the tale, Geppetto, is a carpenter, as was Joseph, the father who raised Jesus Christ. As a carpenter, Geppetto is also a demiurge ("creator", "artisan") in the Platonic and Gnostic sense of the term. A little later in the tale, the Blue Fairy descends from heaven to teach Pinocchio free will, and when he asks if he has finally become a real boy she significantly answers: "No, Pinocchio. The vow of your father Geppetto will not fully come true until you deserve it. Set yourself to the test, with courage, sincerity and passion, and one day you will become a real little boy." This is precisely what is said during Masonic initiation, with regard to apprenticeship and the bearing of responsibility. The voice of the Cricket is definitely that of conscience, urging the puppet to go "to school" – another Masonic symbol for conscience and awareness. The initiation of Pinocchio also comprises a series of trials that involve all four elements: air (the presence of numerous birds in the story, and the puppet's flight on the wings of a dove); earth (the coins buried in the ditch); fire (which burns his feet) and water (with various episodes, right up to the final chapter, involving swimming and drowning). Pinocchio is also prey to "sleep", another Masonic metaphor for the non-activity of the uninitiated; and it is precisely when he is asleep that the Blue Fairy gives him a kiss (a kiss also being part of the Masonic rite of the Templars). When hanged, Pinocchio dies, but he is resuscitated through a purge/purification – that is, by elevating himself to a higher level of initiation. Among the other references to Freemasonry there is the island of industrious bees, which recalls Hiram's Temple of Solomon, with its four hundred pomegranates. That is also the exact number of the small bread buns which the Blue Fairy prepares together with cups of coffee and milk (the colour contrast of black and white is another feature of the Temple and a symbol of the contrast between good and evil). The Cat, the Fox and the Firefly all embody the temptations of an easy and profane life, with limping and lameness being other allusions to Masonic symbols. The puppeteer Stromboli and the Land of Toys again represent the vanities of this world, and Pinocchio's transformation into a donkey reveals he has fallen to the level of beasts. To save himself, he must return to the path of enlightenment. The puppet must find his father/demiurge, but he can only do so after passing through a biblical trial: being swallowed by a whale like Jonah, the central figure in a myth that is fundamental in all the great monotheistic religions and all schools of esotericism. Being reunited with Geppetto, who bears him on his shoulders as he swims through the primary element of water, Pinocchio finally becomes a "real little boy", one of the truly "enlightened".

BUILDING AT 35, VIA POERIO

35, Via Poerio
• Public transport: MM1 Palestro; tram 23, 9/29
• List of other buildings: http://www.robbinsbecher.com/770.html

> *One of twelve copies of number 770 Eastern Parkway, Brooklyn, New York*

Walking down Via Poerio, the cosmopolitan traveller may well do a double take: with its Gothic-style pointed gables and bow windows, the building at number 35 seems to belong in the UK or the Netherlands rather than Milan. Even more incredibly, it is actually one of twelve copies of the building which stands at 770 Eastern Parkway, Brooklyn, New York.

That address became home to Rabbi Yosef Yitzchak Schneersohn, head of the Orthodox Jewish movement Chabad-Lubavitch, after he moved there from a Europe ravaged by the Second World War. Thanks to the zealous efforts of his son-in-law, Rabbi Menachem Mendel Schneerson, who inherited his position as the movement's guide (*Rebbe*), the building at 770 Eastern Parkway became a venerable place of worship. Hence it was decided to reproduce it, more or less faithfully, at various places throughout the world.

At the moment there are twelve such copies. Many are in Israel, but there are others in Argentina, Australia, Brazil and Canada. This one at 35 Via Poerio is the only one in Europe.

Since the destruction of the Second Temple, Italy has produced various important Torah scholars. In 1949, on request from the Jewish community, Rav Yaakov Gansburg was sent to Milan to oversee the provision of kosher food. In 1952 – together with Rav Yaakov Perlow – he supervised the work on the *Mikvè* (bath for ritual ablutions) in Via Guastalla, under the personal direction of the *Rebbe* himself. In 1959, the *Rebbe* then sent his first emissaries to Italy: Rav Gershon Mendel Garelik and his wife. Rav Garelik became rabbi of the Ohel Yaakov synagogue in Via Cellini and initiated the activities of Merkos l'Inyonei Chinuch in Italy. For the first couple of years, Mrs. Garelik taught courses to teenagers and adults, with all the activities of the MLC being held in the young rabbi's home in Via Uberti. Subsequently, a school was opened in the Via Poerio building (it was later moved to Via Macconago) and various branches for cultural activities opened in Milan and elsewhere.

HIDDEN TREASURES OF PALAZZO ISIMBARDI ❸

Palazzo Isimbardi
1, Via Vivaio
• Guided tours on Wednesday at 6pm and Friday at 10am
• Free admission but booking required, at the IAT (Informazione e Accoglienza Turistica) offices, 1, Piazza Castello
• Tel: 02 77402895
• Public transport: MM1 San Babila; bus 54, 61

> **A palazzo only open to the public twice a week**

Palazzo Isimbardi, dating from the sixteenth century, has since 1935 housed the Provincia, Milan's provincial government. However, it is open to the public twice a week – its garden, architecture and numerous works of art making it well worth a visit.

The main courtyard itself is in Renaissance style and still paved in the original brick, together with precious decorations in Candoglia marble (the same as that used for the cathedral). The porch over the main entrance is a colonnaded structure painted with frescoes and adorned with grotesques and depictions of mythological creatures.

On the ground floor are three large seventeenth-century frescoes from a villa in Vaprio d'Adda – attributed to the school of the Varese-born artist Pier Francesco Mazzucchelli – and a sculpture by Francesco Messina depicting Eve. The Sala Pedenovi on this floor contains a large sixteenth-century painting by Bernardino Campi and some precious old clocks from the vast collection of timepieces within the palazzo.

The Italian-style garden features twentieth-century statues depicting some of the activities of the region: industry, irrigation and agriculture. You can also see a relic of the last war, the so-called "Siren Tower" (see p. 121).

Inside again, the monumental staircase leads up to a vestibule containing two large seventeenth-century mappemondes produced by the workshop of Jacopo de' Rossi; there is also a banner in silver and gold thread, which was hand-embroidered in 1927 by the nuns of a secluded religious order. In the following rooms are to be found large Murano glass chandeliers dating from the eighteenth century; a secretaire in inlaid wood by the famous cabinet-maker Giuseppe Maggiolini; sculpture by Enrico Butti and Francesco Barzaghi; valuable paintings by Angelo Trezzini, Giacomo Favretto, Francesco Filippini, Leonardo Bazzaro and other nineteenth-century artists; and twentieth-century paintings by Enrico Prampolini, Carlo Carrà, Raffaele De Grada, Aligi Sassu and Lorenzo Viani.

However, the most important work in the building is still the large (6 by 8 metres) canvas gracing the ceiling of the Sala della Giunta, where the provincial government holds its meetings. Entitled *The Apotheosis of Angelo della Vecchia amidst the Virtues*, it was painted by Giambattista Tiepolo.

"AIR SIREN TOWER"

Garden of Palazzo Isimbardi
1, Via Vivaio
• Guided tours of the palazzo and garden on Wednesday at 6pm and Friday at 10am • The bunker is closed to the public
• Admission free but booking required (IAT – 1, Piazza Castello. Tel: 02 77402895)
• Public transport: MM1 San Babila; bus 54, 61

> *Mussolini's bunker*

Tucked away between the building that houses the Provincial Government of Milan and the Police Headquarters, the garden of Palazzo Isimbardi contains a rather strange concrete construction. Standing some 22 metres high, its pointed roof makes it look rather like a huge pencil. Known as the "Air Siren Tower", this building was an air-raid warning station during the Second World War. Although in part covered by ivy, two locked bomb-proof doors are still visible. The underground explorers who have been allowed to visit the site discovered that a number of the door and window openings still had fragments of decoration (no other air-raid shelter was ever decorated), plus surviving painted signs reading *Bunker Comunicazioni*, *Vietato Fumare* (Smoking Forbidden) and *Meglio Allarmati che Bombardati* (Better Alarmed than Bombed).

This garden was in fact the site of the shelter built in 1943 to protect the authorities should there be an air raid. Legend has it that Benito Mussolini himself spent his last days in Milan here, before attempting to flee in April 1945. Even though this has never been proved, the building has as a result become known as "Mussolini's bunker".

The rectangular-plan two-storey structure could house up to 180 people. It was complete with the standard telephone and telegraph links; ventilation and air filters in case of gas attack (powered by a bicycle if the standard supply failed); a special room reserved for the police chief; and plumbed-in toilets and bathrooms.

OTHER AIR-RAID SHELTERS IN MILAN

Milan has more than 15,000 air-raid shelters, most hidden under buildings or within jointly-owned courtyards (usually the letters "R" or "U.S." served to indicate their presence; see p. 197). Apart from the one in the Palazzo Isimbardi garden, the most important of the above-ground shelters include the tower in Via Adriano, at the edge of the Sesto San Giovanni district. Standing some 35 metres high, this was once occupied by the workers at the Magnetti Marelli factory; since then squatters and vandals have wrecked the interior, but among the junk and rubbish they have left traces of graffiti dating from the Second World War. Other bunkers worthy of mention are the pointed-roof shelter in Via Pitteri, the rounded shelter in Via Mecenate, the shellproof screens in Viale Forlanini and the shelter in Parco Cassina de' Pomm.

SHEET-METAL CAT

43, Corso Monforte
• Public transport: bus 61, 54

> *A curious feline observer*

Passers-by are constantly coming and going along this stretch of Corso Monforte near the administrative centre, yet no one ever seems to notice a small and quiet observer. Tucked away in a basement window, next to the door of number 43, a sheet-metal cat with long whiskers and tail curled around the railing waits patiently.

The Art Nouveau building where the cat is hidden dates from the early twentieth century and its façade is a colourful pot-pourri of brick and blind arches. Look up at the third floor and you can see six figures of women, inspired by medieval designs, painted on the sides of the windows.

Perhaps, like the other decorations, even the cat was a detail added to embellish the house. But, like all its kind, it preferred to be out of the limelight, where only the most curious would find it.

NEARBY:

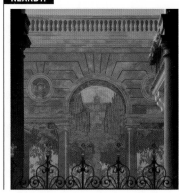

TROMPE-L'OEIL VILLA

If the gate of 7 Via Carlo Pisacane happens to be open, you can glimpse what looks like a colonnade, beyond which a long tree-lined avenue leads to a hilltop villa. It is actually a fine and colourful trompe-l'oeil design, covering the entire wall opposite the gate.

STRETCH OF THE MEDIEVAL CITY WALLS   ❻

7–9, Via San Damiano
• Public transport: MM1 San Babila

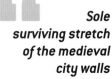

Sole surviving stretch of the medieval city walls

Comprising a base of solid blocks of stone and an upper section of partially overgrown brick, this 30-metre-long stretch of wall is all that remains of the medieval city ramparts built by the military engineer Guiglielmo da Guintellino to protect the city against the forces of Frederick Barbarossa. There is an almost illegible plaque commemorating this.

With the exception of this stretch of wall, all that remains of those

fortifications are two old city gateways: Porta Nuova and Porta Ticinese. However, within Castello Sforzesco you can see the friezes that used to adorn Porta Romana (a city gateway whose remains are to be seen in the basement of two buildings at the junction of Via di Porta Romana and Via Francesco Sforza), as well as the bas-relief of the she-wolf from Porta Orientale (see p. 130).

NEARBY

MILAN'S FIRST LETTERBOX   ❼

To the left of the large doorway to the building which now houses the State Archives but which was once home to the Swiss College is a letterbox. This is not just any old letterbox: as it dates from the Napoleonic era, when this palazzo was the premises of the Senate of the Kingdom of Italy, it is in fact the very first letterbox installed in Milan.

DIALOGUE IN THE DARK

8

Istituto dei Ciechi
7, Via Vivaio
• www.dialogonelbuio.org
• Open Tuesday to Sunday, 6pm–7.15pm
• It is advisable to book: call 02 76394478
• Public transport: MM1 San Babila, Palestro

> *A place in which to experience things as the blind do*

A permanent exhibition within the Milan Institute for the Blind, "Dialogue in the Dark" takes the visitor on an hour-long journey through total darkness, revealing how this transforms such simple experiences as walking in the garden or sipping a cup of coffee. Those who have been through the exhibition say that it has a distinctive effect, changing attitudes to visual perception.

The exhibition is unique in that it is totally unlit. In order to explore the various rooms, visitors have to rely solely on the senses of touch, hearing, smell and taste.

In groups of eight, the visitors – each with their own stick – are accompanied by a non-sighted guide as they make their way through totally dark rooms which recreate certain real experiences. The threshold to the room marks the boundary between light and dark. Thereafter visitors finds themselves in a situation never experienced before, which obliges them to learn a new way of "seeing" their surroundings.

The darkness is so total that it may disorient those who have come to rely so totally on their sense of sight. However, it is an opportunity to discover new aspects of perception in an extraordinarily simple manner. This is not a simulation of blindness but rather an invitation to experience how perception and communication can be made even more intense by the very absence of light.

The Institute for the Blind also organises a restaurant in the dark, a theatre in which the performances are held in total darkness and a tactile exhibition offering the opportunity to explore twenty masterpieces of sculpture in an entirely new way.

FLAMINGOS IN THE GARDEN OF VILLA INVERNIZZI

9

3, Via dei Cappuccini
• Public transport: MM1 Palestro

City-centre flamingos

Walking down Via dei Cappuccini, your eye might be caught by movement on the other side of the tall black-and-gold gate at number 3. For a moment you might think you were in the Caribbean: there, amidst the luxuriant foliage, is a colony of wonderful pink flamingos. A very unusual pleasure for those strolling through Milan.

Along with peacocks and ducks, the flamingos make up the population of the garden of Palazzo Invernizzi, a classical-design building whose main entrance is on Corso Venezia. Once the home of the Invernizzi family – a well-known name in the Italian retail food business – the palazzo now houses the Fondazione Romeo ed Enrica Invernizzi, which promotes research in the fields of economics and food science. However, neither the villa nor the garden is open to the public. Fortunately, the flamingos are not shy. Indeed – perhaps because they are left in complete peace – this is a thriving colony and the birds breed without difficulty, in spite of the far from tropical climate. For decades now they have been a joy to behold for unsuspecting passers-by.

NEARBY

ENTRYPHONE EAR

10

About 200 metres from the flamingo colony – at 10 Via Serbelloni – stands Palazzo Sola-Busca, a gem of Art Nouveau architecture. Next to the entrance

is a large ear sculpted in marble; in fact, the building is familiarly known to the Milanese as *Ca' de l'orèggia* (The House with the Ear). This masterly ear was sculpted in 1930 by the Milanese artist Adolfo Wildt, whose pupils included Lucio Fontana and Luigi Broggini. Accurate to the slightest detail, it is complete with tympana and stirrup and hammer bones. In the thirties – due to the transmission of sound along a pipe inside the building – it actually served as a very original form of entryphone. Nowadays it is no longer in use.

PALAZZO BERRI MEREGALLI

⓫

8 Via Cappuccini
• Public transport: MM1 Palestro

> *A corner of Barcelona*

Among the eighteenth- and nineteenth-century buildings in this district, Palazzo Berri Meregalli is a masterpiece built between 1911 and 1914 by the architect Giulio Ulisse Arata. The extraordinary building brings to mind Coppedè's Art Nouveau decoration and Gaudi's Catalan Modernism, recreating a corner of Barcelona in Milan's city centre.

The building stands out as a monument, almost an open-air museum of styles. Arata's eclecticism led him to mix elements drawn from Romanesque (stonework, brick facings, arches, loggias), Gothic, Renaissance and partly from late Art Nouveau, recognisable by Angelo Mazzucotelli's (see p. 23) concrete putti, gargoyles, frescoes, mosaic inserts and twisted wrought-ironwork. If you ask permission from the caretaker, you can usually go through the wrought-iron grille reminiscent of a medieval castle, and marvel at the spectacular entrance hall embellished with marble, bosses, brick arches, beamed ceilings and multicoloured mosaics by Angiolo D'Andrea: almost like a Byzantine cathedral.

At the far end of the hall, an exquisite sculpture by Adolfo Wildt is preserved: a veiled woman's head with a set of wings known as *Vittoria alata* (Winged Victory).

SHE-WOLF BAS-RELIEF IN CORSO VENEZIA ⑫

21, Corso Venezia
• Public transport: MM1 San Babila, Palestro

Milan too has its she-wolf

Rome is not the only place that can boast a statue of a she-wolf suckling its young; Milan has one too. Certainly, the wolf here is not as imposing as that in Rome – it is simply a bas-relief – but it does have its charm. And yet, even though this work is not shut away in a museum but is there for all to see, it passes largely unnoticed.

The origins of the bas-relief are unclear. It is said to come from a pagan tombstone that was incorporated within the city's Porta Orientale. Also known as Porta Renza, that gateway was part of the Roman walls of the city and stood in the San Babila area. It served to separate the citadel of Mediolanum from the gardens, fields of crops and the uncultivated land beyond. As the city grew, the gateway was moved – and the she-wolf along with it – to the circle of walls within the Navigli canals (to what is now the junction of Corso Venezia and Via San Damiano). Then, in 1818, Porta Orientale was demolished altogether, and the few surviving traces include the lion in Piazza San Babila and the she-wolf suckling her young.

Now protected by a sheet of glass, the she-wolf of Corso Venezia is often overlooked, and the badly-worn inscription in Latin is almost illegible. However, the figure of the animal is still clearly recognisable – a reminder of the days when the co-existence of man and wolf was a serious problem.

TRACES OF THE "FIVE DAYS"

Corso Venezia and Via della Spiga
• Public transport: MM1 San Babila, Palestro

❸

> *Cannon fire in Via della Spiga*

If you know where to look, Milan is still full of traces of past invasions, occupations, battles, wars and street fighting. Look, for example, at the corner of Casa De Maestri at 13 Corso Venezia, or – slightly further on – at the corner of Via della Spiga. As the inscriptions alongside state, these cracks in the marble were made by the cannons fired during the "Five Days" of fighting in Milan from 18 to 22 March 1848.

Exasperated by Austrian rule, the Milanese rose up in revolt, invading the government building and taking the vice-governor, Moritz O'Donnell, prisoner. Trapped within Castello Sforzesco, General Josef Radetzky set about organising the Austrian armed forces, but barricades continued to be raised throughout the city – all in all, a total of 1,600 were built using everything to hand (carts, wagons, furniture, barrels, etc.).

The Austrian response was ruthless, with cannons trained on the rebels to force them to disperse. The marks left in Corso Venezia were made when those cannons were fired. However, the rebellion – which involved all classes of Milanese society and even saw women and children take to the streets – was not so easily put down. Ultimately, the seizure of Piazza dei Mercanti and Porta Nuova, the establishment of a war council and a provisional government and the arrest of leading Austrians led Radetzky to propose a truce. However, the offer was rejected, and on 22 March the imperial troops were defeated in a last clash at Porta Tosa (thereafter called Porta Vittoria) and had to leave the city.

"IT'S A REAL 48!"

Ever since, the expression "It's a real 48" has been used by the people of Milan and elsewhere to refer to a situation of chaos and upheaval.

PALAZZO SERBELLONI

16, Corso Venezia
• The *piano nobile* ("noble floor") apartments are open to the public during exhibitions organised by the Sito Serbelloni Foundation
• www.serbelloni.it
• Public transport: MM1 San Babila, Palestro

> **The hidden opulence of a Napoleonic palazzo**

Built in the eighteenth century, Palazzo Serbelloni is one of the most remarkable expressions of neoclassicism in Milan. Beyond the main doorway is a dazzling hall decorated with stuccowork and frescoes. Passing through the arcades that then lead towards the garden, a varied collection of archaeological material (tombstones and Roman and medieval remains) can be discovered, as well as a number of portrait busts and imposing fireplaces carved in stone from the Serbelloni family estates.

On the first-floor *piano nobile* is a wonderful ballroom, rich in gilded stuccowork, columns, bronzes and mirrors. It is known as the Napoleon Ballroom in honour of one of its most famous guests (others included Prince Metternich, Cesare Beccaria and King Vittorio Emanuele II of Italy).

As Stendhal recounts at the beginning of his novel *La Chartreuse de Parme*, when Napoleon entered Milan at the head of his troops in 1796, his great admirer Gian Galeazzo Serbelloni was anxious to receive the young general as a guest in his brand-new palazzo. The hero of the Italian campaign remained

there for three months, while his wife Josephine stayed almost a full year: you can still see the sumptuous decorations of her bathroom with its vaulted ceiling and her vestibule (nowadays housing offices). One should also not miss the room which contains a fine old marble fireplace and a frescoed ceiling which, like the rest of the palazzo, partly survived the bombing raids of 1943. Long the premises of the Press Club, the palazzo has recently become a cultural events centre.

NEARBY

PLAQUE COMMEMORATING MARINETTI'S ASSAULT UPON "MOONLIGHT"

At 21A Corso Venezia, a plaque recalls that this building was home for a time to Tommaso Marinetti, one of the founders of the Futurist movement. It was here that he published his review *Poesia* and announced his symbolic defiance of "the moonlight reflected in the Naviglio".

GIOVANNI LORENZI COLLECTION

9, Via Montenapoleone
• Visits by appointment: call 02 76022848 (www.lorenzi.it)
• Public transport: MM1 San Babila, MM3 Montenapoleone

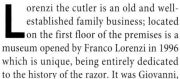

A unique collection of razors

L orenzi the cutler is an old and well-established family business; located on the first floor of the premises is a museum opened by Franco Lorenzi in 1996 which is unique, being entirely dedicated to the history of the razor. It was Giovanni, Franco's father, who first began collecting razors in the 1930s and though the museum does contain some very old pieces – for example, blades of sharpened obsidian, the ancient forerunners of modern shaving equipment, together with numerous "cut-throat" razors dating from the eighteenth and nineteenth centuries – the main body of the collection is made up of the safety razors produced in the last hundred years; all in all, the forty-eight showcases in the two rooms of the museum contain 4,060 models. And each is unique. For example, there are more than 500 types of Gillette razor blade, all different.

Among the more curious exhibits are musical razors, which play a tune as soon as the blade touches the skin; vibrating razors, both manual and electric; razors with a fitted light or a rotating head (for easy cleaning under running water); rare examples of razors made of galalith, an early type of plastic made from lactose protein. There are also ladies' razors and razors for soldiers; razors in cases made from leather, suede or bakelite; razor kits complete with blade-sharpener, shaving brush and a small mirror (even small electrically-heated bowls in which water could be warmed). The museum also has razors that once belonged to famous figures – for example, D'Annunzio – and joke razors (one, supposedly driven by farts, has a little rubber tube for the "power supply").

The Lorenzi collection also contains reproductions of more than 3,000 razor patents, and numerous photographs of barber's shops from all over the world. Other material includes engravings, etchings and period prints; advertising and film posters; barber shop calendars and two dioramas (to a scale of 1 to 10) that illustrate the barber's trade.

Part of the charm of the visit is undoubtedly due to the presence of the museum's original creator, Franco Lorenzi, who acts as guide. A man with a passionate interest in the history of blade-making, he is the author of a rare encyclopaedic work on razors. His enthusiasm, sense of humour and readiness to answer all questions turn this simple museum visit into a real show.

In Rome there is also a private collection of 27,000 different razor blades (see *Secret Rome* in this series of guides).

MUSEUM OF MARIO BUCCELLATI, JEWELLER

23, Via Montenapoleone
• Visits by appointment only; tel: 02 795059
• Public transport: MM1 San Babila, MM3 Montenapoleone

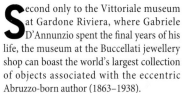

> *Museum dedicated to Gabriele D'Annunzio*

Second only to the Vittoriale museum at Gardone Riviera, where Gabriele D'Annunzio spent the final years of his life, the museum at the Buccellati jewellery shop can boast the world's largest collection of objects associated with the eccentric Abruzzo-born author (1863–1938).

Housed on the third floor of Palazzo Gavazzi, the Buccellati museum begins with a reconstruction of the firm's original jewellery workshop, with a display of various pieces – including those created for the Visconti family and the Royal House of Savoy.

The museum dedicated to D'Annunzio is in the second room, containing a number of pieces which the author of the erotic novel *Il Fuoco* (*The Flame of Life*) himself gave to Buccellati, with whom he had been friends since 1922. There are also numerous photographs, some of them signed by the dandy-cum-prophet; a rare one shows D'Annunzio as an adolescent, and another is one of the few images showing him alongside Mussolini. Other objects include cigarette cases inscribed with his famous mottoes – *IO HO QUEL CHE HO DONATO* (I have that which I have given) and *ARDISCO NON ORDISCO* (I dare, I don't contrive) – handkerchiefs painted by the writer himself, and a whole range of bric-a-brac that will fascinate his admirers. There is also a chest containing the hundred-plus letters which D'Annunzio wrote to Buccellati over the years of their friendship, and which the jeweller then collected in a volume entitled *Caro Mario…Gabriele D'Annunzio al suo gioielliere* (Dear Mario … Gabriele D'Annunzio to his Jeweller). The museum possesses a full library and a number of cases for the bracelets, necklaces and other items which the poet had made for his friends and, above all, his innumerable mistresses (the most famous of whom was Eleonora Duse).

The room with the archives used to be a bathroom. Don't miss the original ceiling, painted in the style of an ancient Roman fresco.

SUITE 105
AT THE GRAND HOTEL ET DE MILAN ⓲

29, Via Manzoni
• Verdi's apartment is usually reserved solely for hotel guests, but it is open to the public during special ceremonies or on such occasions as the 'Spring Days' organised by the FAI (Italian Environmental Defence Agency)
• Public transport: MM3 Montenapoleone

> ***The hotel suite where Giuseppe Verdi died***

Suite 105, on the first floor of the Grand Hotel Et De Milan, is the apartment where Giuseppe Verdi spent his time in Milan for almost thirty years, right up to his death in 1901. The *Maestro* first chose to stay at what was then simply called L'Albergo di Milano in 1872, in part because it was just a short walk from the Scala Opera House, in part because it was the only hotel in the city that had a postal and telegraph service. The place thereafter became the residence of the composer and his wife, Giuseppina Strepponi, during their long stays in Milan.

Nothing has been changed in the suite since it was occupied by Verdi and you can still see the composer's bedroom and sitting-room as they were at the time. In this room, which once held the desk at which Verdi composed *Otello* and *Falstaff*, there is a portrait of the composer by the Romantic artist Giuseppe Barbaglia, as well as a handwritten message by Giuseppe Manzoni on one of his own calling-cards.

The Grand Hotel witnessed some of Verdi's greatest triumphs. After the premiere of *Otello* (on 5 February 1887), the joyful crowd unhitched the horses from the composer's carriage and drew him to the hotel themselves; once he had retired to his apartment, Verdi then had to step out onto the balcony to receive the cheers of the crowd until late into the night. And after the premiere of *Falstaff* he was met in the hotel hall by a group of his ardent admirers, who crowned him with a laurel wreath cast in bronze.

STRAW SCATTERED SO AS NOT TO DISTURB THE DYING *MAESTRO*

When Verdi lay dying in January 1901, the Milanese once more showed their profound affection for the great composer by scattering straw on Via Manzoni to deaden the noise of passing carriages. Nothing was to be allowed to disturb the repose of the fading *Maestro*.

THE ROOF OF THE ARMANI HOTEL

31, Via Manzoni
• Tel: 02 88838888
• www.armanihotels.com
• Public transport: MM3 Montenapoleone

Giorgio Armani's five-star hotel in Milan fills an entire block between Via Manzoni and Via dei Giardini. Eight elegant floors, over three floors of shops, restaurant and bars, all of the Armani brand.

> *An ingenious advertisement*

However, the hotel's most extraordinary feature, when seen from above (for those lucky enough to fly over it in a helicopter or hot-air balloon ...), is its shape. The designer has managed to brand the building, now firmly ingrained in the fabric of urban Milan, as a giant "A" – perhaps unique in the marketing world.

ROMAN WALLS UNDERGROUND

Nearby, in the wine cellar of the Don Carlos restaurant, connected to the Grand Hotel et de Milan (29 Via Manzoni), are the foundations of Roman walls from the Maximian era, consisting of mortar-bound pebble and brick fragments. As the foundations had to be 4 metres wide, it is thought that this section, which is around 1 metre thick, is all that remains, and that the rest was dug out to construct the cellar. Reusing materials was a widespread practice in late antiquity, as in the fourth century when a defensive wall had to be built quickly and cheaply against barbarian invasions. Other evidence of recycling sections of foundation and architectural fragments, relating to funerary monuments, have been found in Via Montenapoleone, Via dell'Orso at the corner of Via Verdi, Via Bigli, Via Monte di Pietà and Via Manzoni.

Other parts of Maximian walls can be seen in the basement rooms of numbers 21 (Casa Dozzio) and 27 Via Montenapoleone. At the gate at the junction of Via Bigli, at number 25, are ashlar blocks for reuse with markings that may be Roman.

STATUE OF ST EXPEDITUS

Santa Maria del Carmine
2, Piazza del Carmine
• Open Monday to Friday, 7.15am–12 noon and 4pm–7.15pm
• Public transport: MM2 Lanza; tram 2, 12, 14; bus 61

> ## *The quick miracle worker*

It is difficult to imagine a more "Milanese" saint than St Expeditus; his statue is in the Church of Santa Maria del Carmine and the saint is said to "deliver" 24/7.

A Christian martyr of the first to second centuries AD, Expeditus is the patron saint of urgent and desperate causes. The classic iconography shows him crushing underfoot a crow that croaks *cras* (Latin for "tomorrow") whilst he himself holds a cross bearing the word *hodie* ("today"). In other words, St Expeditus seems to be saying: Do not put off until tomorrow what you can do today. In Germany, where he is also venerated, he is actually depicted holding a watch.

The statue of St Expeditus in the Church of Santa Maria del Carmine always has candles burning before it, with students preparing for exams often turning to the saint for some quick "help".

GESSO MODELS OF THE STATUES ON THE CATHEDRAL SPIRES

Santa Maria stands on a site which as early as 1250 was a place of worship run by the Carmelite Order.

The present church was built in 1447 using material taken from Castello Visconteo (now Castello Sforzesco), which had been damaged during the period of the Golden Ambrosian Republic. The church has subsequently been altered a number of times.

It is interesting to note that the statues in the wooden choir stalls are gesso models of originals that now grace the spires of the cathedral.

The Baroque-style sacristy has cabinets designed by Gerolamo Quadrio in 1629; it was these rooms that received the body of Giuseppe Prina, the State Finance Minister who was massacred at Palazzo Carmagnola by a mob furious at his increase in the salt tax.

You can also visit the remaining two sides of the monastery's cloister (entrance from the side aisle on the left).

These feature parts of Roman and medieval plaques as well as fragments from the patrician tombs that once stood inside the church.

SAINT BY MISTAKE?

Nothing is known for certain about St Expeditus; it is not even sure that he existed. However, the saint is the object of popular devotion that has spread throughout the world, and was already flourishing in the sixteenth century (at least in France). There are various legends regarding the saint. One says that his name comes from the *expeditus* (sent) written on a package that arrived in Rome, the term then taken as identifying the unknown saint whose remains it contained. As for the veneration of the saint, undoubtedly the name Expeditus has led to all sorts of puns, with the figure becoming the patron saint of expedition. Initially, his intercession was sought for urgent causes, but then Expeditus became the patron saint of shopkeepers (well known for their dispatch in business) and sailors; his help is also sought by students taking exams or by those awaiting a court verdict. In Milan, a second statue of St Expeditus can be seen in the Church of San Nicolao.

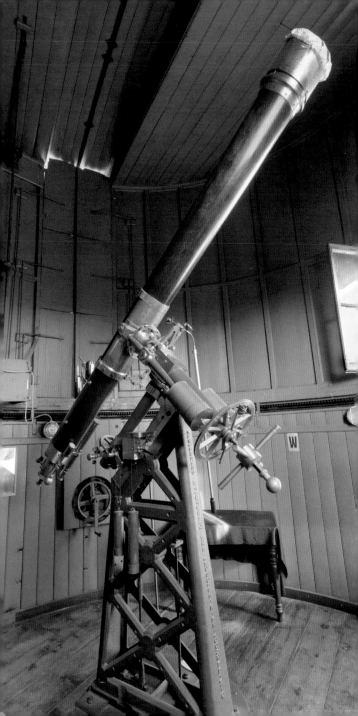

SCHIAPARELLI'S CUPOLA

Brera Astronomical Museum
28, Via Brera
• Open Monday to Friday, 9am–4.30pm
• Admission free
• Visits to the cupola by appointment: infobrera@unimi.it
• Public transport: MM2 Lanza

The cupola from which Schiaparelli "saw" the canals of Mars

On the last floor of the building now housing the Brera Astronomical Museum, the tower at the north-east of the Observatory is surmounted by a cupola built at the behest of Giovanni Virginio Schiaparelli, director of the Observatory in the second half of the nineteenth century. Built by the German Georg Metz, the astronomical telescope here has a lens of a diameter of 218 millimetres and a focal length of 3.15 metres, which is still in very good condition.

It was using this telescope that Schiaparelli observed what he took to be "canals" on the surface of the planet Mars; these would subsequently become famous as some took them to prove the existence of life on Mars. It was not until the photographs taken by the Mariner 4 space probe in 1965 – and the first map of the planet based on information from Mariner 9 in 1971 – that such speculation could be put to an end: it is now clear that there are no "purpose-built" canals on the planet, nor are there any signs of life.

NEARBY

BRERA ASTRONOMICAL MUSEUM

Housed within the building that also contains the Brera Academy

and Art Gallery, the Astronomical Museum has a collection of scientific instruments that once belonged to the Astronomical Observatory, the city's oldest institution for scientific research. It was thanks to the efforts of Schiaparelli, director of the Observatory from 1862 to 1900, that the enormous historic heritage of this institution was preserved. This includes a library of ancient texts, a historic archive and a collection of scientific instruments that includes a Gauss magnetometer manufactured by Meyerstein (1835) and Poggiali's spectrograph (1865).

OVIDIO SCOLARI COLLECTION ㉓

Biblioteca Nazionale Braidense
28, Via Brera
• Open Monday to Friday, 8.30am–6.15pm and Saturday 9am–1.45pm
• Public transport: MM2 Lanza; bus 61; tram 2, 12, 14

Collection of books on magic at Braidense Library

On the small balcony that runs around the entrance hall of Braidense Library, the sharp-eyed will see that certain books are in fact reproductions in wood which serve as secret doors. Behind one of these is concealed the Ovidio Scolari Collection of books on magic. Most fittingly, books on the "secrets" of magic are kept in a secret place.

Comprising 227 publications, this collection encompasses the quintessence of the knowledge available to early twentieth-century adepts of magic. As the name suggests, it was put together by one Ovidio Scolari, a passionate supporter of the magical arts who bequeathed it to the Braidense Library at his death in 1934.

Among the more prestigious volumes are an 1881 edition of *Confidences d'un prestidigitateur*, an autobiography in the form of a novel by the famous French illusionist Jean Eugène Robert-Houdin; the 1876 *Modern Magic*, a classic handbook of magic by "Professor Hoffmann"; the rare 1899 *Isn't it Wonderful?* by Charles Bertram; a copy of Will Goldston's 1912 *Exclusive Magical Secrets*, which is actually padlocked; and Harry Houdini's

controversial 1908 *The Unmasking of Robert-Houdin*. Other books include the classic *Our Magic* (1911) by Nevil Maskeline and David Devant; *La Prestidigitation sans appareils* (1914) by Camille Gaultier and *The Expert at the Card Table* (1905) by S.W. Erdnase, a veritable "bible" of card tricks and similar sleight of hand.

The Italian books include *Frizzi Mefistofelici* by the Milan-born Enrico Longone (more famous as "Frizzo"), and *Confidenze di un prestidigitatore* by Sicilien Romanoff. The one book which is truly precious – in terms of both rarity and material value – dates from 1759: Carlo Antonio's *Trésor des jeux*.

MILAN MAGIC CLUB

There is a long tradition of magicians and illusionists in Milan, the city now being home to the CLAM (Club Arte Magica) which was founded in 1972 by Pierino Pozzi, better-known under his stage-name of "Karton". At the premises of the old Napoleonic ironworks at 21 Via Thaon di Revel (see p. 305), the members meet every Friday to hold a school of magic and organise shows and conferences on specific subjects. To join or participate, consult the site www.clubartemagica.org.

LAUDIBUS NOSTRIS NON CRESCIT DEUS SED NOS

CRYPT OF THE *ANAUNIA* MARTYRS

Basilica of San Simpliciano
7, Piazza San Simpliciano
• Open Monday to Saturday, 7am–12 noon and 3pm–7pm (Sunday 4pm–7pm)
• Public transport: MM2 Lanza; bus 61; tram 2, 4, 12, 14

> **Legend of the three saints who defeated Barbarossa**

L egend has it that, after razing Milan to the ground, Frederick Barbarossa was defeated by the "spiritual" intervention of three saints whose mortal remains were at the time buried at San Simpliciano. Towards the end of the fourth century, St Ambrose had sent three young missionaries – Alexander, Martyrius and Sisinius – to preach the gospel in the ancient region of *Anaunia* (the present-day Val di Non in the Trentino area). However, the mission ended badly: the three young men were burned at the stake in 397, their bodies later being returned to Simplicius, Ambrose's successor, who having finished work on this church in 401 then had them buried in the crypt. Seven centuries later, just before the battle of Legnano (29 May 1176), which saw the Milanese defeat the forces of Barbarossa, three white doves flew out of San Simpliciano and settled on the *Carroccio* (War Wagon) of the Lombard League, which was waiting there to receive a blessing. After the victory, the Benedictine monks of San Simpliciano added three doves to their crest in commemoration of the event; in fact, 29 May is still celebrated here every year in an official ceremony.

Upon application to the sacristan, you can now visit the *sacellum* which used to hold the bodies of the three martyrs. (In 1927 they were moved to the

Basilica of Sanzeno in Trento, which is dedicated to them.) The entrance is in the transept to the left of the altar; it is actually the base of the organ itself and is richly decorated with paintings of male and female saints by Aurelio Luini. Recently restored, the interior of the *sacellum* is very simple, with some of the original walls and paving. It is now used as a Chapel of the Blessed Sacrament.

Together with San Nazaro Maggiore, Sant'Ambrogio and the (no longer extant) San Dionigi, San Simpliciano was one of the four fourth-century churches founded by St Ambrose and was known at the time as the *Basilica Virginum*. Although it has subsequently undergone numerous changes, the church still has its original palaeo-Christian outside walls, which reach to a height of 22 metres.

CLOISTERS OF SAN SIMPLICIANO

3, Via dei Cavalieri del Santo Sepolcro
• Open during conferences, concerts of Baroque music and sessions of musical meditation, organised regularly and advertised on www.sansimpliciano.it and www.teologiamilano.it
• Public transport: MM2 Lanza; bus: 43, 61, 94

> **In the heart of the Brera district, two peaceful cloisters**

A s soon as you enter the cloisters of San Simpliciano and stroll along the gravel paths edged with plant beds you have the impression of being in the heart of the countryside, far from the centre of Milan.

No sign in the street indicates the presence of these "invisible" cloisters, tucked away within a building that now houses the North Italy Theology Faculty. However, during conferences, concerts of Baroque music or the regular sessions of musical meditation (see above), the place is open to the public.

Of these two superb cloisters located just behind the basilica of San Simpliciano, the larger dates from the sixteenth century and the smaller from the fifteenth. Both were recently restored, with great care taken to respect the original architecture – in particular, the open arcades. The monks' cells on the first floor, which give directly onto this open gallery, have now been restored as fully functional rooms. The cellar, too, has undergone extensive and painstaking restoration work; it now houses the archives, containing the 170,000 books of the institution's academic library.

The restoration also included the façades and the walls within the cloisters. Those in the larger cloister have recovered their muted straw colour; and while the cycle of frescoes painted by Borgognone in the smaller cloister has been lost, the restoration did repair the cracked wall surfaces and save the floral decoration of the vaulted ceiling. Equal care was taken to conserve the brick paving and the well-head at the centre of the cloister.

NEARBY

PLAQUE COMMEMORATING QUASIMODO

Located within the porch at number 16 Corso Garibaldi, this recalls that Salvatore Quasimodo, winner of the Nobel Prize for Literature in 1959, lived here. The poet is buried in the Tempio della Fama (Temple of Fame) in Milan's Monumental Cemetery.

ROMAN PEDIMENT

Set within a nearby building (7 Via del Lauro) are various individually lit fragments of Roman pediments. These remains date from the first century AD and were unearthed on this site during construction work on the building.

DISFIGURED TOMBSTONE IN SAN MARCO CHURCH

2, Piazza San Marco
• Open daily, 7am–12 noon and 4pm–7pm
• Public transport: MM2 Lanza; bus 61

A case of "damnatio memoriae"?

If you go down the aisle of San Marco to the transept, just to the right of the main altar you'll find a strange tombstone decorated with the bas-relief of a man whose face has been deliberately disfigured.

Set upright, this work is all that remains of a sarcophagus which, in all

likelihood, once contained the body of the man whose portrait has been erased. Dressed in Renaissance garb, he is shown with his hands crossed on his chest and his head resting on a cushion. Clearly this was a nobleman – or at least some well-known local figure – and, for one reason or another, his effigy was "punished". In all likelihood, this is an example of the practice of *damnatio memoriae*, a post-mortem condemnation to oblivion. The practice, dating back to Roman times but still followed in the Middle Ages (in some countries, it still goes on), involved the deliberate elimination of all trace of the offender: any public monument to him was removed and all record of his honours destroyed. The punishment was generally inflicted upon those who had committed a serious crime against the Church. In the present case there is absolutely nothing to identify the man on the tombstone: his face has been thoroughly destroyed using a hammer, and any dates that there might have been around the edge of his tomb have been erased.

STAR ON THE FAÇADE OF SAN MARCO BASILICA

2, Piazza San Marco
- Open daily, 7am–12 noon and 4pm–7pm
- Public transport: MM2 Lanza; bus 61

> *A Star of David on a Catholic church*

If you carefully examine the imposing façade of San Marco basilica, you'll notice – centre top – a rose window adorned with a rather rare symbol for a Roman Catholic church: the six-point Star of David, which is also called the Seal of Solomon and is associated with alchemy and Freemasonry as well as being the symbol of Judaism. From the seal, a total of sixteen rays emerge, rather like an old "wind rose".

Although its presence here has stimulated the imagination of any number of conspiracy theorists, the symbol does not reveal the existence of any sort of universal conspiracy: right up to the nineteenth century, the Star of David was often used to adorn places of Christian worship. As a decorative motif, the star appears, for example, on the neo-Gothic façade of Santa Croce basilica in Florence. It was only after that date that the symbol ceased to be used, as it became more closely associated with Judaism, or with Occultism and Freemasonry.

For further information on the Star of David and its symbolism, see the double page overleaf.

THE STAR HEXAGRAM: A MAGICAL TALISMAN?

The hexagram – also known as the Star of David or the Shield of David – comprises two interlaced equilateral triangles, one pointing upwards and the other downwards. It symbolises the combination of man's spiritual and human nature. The six points correspond to the six directions in space (north, south, east and west, together with zenith and nadir) and also refer to the complete universal cycle of the six days of creation (the seventh day being when the Creator rested). Hence, the hexagram became the symbol of the macrocosm (its six angles of 60° totalling 360°) and of the union between mankind and its creator. If, as laid down in the Old Testament (*Deuteronomy* 6:4–9), the hexagram (*mezuzah* in Hebrew) is often placed at the entrance to a Jewish home, it was also adopted as an amulet by Christians and Muslims. So it is far from being an exclusively Jewish symbol. In both the Koran (38:32 et seq.) and *The Thousand and One Nights*, it is described as an indestructible talisman that affords God's blessing and offers total protection against the spirits of the natural world, the djinns. The hexagram also often appears in the windows and pediments of Christian churches, as a symbolic reference to the universal soul. In this case, that soul is represented by Christ – or, sometimes, by the pair of Christ (upright triangle) and the Virgin (inverted triangle); the result of the interlacing of the two is God the Father Almighty. The hexagram is also found in the mediated form of a lamp with six branches or a six-section rose window.

Although present in the synagogue of Capernaum (third century AD), the hexagram does not really make its appearance in rabbinical literature until 1148 – in the *Eshkol Hakofer* written by the Karaite* scholar Judah Ben Elijah. In Chapter 242 its mystical and apotropaic (evil-averting) qualities are described, with the actual words then often being engraved on amulets: "And the names of the seven angels were written on the *mazuzah*: The Everlasting will protect you and this symbol called the Shield of David contains, at the end of the *mezuzah*, the written name of all the angels."

In the thirteenth century the hexagram also became an attribute of one of the seven magic names of Metatron, the angel of the divine presence associated with the archangel Michael (head of the heavenly host and the closest to God the Father).

The identification of Judaism with the Star of David began in the Middle Ages. In 1354 King Karel IV of Bohemia granted the Jewish community of Prague the privilege of putting the symbol on their banner. The Jews embroidered a gold star on a red background to form a standard that became known as the Flag of King David (*Maghen David*) and was adopted as the official symbol of Jewish synagogues. By the nineteenth century, the symbol had spread throughout the Jewish community. Jewish mysticism has it that the origin of the hexagram was directly linked with the flowers that adorn the *menorah***: irises with six petals. For those who believe this origin, the hexagram came directly from the hands of the God of Israel, the six-petal iris not only reassembling the Star of David in general form but also being associated with the people of Israel in the *Song of Songs*.

As well as offering protection, the hexagram was believed to have magical powers. This reputation originates in the famous *Clavicula Salomonis* (Key of Solomon), a grimoire (textbook of magic) attributed to Solomon himself but, in all likelihood, produced during the Middle Ages. The anonymous texts probably came from one of the numerous Jewish schools of the Kabbalah that then existed in Europe, for the work is clearly inspired by the teachings of the Talmud and the Jewish faith. The *Clavicula* contains a collection of thirty-six pentacles (themselves symbols rich in magic and esoteric significance) which were intended to enable communication between the physical world and the different levels of the soul. There are various versions of the text, in numerous translations, and the content varies between them. However, most of the surviving texts date from the sixteenth and seventeenth centuries – although there is a Greek translation dating from the fifteenth.

In Tibet and India, the Buddhists and Hindus read this universal symbol of the hexagram in terms of the creator and his creation, while the Brahmins hold it to be the symbol of the god Vishnu. Originally, the two triangles were in green (upright triangle) and red (inverted triangle). Subsequently, these colours became black and white, the former representing the spirit, the latter the material world. For the Hindus, the upright triangle is associated with Shiva, Vishnu and Brahma (corresponding to the Christian God the Father, Son and Holy Ghost). The Son (Vishnu) can be seen to always occupy the middle position, being the intercessor between things divine and things earthly.

*qara'im or *bnei mikra*: "he who follows the Scriptures". Karaism is a branch of Judaism that defends the sole authority of the Hebrew Scripture as the source of divine revelation, thus repudiating oral tradition.
**Menorah – the multibranched candelabra used in the rituals of Judaism. The arms of the seven-branched menorah, one of the oldest symbols of the Jewish faith, represent the seven archangels before the Throne of God: Michael, Gabriel, Samuel, Raphael, Zadkiel, Anael and Kassiel.

WOODEN BOOKS IN MUSEO CIVICO DI STORIA NATURALE

55, Corso Venezia
• Info point: 02 88463337
• www.comune.milano.it/museostorianaturale
• Open Tuesday to Sunday, 9am–5.30pm; admission free on Friday after 2pm and daily for the last hour
• Public transport: M1 Palestro

> *The Austrian archduke's extraordinary herbaria*

Among the vast number of objects, mineral samples, fossils and stuffed animals on display in the Museo Civico di Storia Naturale, you might come across two wooden boxes in the form of books, one open and one closed.

In a display case just inside the entrance, these are only two of over 400 examples of such pieces within the museum collection. Known as the "Books of Monza" – because they come from the Villa Reale in Monza – they are some of the most historically valuable exhibits in the museum. There is only one other comparable series in Italy, now in San Vito di Cadore.

These containers, designed to open just like real books, held specimens of all the various species of shrub, tree and plant in the gardens of the Villa Reale. They are in fact herbaria containing all the classic components of each species: stem, leaf, blossom, fruit, seeds. However, they also have cross-sections of branches, pollen samples, wood cinders, wood shavings, a cube of fossilised wood, examples of malformations, etc. A compartment within the binding of the "book" contains a sheet of paper with a list (in French) of its various contents. We do not know the origin of this collection nor who put it together. However, it is thought that the books may have been commissioned by Archduke Ranier Joseph of Austria in 1815.

These books are only one of the numerous curiosities which an attentive visitor can discover within the forbidding walls of what is considered the greatest Natural History Museum in Italy. For example, there is a rare example of a quagga, a now extinct breed of South African zebra; the world's largest sulphur crystal; atmospheric dioramas depicting all sorts of animals in their natural habitat; and "Ciro", the first dinosaur discovered in Italy. Ciro's scientific name is *Scipionyx samniticus*, an unknown species before these remains were found. Scientists now say this is one of the best-preserved and most important vertebrate fossils yet to come to light.

MILAN'S MERMAID

Museo Civico di Storia Naturale
55, Corso Venezia
• Info point: 02 88463337
• www.comune.milano.it/museostorianaturale
• Open Tuesday to Sunday, 9am–5.30pm; admission free on Friday after 2pm and daily for the last hour
• Public transport: M1 Palestro

I t is not certain how it got there, but it is there. In Milan's Museo Civico di Storia Naturale there is what looks like a mummified mermaid. It came to light in the 1980s, in the midst of a load of objects left in the basement. One explanation is that it was given to the museum in the first half of the nineteenth century by the Villa brothers, passionate collectors of scientific curiosities.

A realistic fake that fooled them in the nineteenth century

Some documents seem to suggest that they paid the equivalent of something like 40,000 dollars for what is undoubtedly a fake. When you look closely, it seems to have been modelled (perhaps from papier mâché) with details from real animals added later: the teeth come from a fish, while the nails could be the claws of a bird. The whole thing is a fake – from the down intended to represent hair to the "scales" along its spine (which seem to come from some plant).

These would-be mermaids – monstrous creatures that aroused widespread curiosity – were a regular feature of *Wunderkammern*, nineteenth-century "cabinets of curiosities". One of the most famous was the so-called "Fiji Mermaid", which in 1842 became part of P.T. Barnum's travelling show. That mermaid was destroyed in a fire, but would be imitated by many others. One such example was exhibited in 1961 in a British Museum show dedicated to fakes and forgeries of all kinds. The one in the Milan museum is one of the few original survivors from the period.

Sometimes, the mermaid is put on public display, in exhibitions of fakes, etc. However, generally it is kept in the curator's offices, in a small cabinet of "wonders" that include a one-eyed cat and a three-legged bird.

COLUMNS IN PIAZZA OBERDAN

• Public transport: MM1 Porta Venezia

A disguised chimney

Far from being the remains of some ancient monument or an unfinished temple, the two mysterious columns in Piazza Oberdan are in fact there to disguise a chimney.

Beneath the piazza are the "Venezia" public baths (Albergo Diurno Venezia), reached by the metro entrance at the corner of Corso Buenos Aires and Viale Vittorio Veneto. There used to be two canopied entrances – one on the Via Tadino side and the other at the site of the present entrance – but they fell victim to work on the metro line.

The public baths were built in 1925, with a licence to operate for thirty years. In 1955, when the licence ran out, Milan City Council took over an establishment whose original designs had envisaged the following facilities: thirty individual bathrooms, six shower cubicles with wardrobe, ten toilets, a cloakroom, laundry room, bank, offices, telephone boxes, storage space for bicycles and areas reserved for shoe-shiners.

The entire space was heated by a boiler whose chimney was disguised as one of the two columns in the square above. To make this addition to the urban fabric more aesthetically pleasing, it was flanked by another purely decorative column. Originally, there had also been plans to build some sort of monument in the square, but these came to nothing.

Posters pasted to the glassed-in partition walls generally make it difficult to see into the main hall of the public baths. However, if the glass-panelled door to the left of the metro entrance is open, you can sometimes glimpse the interior, where the humidity and rainwater seeping in from the street above have gradually damaged the walls, panels and decorations.

NEARBY
CLOCK BALCONY

The porch over the central doorway of the late nineteenth-century building at 1 Via Tadino houses a beautiful yet curious-looking clock flanked by pots of plants and two life-size painted statues of a little girl and a little boy dressed as shepherds.

COURTYARD OF PALAZZO LURASCHI

1, Corso Buenos Aires
• Public transport: MM1 Porta Venezia

I f you peep through the entrance of Palazzo Luraschi at 1 Corso Buenos Aires, you'll see a small but atmospheric courtyard unique for two specific features: the four marble columns from the old lazaretto (see p. 169) and twelve carved busts of the main characters from Manzoni's novel *I Promessi Sposi*. These include Renzo, Lucia, Don Rodrigo, Cardinal Borromeo, Father Cristoforo, Agnese and the Nun of Monza.

The Promessi Sposi courtyard

The palazzo, designed by and named after the engineer Ferdinando Luraschi, was built in the years 1881–1887 (master builder: Angelo Galimberti). It was one of the first to be constructed in this area (on what was then called Corso Loreto) after the demolition of the lazaretto. Saving material that would otherwise have been destroyed, Luraschi decided to incorporate within his building four of the columns that had originally made up part of the internal perimeter within that lazaretto (another eleven can be seen at 5 Via San Gregorio).

The reason for the twelve busts of characters from *I Promessi Sposi* is rather different. The building regulations of the day imposed what was called *la servitù del Resegone* (servitude of Resegone): in fact, no building in the north of the city was allowed to stand more than two or three storeys high, so as not to obstruct the landscape visible from the city bastions (a view that included Mount Resegone and the alpine foothills). Palazzo Luraschi, one of the first eight-storey buildings in Italy, was also the first in Milan to break this *servitù*.

Perhaps the fact that his building stood in the area of the old lazaretto – which figures so largely in Manzoni's work – and also obstructed the view of a mountain that is often mentioned in the famous novel, inspired Luraschi to install these twelve sculpted busts as an act of homage to *I Promessi Sposi*.

NEARBY

COLUMN OF SAN DIONIGI

A plaque at 50, Corso Venezia bears this quote from Chapter XI of *I Promessi Sposi*: "Here there was a column with a cross on top, called St Dionysius's column". This votive monument had been raised in 1577 at the time of the plague, and in the novel it is here that Renzo stops to collect bread. The column was demolished in the eighteenth century – together with the church dedicated to the same saint – in order to make way for the Porta Venezia public gardens.

GERENZANA IRRIGATION CANAL

10, Via Spallanzani
• Public transport: MM1 Porta Venezia; tram 5, 9, 29/30, 33

> *Exposed stretch of an old watercourse*

Drawn off the River Seveso, the Gerenzana irrigation canal (Roggia Gerenzana) is a watercourse that runs north-south through the city. Nowadays, it is built over for most of its length, with the exception of the short stretch that can be seen within the courtyard of Casa Galimberti or from the courtyard of the supermarket at the corner of the street (you must ask for permission to enter).

These few metres of canal, almost totally neglected and often dry, bear witness to a watercourse which played a fundamental role in the life of this district of Milan.

Originally, the canal was owned by the Marchesi Brivio-Sforza, serving to irrigate their estate at San Guiliano Milanese (where a stretch of the canal can still be seen near Piazza Insubria). When the canal reached the city's Porta Orientale (now Porta Venezia), the water passed through a series of ad hoc filters made using gravel and sand, and the subsequently purified waters served to fill the Bagno Diana (Diana Baths), the first open-air swimming pool in Italy.

The stretch that ran along Via Sirtori, on the other hand, supplied the premises of the Società Anonima Omnibus e Tramways. Dating from 1861, this was a building with coach house and stables, where the company's 500 or so horses had to be provided with drinking water.

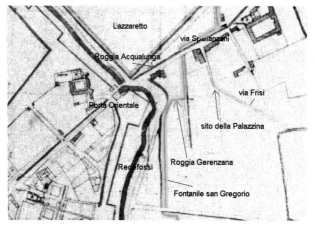

HIDDEN GARDEN OF THE SHERATON DIANA MAJESTIC HOTEL ⓷⓸

42, Viale Piave
• Open daily: 10.30am–1am
• Public transport: MM1 Porta Venezia; tram 9

> **A statue that graced Milan's first public swimming pool**

Although in the city centre it is easy enough to find some pleasant courtyard beyond a gate, the gardens of historic palazzi are less obvious, hemmed in by other buildings or protected by impenetrable railings that give little away. The Porta Venezia district, not far from the large public park of Giardini Montanelli, has just such a garden – well worth a visit.

The entrance is via the Sheraton Diana, at number 42 of the busy Viale Piave where, once through reception, access to the hotel terrace is free. From the large bay window in the bar, you can look out on the dense foliage of the garden, in the midst of which a statue of Diana stands in a small pool.

The statue of the goddess, protector of springs and woods, used to grace the entrance to Milan's first public swimming pool, opened in 1842 in a green space just outside the Bastioni di Porta Orientale (now Piazza Oberdan). The Bagni di Diana (as the baths were named in honour of the goddess) were only open to men, who had the use of a huge swimming pool, diving boards, cabins and a balcony from where they could watch other bathers. The water came from the nearby Roggia Gerenzana, a channel that branched off the Naviglio della Martesana.

The basin was permanently covered over in 1908, when the architect A. Manfredini, following the French fashion of the time, planned to replace it with a leisure centre that was also very successful. The new Kursaal Diana included a restaurant, ballroom, modern hotel with electric lighting, rooms with baths, telephone on all floors, and a double lift to carry guests and baggage separately. An additional feature was a *sferisterio* (pelota court), which was later converted into a brand-new ice rink.

The Kursaal, to which Mussolini later gave the name "Diana Maestoso", is well known for the 1921 bombing that devastated the great theatre that now borders the garden on one side, half hidden by the branches of a spectacular and heavily perfumed wisteria.

CELLS OF THE MILAN LAZARETTO

San Nicola al Lazzaretto church
5, Via San Gregorio
• Public transport: MM1 Porta Venezia

The original building, covering 140,000 square metres, was demolished more than a century ago. However, the lazaretto still occupies a vivid place in the city's memory – both because of its leading role in Chapter XXXI of Alessandro Manzoni's *I Promessi Sposi*, and because of the terrible events with which it was associated during the course of its history.

> *Extant traces of the lazaretto in Corso Buenos Aires*

Given how huge it was, the remaining traces of the building are surprisingly sparse: the most substantial remnant comprises the five and a half rooms in Via San Gregorio, which since 1974 have belonged to the Greek Orthodox Church of the Ancient Calendar.

From the street, you can still see the original Renaissance-style windows and the five chimneys (each room had its own fireplace). Then, upon entering the courtyard, you come to an arcade of eleven columns and ten arches, complete with terracotta decoration. Amidst the foliage on the street side of this courtyard runs a stretch of the original moat, known at the time as the *fontanile della sanità* ("fountain of health"). The wall inside the arcade bears a plaque with a Latin inscription which translates as: "O traveller, pause as you pass but do not pause in your tears."

OTHER TRACES OF THE MILAN LAZARETTO

In the courtyard of 1 Corso Buenos Aires, where some of the original columns from the lazaretto – identical to those in Via San Gregorio – were incorporated by the engineer Luraschi in the portico of his palazzo (see *Promessi Sposi* courtyard, p. 163).

Hidden among the neighbouring houses, the small church at **1 Largo Bellintani Fra Paolo** was originally part of the lazaretto. Initially dedicated to San Gregorio (but now named after St Carlo Borromeo, at whose behest it was built), this stood in the centre of the lazaretto complex. It has been closed for some time because the ceilings are unsafe.

Finally, at **29 Via Castalia** is the **Antica Farmacia del Lazzaretto**. Established in 1750, this is still open for business. As well as being one of the oldest apothecaries in Milan, it is also well-known for its "Amaro Medicinale Giuliani", a herb-based liqueur created in 1905 by the then owner Germano Giuliani. The liqueur, initially intended as a gift for regular customers, was later produced commercially.

For the history of the Milan lazaretto, see the following double-page feature.

IL LAZZARETTO DI MILANO

From the fifteenth to the seventeenth centuries, Europe was regularly devastated by the plague: 25 million people – about a third of the European population at the time – died from the disease. Like the rest of Italy, Milan was one of the first places in Europe to be hit by the plague, which is first recorded in fourteenth-century China. The most devastating epidemics in the city were in 1576–78 and 1630–1632, the last serious outbreak, which killed more than 50,000 people (half of Milan's population).

Isolation was the only way of halting the spread of the disease, and to achieve this purpose – as well as provide a minimum of care for those afflicted – Ludovico il Moro had a special lazaretto built. The site chosen was outside the built-up area of the city, near the Porta Orientale; this eastern location meant that the wind – which in Milan generally blows from the west – would not carry infected air over the healthy parts of the city.

The lazaretto was designed by the engineer Lazzaro Palazzi and built in the years 1488–1513. A rectangular structure measuring 378 by 370 metres, it stood on a site that is bound by the modern-day Corso Buenos Aires, Via San Gregorio, Via Lazzaretto and Via Vittorio Veneto. A depiction of what the lazaretto looked like can be seen in the painting on the wall of 2 Via Laghetto (see p. 255).

The structure, which was originally known as the Edifico di Santa Maria della Sanità, had brick walls with terracotta decorations. Each cell had small windows surmounted by tympana and the overall architecture was similar to that of the Ospedale Maggiore, which ran the lazaretto. The whole was surrounded by a sort of moat, known as the "fountain of health", and contained a total of 288 "cells", each measuring around 20 square metres and complete with two windows, fireplace, latrine and straw mattress. Each such cell could contain up to thirty plague victims, so we can only begin to imagine the filth and smell when so many sick and dying people were crammed together in such a small space. It was no accident that the doctors themselves never went near the lazaretto, sending assistants – apothecaries and barber-surgeons – so that they could keep an eye on the situation from a safe distance and make the necessary diagnoses and prescriptions.

The perimeter wall of the building enclosed a large central courtyard with a chapel dedicated to Santa Maria della Sanità. This was demolished in 1576 and its place taken by a church built at the behest of St Carlo Borromeo and dedicated to San Gregorio (but nowadays dedicated to St Carlo Borromeo himself). The octagonal structure was chosen to symbolise the "doubling" of the walls of the lazaretto itself; it was also an allusion to the Eighth Day, that of Christ's Resurrection. Now bricked in, each side of the original structure was open, so that the patients could see the celebration of mass from inside their cells. Begun in 1580, work on the church was only completed after the death of St Carlo Borromeo, and now houses a painting by an anonymous artist which shows the saint visiting the sick. With the arrival of Napoleon's forces in 1796, the church was given over to pagan worship, and was only reconsecrated at the end of the nineteenth century. When epidemics of the plague came to an end, the lazaretto was disinfected and then made available for use by the Ospedale Maggiore. Over time it served as a barracks, military hospital, military prison, storehouse, cannon foundry and grazing ground for flocks. The structure also housed a veterinary school and served as a venue for celebrations and tournaments held in Napoleon's honour. During the period of Austrian rule, the cells were used for paupers and the homeless, while the church was turned into a barn. The Ospedale Maggiore also rented out space to railway workers, market gardeners, artisans, pedlars, washermen, farriers and icemen.

Ultimately, the building was bought – for 1,803,690 lire – by the Banca di Credito Italiano, which intended to use the site for new housing developments. The lazaretto was demolished between 1882 and 1890.

ORIGIN OF THE ITALIAN TERM *LAZZARETTO*

There are two hypotheses. One claims that the name comes from that of Lazarus, the leper Christ raised from the dead who would then be worshipped as the patron protector of all lepers.

The second says that the term comes from the name of the very first lazaretto, which was in Venice and dedicated to Santa Maria di Nazareth; the word Nazareth being corrupted to *nazaretto* and then *lazzaretto*.

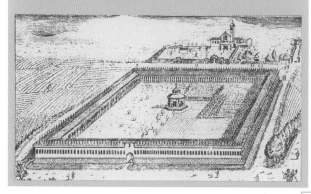

SHRAPNEL MARKS ON THE TRAM PYLONS ㊴

Piazza della Repubblica
• Public transport: MM3 Repubblica; tram 1, 9, 29/30, 33

Bomb-damaged tram pylons

The pylons carrying the tram cables in Piazza della Repubblica show amazing signs of bomb damage; there are even some holes blasted right through them. The air raids that hammered Milan in August 1943 left traces of bomb blasts and shrapnel damage all over the city. However, whereas buildings, road surfaces, gardens and monuments have been repaired or replaced, these pylons have been left as they were, simply being repainted every now and again.

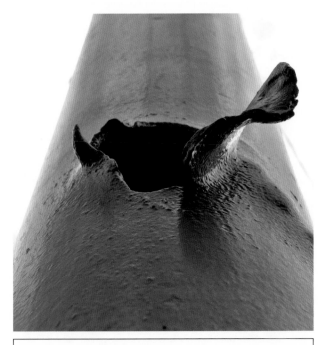

Other "lesser" signs of bomb damage dating from the Second World War can be seen in Via Palestro and Piazza del Duomo.

SANTA TERESA MEDIA LIBRARY AND ARCHIVE ④⓪

Former Church of Santi Giuseppe e Teresa
28, Via Moscova
• www.mediabrera.it (02 8739781) • For free transfer of home movies to
DVD, write to homemovies.milano@gmail.com
• Public transport: MM2 Moscova; MM3 Turati

> *Have
> your home movies
> transferred to DVD,
> free of charge*

The Santa Teresa Media Archive is part of the Braidense National Library of New Media. Here, you can watch all the programmes broadcast by the Italian state television and radio service (RAI) since the 1950s (at least, those of which the archive has recordings) as well as the programmes broadcast by Mediaset TV channels and the independent seventh channel ("La 7") since 2000. Along with these television archives there are also archives of RAI radio programmes, a vast collection of films on DVDs and VHS, music CDs and recordings of the shows put on at Milan's Teatro Piccolo. All the digital collections within Braidense Library (Sommariva, Manzoni collection, a newspaper and periodicals library and a collection illustrating the art of book-binding) can be consulted via databases available online or on CD-ROM.

The Media Library and Archive also provides a very special service: the free transfer of old home movies (for example, those shot on Super-8) to DVD, upon the single condition that the Archive is itself allowed to keep a copy. For information write to homemovies.milano@gmail.com. Such material will one day prove invaluable for future sociologists and researchers.

Another attractive feature of the Media Archive is its premises: the former church of Santi Giuseppe e Teresa, which dates from the seventeenth century and was part of the monastery of the Discalced Carmelites. The building, in the form of a Greek cross, has been restructured several times to fulfil the different roles it has played since deconsecration. After the suppression

of the monastery in 1782, it housed (in chronological order): a tobacco factory, a military barracks, a Mint, a cooperative and finally an institution that organised leisure activities for workers. Having survived the bombs of the Second World War intact, the building was (in 1959) modified in accordance with new building regulations and then repurchased by Milan City Council in 1974. The project for restoration as a media archive and library dates back to the 1990s.

Note in the central hall of the building an eighteenth-century *Map of Italy* by Matteo Greuter.

WOODEN GATES OF THE INCORONATA LOCK 🄸

Via San Marco
• Public transport: MM2 P.ta Garibaldi, Moscova; tram 2, 23/30; bus 43

> *A lock designed by Leonardo da Vinci*

The lock at the end of Via San Marco, below Viale Monte Grappa, once marked the arrival-point for those coming into the city from the north along the Naviglio Martesana (NM); now emptied of water, it still has the decaying wooden lock gates which are identical to those in a drawing from Leonardo's Atlantic Codex.

Water was abundant in Lombardy, and Leonardo was fascinated by it, beginning to study the Navigli canals as soon as he arrived in Milan; the first visual record of the linkup of the NM with the circle of the Navigli is a 1463 drawing by Leonardo himself. NM was in fact linked with the city's moat in 1496, in a project carried out by Giuliano Guasconi. Leonardo, at the time engineer to the court of Ludovico il Moro, served as consultant. One problem that had to be resolved was the difference in level between the Naviglio Grande, which reaches the city from below, and the NM, which reaches it from above. Hence the resort to a system of lock gates, which had already been used in Milan from the first half of the fifteenth century. As can be seen from

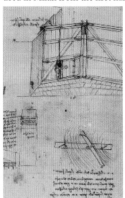

an autograph drawing in the Atlantic Codex, dated between 1506 and 1513 (see below), Leonardo developed an improvement on the lock-gate mechanism with the addition of a lower opening; operated by a specially designed "off-centre" hinge, this allowed for gradual opening in response to the increasing flow of water and easier regulation of the pressure exerted on the lock gates.

In 1967, the Chiusa della Gabelle (Tax Lock, so called because here barges paid customs duties; there is even a cabin for the customs officers) was recognised as a protected structure. At the time it was described as "the sole trace of the urban stretch of the Naviglio Martesana, complete with the last of the old bridges over the Naviglio, the last surviving lock and cabin, and remains of the original equipment used by those travelling along the canal".

BIBLIOTECA UMANISTA DELL'INCORONATA ㊷

Chiesa di Santa Maria Incoronata
112, Corso Garibaldi
• Visits by appointment; call the parish on 02 654855
• Public transport: MM2 Moscova

A fifteenth-century library

The Libraria Agostiniana dell'Incoronata is one of the hidden gems of the city. Founded in 1487 by Augustinian friars immediately after the construction of the church itself, it is one of eight such libraries in Italy and probably the only one in Milan to be decorated with frescoes. Located on the first floor of the imposing building which once extended around four courtyards and cloisters (only one survives), this library is laid out in three aisles separated by granite columns; the vaulted ceiling is frescoed with images of the *Magistri Sacrae Paginae* (i.e. Masters of the Bible), illustrious Augustinians. These are also to be seen in the lunettes between the arches of the arcade and on the small pedestals of the vault groins, which are flanked by oculi rendered in perspective.

The library used to contain a large number of manuscripts, which – thanks to the wonderful light flooding in through the windows – the brothers could easily consult seated at the wooden desks. However, nowadays the room is bare. One reason is that, with a view to the establishment of the Biblioteca Ambrosiana in 1609, Federico Borromeo collected manuscripts from various city monasteries, convents and private collections, intending to create the first library in Milan whose works could be consulted and studied by the public at large. Much of the collection from the Incoronata found its way into the Ambrosiana; however, other works were dispersed during the suppression of the monastery and the confiscation of books which Napoleon ordered in 1797. The only example in Italy of a humanist library contemporary with La Incoronata which has preserved its original furnishings and collections is the Biblioteca Malatestiana in Cesena.

WHY *INCORONATA* (VIRGIN ENCROWNED)?

When the Augustinian monastery was built here at the beginning of the fifteenth century, the church alongside was restored in the Late Gothic style then in fashion. As the work was completed around the time when Francesco Sforza had just been crowned duke (in 1451), it was decided to dedicate the new church to the Virgin Encrowned, an indirect dedication to Sforza himself.

CENTRO SOCIO RICREATIVO ANZIANI

8/A, Viale Monte Grappa
• Open 8.30am–12.30pm and 1.30pm–4.30pm
• To visit, call 02.6592362
• Public transport: MM2: Porta Garibaldi, Moscova; tram: 2, 23/30;
bus: 43

> *The old soup-kitchen building*

T he inscription *CUCINE ECONOMICHE* (low-cost soup kitchen) on an old building near Ponte delle Gabelle (see p. 175) identifies this as the site of a facility set up in 1883 by the "Committee for the Promotion of Low-Cost Soup Kitchens and Communal Bakeries".

Intended to provide basic nourishment for the ever harder-pressed working – or unemployed – classes, these *cucine economiche* supplied food cheaply. They were the product of the ideological ferment generated by the various debates and congresses on poverty that had accompanied the National Exposition held in 1881 in the city's Public Gardens.

These soup-kitchen buildings, designed by the architect Luigi Broggi, are a good example of neo-romantic architecture in Milan. The rational layout and simplicity of the interior, over two floors, responds perfectly to the function of the building: on the ground floor was the kitchen and a canteen that could seat 160, on the upper floor the administrative offices. The external decoration consists of a series of openings under surbased arches, with alternating horizontal strips of brickwork or plaster, plus simple motifs created using idiosyncratically aligned bricks.

In the small, now overgrown, courtyard stands a small chapel, which before renovation contained dozens of ex-votos dating from the end of the

nineteenth/beginning of the twentieth centuries. These thanksgiving offerings from tramps and vagabonds have all now disappeared.

Having fallen into disuse, the building was refurbished in 2000 to house the Fondazione Bettino Craxi, set up by Stefania Craxi in memory of her father. Nowadays it is the premises of the Centro Socio Ricreativo Anziani (Social and Recreational Centre for the Elderly) run by the Milan Social Services Department. Pensioners can gather here for recreational activities, dances or just for a chat.

SOUTH-WEST

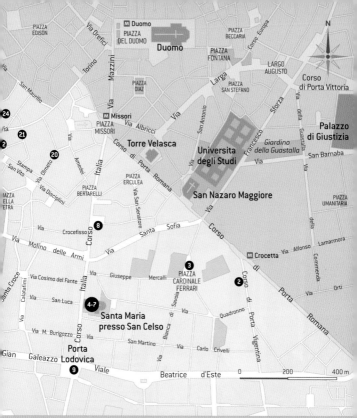

SAUNA IN A TRAMCAR

1

Terme di Milano
2, Piazzale Medalie d'Oro
• Open daily: 9.30am–11pm
• Tel: 02 55199367
• www.termemilano.com

*A proper
sauna
in a historic
ATM tramcar*

Sauna in a tram? That might be what happens in the heat of summer, when the cars are full of tourists … but the Terme di Milano came up with the idea of offering just such an experience throughout the year.

Having lost its ancient Roman baths, of which only a few ruins remain in Largo Lane dei Servi, Milan was once again equipped with a thermal spa in 2007. The spa is in an Art Nouveau complex surrounded by a section of the original Spanish Walls. The set-up has a unique special attraction: a tram.

Known as the "Wellness Tram", this is a proper sauna within a historic tram belonging to the Azienda Trasporti Milanesi (ATM). You enter through the back door and, once on board, sit on the polished wooden benches and breathe in the atmosphere of the past, thanks to the background sounds and images of old trams. In the middle of the tramcar is a large brazier around which various treatments are on offer to the sound of the tram's bell, starting with the *Aufguss* (steam jet) enriched with perfumed essences. Compared with the classic Finnish sauna, however, the tram is a "softer" option – the temperature is set at 70° and humidity is 35%.

Only a few well-preserved sections remain of the Mura Spagnole (Spanish Walls) that once surrounded the city. Built between 1546 and 1560 by order of Ferrante I Gonzaga, city governor during the Spanish rule of Milan, the fortifications had a perimeter of 11,216 metres with an opening for each of the eight main gates: Comasina, Lodovica, Nuova, Orientale, Romana (the sole survivor), Ticinese, Vercellina and Vigentina. These ramparts, which were among the most famous in Europe, consisted of a curtain-wall of bricks edged with flint set against a sloping embankment planted with trees. In 1750, having lost their military purpose, the walls were used for a public promenade (as described by Stendhal in his travel diary *Rome, Naples and Florence*), then condemned in the 1884 town plan as a traffic obstruction. Demolition began in 1899 and continued until the end of the Second World War.

Today the remnants of the walls can be seen in Piazzale Medaglie d'Oro and along the adjoining esplanade bordered by private residences, as far as Piazza XXIV Maggio. Two short sections, converted into small public gardens, are located in Viale Monte Nero, with another section in Viale Vittorio Veneto, near Porta Venezia. The inner ring road is still named after the Spanish Walls because it follows the same trajectory.

DIE XIII MARTII ANNO DOMINI LI

. BARNABAS APOSTOLVS EVANGELIVM CHRIST

OPVLO MEDIOLANENSI PRAEDICANDO IN LOC

... MOENIA ATE MARXAE PORTAE ORIENT

HOC LAPIDE FVNDANS EIMEDIAM CLAVSTIN

THE ROUND STONE IN SAN BARNABA ❷

Church of Santa Maria del Paradiso
10, Corso di Porta Vigentina
• Open daily, 8.30am–12 noon and 3pm–6pm
• Public transport: MM3 Crocetta
• www.tredesindemarz.org

> *The stone commemorating 13th March*

The Church of Santa Maria del Paradiso was founded in 1590, and within the floor of the nave is set a circular stone that appears to depict the Sun, with a central hole surrounded by thirteen rays. Tradition has it that on 13 March of 52 AD, St Barnabas (Joseph of Cyprus) arrived to preach the Gospel in what was still a pagan city. The saint stopped first at the Eastern Gateway, making a number of converts; and as he proceeded on his way, the snow melted, flowers bloomed and the statues of pagan deities crumbled. The story goes that one day he took his wooden crucifix and miraculously struck it deep into a round stone; then, using only his finger, he traced within the stone the thirteen radiating grooves that commemorate that day.

The Latin inscription beneath reads: "On the thirteenth day of March in the Year of Our Lord 51, St Barnabas the Prophet, while preaching the Gospel of Christ to the people of Milan near the city walls of Via Marina at the Porta Orientale, raised the standard of the Cross in this round stone."

Historical research has revealed that the tradition of the saint and his "passage" through Milan is unfounded: St Barnabas never left Turkey, and the Milanese actually converted to Christianity three centuries later.

While it may seem medieval, the stone is in fact much older – probably Celtic in origin. Brought to the Santa Maria del Paradiso by the Servite Fathers, it was originally in the Basilica of San Dionigi, which St Ambrose had built in the fourth century to honour the city's eleventh bishop, Dionysius. The basilica was demolished in the eighteenth century to make way for the Public Gardens of Porta Venezia.

CUT A CHILD'S HAIR ON 13TH MARCH, IT GROWS BACK THICK AND STRONG

Despite the findings of historical research, the *Tredesin de Marz* remains a special feast day for Milan (www.tredesindemarz.org). In commemorating St Barnabas, the city brings forward the advent of spring by a week. Around Corso di Porta Vigentina there is a flower market, complete with games, shows, Celtic events and parades in period costume. This is undoubtedly one of the oldest – and still eagerly awaited – popular fairs in Milan. Local tradition has it that if a child's hair is cut on this day, it grows back thick and strong.

THE WELL IN WHICH ST CALIMERUS WAS MARTYRED

❸

Crypt of San Calimero basilica - 11, Via San Calimero
• The crypt can be visited on application to the parish of Santa Maria al Paradiso • Tel: 02 58314028; e-mail: parrocchia.paradiso@tiscali.it
• Public transport: MM3 Crocetta; tram 16, 24; bus 94

> *A miracle-working well?*

The ancient church of San Calimero, modernised in 1882, was built in the fifth century on what was undoubtedly the site of a Temple of Apollo. Inside, on the far side of the main altar, there are two gates which lead through to a sixteenth-century crypt. Covered entirely in frescoes by the Renaissance painters Giovanni Mauro and Giovanni Battista della Rovere – two brothers who were known as *I Fiammenghini* (The Little Flemings) – this space contains the altar-tomb of St Calimerus, the fourth bishop of Milan and a man of which almost nothing is known.

When, at the behest of Bishop Tomaso, the crypt containing these mortal remains was opened up in the eighth century, it was found to be flooded, which is hardly surprising given the number of underground canals in Milan. It was perhaps Tomaso himself who had the well constructed that is still in use today to drain away water. A wall-plaque behind the well recounts all this, although it does not say that Calimerus was a martyr: the legend according to

which Calimerus was tortured by the pagans and then thrown into a well – as a gesture of contempt for the sacrament of baptism which he required of all citizens, Romans and pagans alike – dates from much later.

It was around the same period that the story began that the water of this well worked miracles. This is why, on St Calimerus' feast day (31 July), water from the well used to be given to the sick and diseased to heal them. Furthermore, during periods of drought the priest might draw water from the well during Mass and then pour it onto the forecourt of the church as a sort of propitiatory ritual.

COURTYARD OF SANTA MARIA DEI MIRACOLI SOPRA SAN CELSO

4

37, Corso Italia
• Open 7am–12 noon and 6pm–4.30pm
• Public transport: MM3 Missori

A hidden meridian

Unknown to many Milanese, the courtyard of the sanctuary of Santa Maria dei Miracoli sopra San Celso contains a surprising wall meridian. Within the arcade on the left wall, the first brick-built niche, which houses an icon of Santa Maria dei Miracoli (see p. 191), is marked with vertical striations. Seen from a distance, these look like the divisions between the bricks, or are simply attributed to the damage caused over time. However, a closer look reveals that these lines do not run parallel but fan out from each other, with various signs of the zodiac being inscribed within the terracotta of the brick; Scorpio, Sagittarius, Capricorn, Aquarius and Pisces are clearly recognisable. This is in fact a wall meridian which, like all those of the day, was placed within a south-facing wall, thus it could only be used in the period from October to March.

The gnomon – the raised object whose cast shadow made it possible to read off the time – is now missing; however, the presence of three holes within the wall show there must once have been one.

NEARBY
GARDENS OF SAN CELSO

5

Although closed to the public, this garden stretching in front of the small Romanesque church of San Celso (rebuilt in 996) is much appreciated in springtime because of the heavy perfume of its flowers. Few know, however, that in Via Vigoni behind the small church and the sanctuary is a second smaller garden which is open to the public. Quiet and secluded, this is decorated with a few statues, a fine fountain and a beautiful tulip tree. It also offers a view of the apses of the two churches alongside.

THE VIRGIN'S VEIL

6

Santa Maria dei Miracoli sopra San Celso church
37, Corso Italia
• Open 7am–12 noon and 4pm–4.30pm
• Public transport: MM3 Missori; tram 16, 24; bus 94

> *Veil and icon recalling a miraculous apparition of the Virgin*

The sanctuary of Santa Maria dei Miracoli sopra San Celso houses two mementos of a famous miracle: an ancient icon of the Virgin and the veil that once covered it. The veil is placed on public display once a year, on 30 December during the Mass held to celebrate the anniversary of the event. The icon, on the other hand, can be seen all year round: it is on the altar to the left of the presbytery, but is badly damaged due to the custom of the faithful touching it when offering prayers. However, the face and silhouette of the Christ Child are recognisable. A replica of the icon can be seen much more easily in the arcade of four bare-brick arches opposite the sanctuary.

According to legend, it was on 30 December 1485, when the Black Death raged within the city, that the Milanese flocked to their churches to beseech an end to the plague. One mass was held at San Nazaro in Campo, the church that once stood in this district; its exact site is that of the current high altar. The apse of that earlier church was decorated with a veiled painting that depicted the Virgin and Child; it was said that St Ambrose himself had commissioned the work as a sort of stele to commemorate the place where he had found the bodies of the early martyrs St Nazarius and St Celsus. On that 30 December the veil covering the painting was sudden pushed to one side by the hand of the Virgin herself, who then smiled at the faithful and held up the Christ Child for them to see. The legend continues that from that day forth the plague began to abate. The image thereafter attracted large numbers of pilgrims and that is why the large sanctuary was built on this site. Some claim that the veil displayed each 30 December is the one that originally covered the painting.

ANOTHER MIRACLE

Inside the church, in the second chapel on the left, is a fourteenth-century fresco from the small church that used to stand on this site. Depicting the Virgin and Child flanked by St Nazarius and St Celsus, this work too figures in the story of a miracle: it is said that on 13 and 14 July 1620 the worshippers then in the church saw the Virgin in the fresco open and close her eyes. One even claimed to have seen a tear, with the result that the image became known as the *Madonna del Pianto* (Virgin of the Tears). Later, a number of the faithful who were afflicted with eye diseases would say that this Virgin had cured them.

ST PAUL ON THE ROAD TO DAMASCUS

Church of Santa Maria dei Miracoli sopra San Celso
37, Corso Italia
• Open 7am–12 noon and 4pm–4.30pm
• Public transport: MM3 Missori

**The source
of Caravaggio's
inspiration**

In the ambulatory of the church of Santa Maria dei Miracoli sopra San Celso, to the left of the high altar, hangs Moretto da Brescia's painting of *Paul on the Road to Damascus*. This work undoubtedly had a profound effect on the imagination of Caravaggio: painted in 1542, it is innovatory because it eschews the usual view of St Paul from above and depicts the scene from the point of view of the saint, on the ground after he has been thrown from his horse. The animal, in fact, dominates the composition, just as it does in Caravaggio's masterpiece depicting the same scene in the Cerasi Chapel in the Roman church of Santa Maria del Popolo.

CARAVAGGIO IN MILAN

Although Michelangelo Merisi da Caravaggio, better known simply as Caravaggio, painted most of his masterpieces when in Rome, he is still one of Milan's most famous citizens, having been born here on 29 September 1571 and then baptised in the Basilica of Santo Stefano Maggiore (see p. 257); his certificate of baptism was rediscovered within the diocesan archives in 2007. He was the son of Lucia Aratori and Fermo Merisi, who was an architect and administrator in the household of Francesco Sforza, a member of the younger branch of the great Milanese dynasty and Marchese di Caravaggio (a village just a few kilometres from Milan).

The Merisi family was quite well-off, enjoying a fixed income from the Sforza and owning various areas of land (when sold, these would provide the young painter with an income during his first difficult years in Rome). At the age of 13 Caravaggio entered the studio of the Bergamo-born painter Simone Peterzano, who used to sign his works *Titiani Alumni* ("pupil of Titian"). The contract for what turned out to be a four-year apprenticeship was signed on 6 April 1584 by the boy's mother – his father had died during an epidemic of the plague in 1577.

Peterzano's art was a mix of the Late Mannerism typical of the Lombard School and the more realist style championed by the Counter-Reformation, the whole with a sense of light that was obviously influenced by Venetian art. Throughout his life, Caravaggio aspired to such realism, faithful to the "true" renditions for which his teacher had taught him the basics.

As was traditional, his apprenticeship also involved the study of the works to be found in Milan and the surrounding area. It is certain, for example, that the young Caravaggio had the opportunity to study Leonardo da Vinci's *Last Supper* (see p. 70) and the masterpieces of Arcimboldo. He also travelled elsewhere in northern Italy, and may even have gone as far afield as Venice, where he would have seen the admirable sense of colour in the works of such masters as Giorgione, Titian and Tintoretto. One undoubted influence was the work of a group of painters from the Brescia area, who have since been labelled "pre-Caravaggesque". Including such figures as Moretto, Savoldo, Foppa and Moroni, these artists paid particular attention to the rendition of the natural world and the reality of everyday life; indeed, the sixteenth-century frescoes by the Campi brothers within the now-deconsecrated church of San Paolo Converso (see p. 195) – painted some thirty years before the artist's birth – might almost be taken as Caravaggio *avant la lettre*. Other clear influences within Milan were Moretto's *The Conversion of St Paul* in the church of Santa Maria dei Miracoli (see p. 191); the Foppa frescoes in the Portinari Chapel (see p. 212) and the paintings by that artist now to be seen in Castello Sforzesco; Ferrari's *Saint Catherine* in the church of Sant'Angelo, which also contains four works by Campi; Callisto Piazza's *Deposition from the Cross* in the church of Maurizio; and, of course, the works by Caravaggio's own teacher, Simone Peterzano, in the churches of San Barnaba and Santa Maria della Passione. Apparently, however, no work attributable to the young Caravaggio survives from this period.

Just after completing his apprenticeship, Caravaggio seems to have been involved in some criminal affair, the first of a long line of shady incidents within the life of this master of light and shade. Soon after the death of his mother he had already gone through his part of an inheritance which he had shared with his sister Caterina and brother Giovan Battista, and

it seems likely that he then moved to Rome in summer 1592; however, some sources argue that he did not arrive there until four years later.

The artist would never return to Milan, dying at Porto Ercole (Tuscany) in 1610, when just 39 years of age. The city now possesses just two of his works, but they are among some of his most extraordinary creations: *Basket of Fruit* in Galleria Ambrosiana and *The Supper at Emmaus* in the Pinacoteca Brera.

FORMER CHURCH OF SAN PAOLO CONVERSO ❽

Piazza Sant'Eufemia
• Accessible only during exhibitions held by the Metropolitan Foundation for Art and Culture, 25, Via Sant'Eufemia
• Public transport: MM3 Missori; tram 15; bus 94

A masterpiece of Lombard Mannerism

Without doubt the old church of San Paolo Converso is one of Milan's best-kept secrets. Now deconsecrated, it serves as an exhibition venue for cultural events organised by the Metropolitan Foundation. This extraordinary double-space church (the model for which was San Maurizio) contains a spectacular collection of masterpieces painted by the two Cremona-born brothers Antonio and Giulio Campi.

By an unidentified architect – who may have been Galeazzo Alessi – the church was built for the Convent of the Angelic Sisters of Saint Paul (itself demolished in 1804). Work began in 1549, and it is likely that the whole project, together with interior decoration, was completed some forty years later. Nowadays, the area that was reserved for use by the nuns is the most badly damaged part of the structure: after the suppression of the order, it was neglected and ultimately used as a storeroom. However, the part reserved for the public is still a veritable gallery of remarkable work by the Campi brothers.

The whole space is decorated with frescoes, stucco-work, friezes, bas-reliefs and other decorations, revealing that *horror vacui* (abhorrence of empty space) characteristic of Late Renaissance architecture. Behind the presbytery are four frescoes that depict *Scenes from the Life of St Paul*, undoubtedly the first in the church to be painted. In the side chapels, note a remarkable *Beheading of St John the Baptist* and a *Martyrdom of St Lawrence*, both of which must have influenced the future work of Caravaggio (see p. 192), a *Martyrdom of St Euphemia* (by an unknown artist) and *Christ Giving the Keys to St Peter*. One of the real gems in the church, however, is the remarkable frescoed vault, covering almost 500 square metres. In spite of the damage to the frescoes caused by water seeping through the roof, this church as a whole still remains one of the masterpieces of Lombard Mannerism.

The church acoustics are so special that, up to the 1960s, it was used for recording sessions by such artistes as Maria Callas and Mina.

OTHER AIR-RAID SHELTER PANELS

The following is an incomplete list of places where you can still find signs marked with "R" and "U.S.": Via Vasari, Via Seneca, Piazza Cesare Beccaria, Corso Indipendenza, Via Ripamonti, Via Tirso, Via Melloni, Via Paganini, Via Archimede, Piazza Bertarelli, Via Caradosso, Via Marco Aurelio, Via Soave, Via Tamagno, Via Crivelli, Via Marcona, Via Luosi, Via Beato Angelico, Via Mercadante, Via Belfiore, Via Volterra, Via Porpora, Via Elba, Via Monteverdi, Via Cimarosa, Via Washington, Corso di Porta Vittoria, Via Cesare Battisti, Via Cenisio, Via De Grassi, Via Valtellina, Via Spartaco and even in Piazza Duomo (on two columns of the arcade, opposite an entrance to the metro).

SIGNS IDENTIFYING AIR-RAID SHELTERS ❾

2, Piazzale di Porta Lodovica
• Public transport: tram 15, 29, 30

Unusual signposts to possible survivors

On either side of the doorway to an old building in Porta Lodovica a white arrow can be seen against a black background marked with a capital "R". These markings date from the Second World War and on various buildings in the city – not only here at Porta Lodovica – they have survived wartime bombing and subsequent rebuilding.

The large "R" stands for *rifugio* (air-raid shelter), large numbers of which were created throughout the city during the war. Most of them were later converted to cellars or garages. Not far from these arrows others can generally be found in two colours, marked with the initials "U.S."; this does not stand for "United States" but for the *uscita di sicurezza* (emergency exit) from the air-raid shelter. As they are outside, these indications were obviously not meant for those who were already inside the shelters. They were there for rescue workers: if the building had taken a direct hit during a bombing raid, they showed the easiest route to possible survivors.

On the Porta Lodovica building, these indications are to the right of the main doorway; there is also another, perfectly preserved "R", at the corner of the street.

Less frequent are large white "I"s against a black background (two

examples can be seen in Via Caccialepori and Via Piolti de' Bianchi) and rarer still are large black "I"s against a white background: these were set up by order of the city's fire service and local air-raid protection committee and indicated the location of a fire hydrant (*idrante*) from which firemen could pump water.

On the walls of the first pavilion of the Polyclinic, at 9 Via Pace, there is a white circle enclosing a red square, which indicated a hospital equipped with an air-raid shelter.

MUSEO DEL CAVALLO GIOCATTOLO "LORENZO PIANOTTI"

30, Alzaia Naviglio Pavese
• Visits on request, call 02 8323225 or 328 941 3716
• Every 13 December (St Lucy's Day) the house is open all day, with no need to book • Admission free
• Public transport: tram 3, 29/30

Toy horse heaven

This must be the world's largest collection of wooden horses. The "Lorenzo Pianotti" Toy Horse Museum has more than one thousand of them, of all shapes and sizes, dating from a variety of periods. Artist and collector Pianotti actually lives in the building that houses the museum, making the collection readily available to visitors (on reservation) and providing a very personal guided tour.

Since putting together the core collection (that is, 500 wooden horses) and designing the original layout of the Museum of the Toy Horse established by the Chicco company in Grandate near Como (see www.museodelcavallogiocattolo.it), Pianotti's passionate interest in collecting toy horses is unabated. The pieces in his collection date from the eighteenth century up to the present day, and range in size from small equine figurines used as games pieces to massive steeds. There are rocking horses, horses on wheels and horses in the form of bottles or lamps. Painted or sculpted, modelled in plaster or papier mâché, there are horses for children and adults. Each corner of the museum has some form of our noble four-legged friend.

This exceptional collection also includes more than 200 miniature hats dating from the Napoleonic period, as well as old books of fairytales, period postage stamps and 250 bookmarks dating from the late nineteenth century to the 1960s (all somehow horsy in character). The oldest horse models in the museum – those which the artist did not pass on to the Grandate museum – were also the very first in Pianotti's collection: "Mario" and "Arturo" (each horse in the museum has a name) were bought by Lorenzo as a young child.

NEARBY

FRIDAY NIGHT IS *ROCKY HORROR PICTURE SHOW* NIGHT
Every Friday night since 1981 the Cinema Mexico (57 Via Savona) has screened *The Rocky Horror Picture Show*, Richard O'Brien's cult musical. Just as in Paris (see *Secret Paris* in this series of guides), this is not however an ordinary screening: the public participates in the show, some even dressing up like the characters. Singing and dancing along with the action on screen – as well as taking part in the dialogues, which everyone seems to know by heart – each member of the audience becomes an actor in this strange rock opera parody, which dates from 1975.

THE LONG COURTYARD
OF CORSO SAN GOTTARDO

15, Via Ascanio Sforza (Naviglio side) and 18, Corso San Gottardo
• Free access via gates at either end of courtyard
• Public transport: tram 3

Furmaggiatt district

A long the road that runs from Porta Ticinese to Pavia, a row of social housing conceals some of the rare remaining evidence of the Milan of yesteryear. If you cross the threshold of the house at 18 Corso San Gottardo, you reach a long series of typical interior courtyards that run through the entire block, to emerge on Naviglio Pavese by the front door of 15 Via Ascanio Sforza.

This is one of the few surviving examples of the formerly ubiquitous *casére* (little houses) in this district. There is another, unfortunately no longer accessible, at number 14. All along this courtyard are the typical *linghere*: the long passages leading to people's homes, at the end of which were the only bathrooms. The overcrowding and the spartan facilities were however offset by the vibrant social life of the courtyards, which were also useful for Milanese crooks who used them to make a quick get-away.

The houses of Corso San Gottardo made up the picturesque district of Furmaggiatt. When the Naviglio Pavese was completed in 1819, it was here that the cheeses produced in the countryside south of Milan began to arrive, loaded onto barges. As the land had grown particularly fertile under the Cistercians of Chiaravalle who introduced irrigation by flooding, a common practice in the Po Valley, cattle breeding and the associated dairy products that fed the Milan market had intensified.

The cheese rounds were unloaded into the little houses overlooking the canal, hence the name *casére*, permeated as they were with the acrid smell. As the new cheeses were landed they replaced the previous load, which after three months' maturing was ready to be sold by the cheesemongers on Corso San Gottardo. Sales were brisk thanks to the heavy traffic on this road that linked town and country as well as being on the route of the Gamba de Legn (Wooden Leg), a steam locomotive so called perhaps because of its undulating gait as it seemed to limp along. To prevent the cheeses fermenting and becoming indigestible, the crust was scraped off: the ladies of San Vincenzo de' Paoli charitable organisation took advantage of this to collect some strips while they were still soft, using them to flavour soup for the neighbourhood's poor.

A BARGE TRIP DOWN THE NAVIGLI CANAL

- Leaves from towpath (alzaia) Number 4 on the Naviglio Grande
- Reservations at website http://naviglilombardi.it or phone 02 92273118
- The barge seats fifty
- Public transport: MM2 Porta Genova; tram 2; bus 47, 74

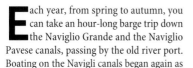

> *From canals to locks*

Each year, from spring to autumn, you can take an hour-long barge trip down the Naviglio Grande and the Naviglio Pavese canals, passing by the old river port. Boating on the Navigli canals began again as an experiment in 2007, but such was the success of the initiative that it has now become a permanent fixture of the tourist calendar.

The excursion on the fifty-seater barge (free for accompanied children under 6) gives visitors the chance to travel the route taken by the cargo boats that supplied Milan in the old days. After casting off, the barge passes in front of the Vicolo dei Lavandai (see p. 204), to reach the landing-stage on the towpath (*alzaia*) at 66 Naviglio Grande; this is near Palazzo Galloni, which houses an Engraving Centre (see below). You then come to one of the most significant architectural complexes along this first stretch of the canal: the church, bridge and wash-house of San Cristoforo. From the double-fronted church of St Christopher, a masterpiece of fourteenth-century architecture, princesses, kings and emperors took ship when they were entering Milan by water. The modern-day barge trip next takes you towards the Vicolo dei Lavandai; then, having passed beyond the Ponte dello Scodellino ("Bridge of the Dishes" – the name refers to a number of hostelries that used to provide food for the bargemen), the barge enters the Darsena. This port for trading vessels from the Lake Maggiore area comprised some 6,000 metres of fully equipped quays and was one of the most important inland docks throughout the Mediterranean. The barge then travels back up the Naviglio Pavese (Pavia Canal) to the first of the locks, the famous Conchetta ("small lock"), which has recently been fully restored and you now see what it would have been like at work. The canal trip ends at the point of departure (Alzaia 4).

For further information on the Navigli, see the double page overleaf.

NEARBY

ENGRAVING CENTRE ⓮

Palazzo Galloni, built in the seventeenth century, has since 1975 housed a Centro dell'Incisione, which was founded by professional etcher Gigi Pedroli and organiser of exhibitions and cultural events Gabriella Casarico. From 4pm to 7pm Tuesday to Saturday (and the last Sunday of each month), the picturesque courtyard of the palazzo is home to the animated activity of a school for engravers.

WHAT REMAINS OF THE NAVIGLI

The Navigli is an old network of navigable canals that run around and across Milan, linking the city with Lake Maggiore, Lake Como and the southern stretch of the Ticino, as well as opening a way to the sea via the River Po. Gradually expanded over the centuries, the network was in use from Roman times right up to 1935, when work to fill in the canals was completed.

Nowadays all that remains are short stretches of open canal, as well as a few bridges, towpaths, locks and wash-houses.

There are three open-air stretches in all. To the south are the **Naviglio Grande** and the **Naviglio Pavese**, which run into the city as far as Piazza XXIV Maggio. These also encompass the old **Darsena** (river port), a large complex of quaysides awaiting restoration. To the north is the **Naviglio Martesana**, which extends as far as the Villaggio dei Giornalisti district, where it continues to flow underground.

Some locks and water basins (*chiuse* and *conche*), originally built to compensate for differences in level within the watercourses, have also been preserved, but solely for their interest as artefacts of industrial archaeology. The most significant are the **Conca de Viarenna** (p. 207) and the **Conca delle Gabelle** (p. 209), as well as the **Conchetta** ("small lock") on the Naviglio Pavese (near Via della Conchetta) and the **Conca Fallata** (in Via della Chiesa Rossa). As the Naviglio Grande was built before the development of the necessary technology, it does not have any locks.

There are also some **89 wash-houses** (*lavatoi*) on the banks of the three Navigli; notably the one near San Cristoforo church, but the best known is the Lavatoio Brellin in Vico dei Lavandai (see p.203).

A total of **187 bridges or walkways** cross the three urban canals and the canals of Bereguardo and Paderno. Within Milan itself, there are eleven such structures over the Naviglio Grande, twelve over the Naviglio Pavese and fourteen over the Naviglio Martesana. Particularly noteworthy are the concrete and iron pedestrian bridges over the Naviglio Grande and the Naviglio Pavese, as well as the **Ponte delle Sirenette** (Bridge of the Mermaids), which was transferred to Parco Sempione; the **Ponte dello Scodellino** (Bridge of the Dishes), located at the point where the Naviglio Grande empties into the Darsena and owing its name to the fact that the barges stopped here so that the bargemen could get a bowl of soup (*scodella di minestra*) at the nearby *Osteria del Pallone*; and the **Ponte del Trofeo**, which links Via Gorizia and Via Scoglio di Quarto and is so named because in the seventeenth century the Count of Fuentes, Spanish governor of Milan, had a "trophy" placed here to celebrate the work on the

Naviglio Pavese. That trophy plaque, removed in 1865, can now be seen in Museo del Castello.

Underneath the city of Milan there is still a network of 250 kilometres of waterways; some 50 kilometres of wide routes and the other 200 kilometres made up of small irrigation canals and streams. This near intact patrimony buried underground periodically leads someone to advance a suggestion dear to many Milanese: that all the covered Navigli should once more be opened up.

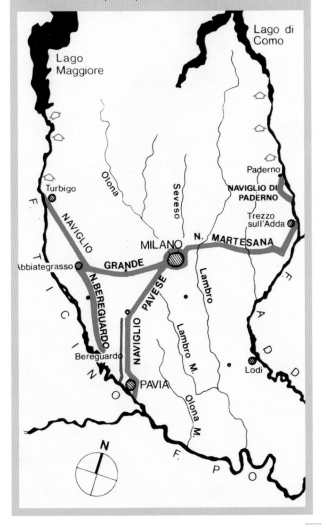

SCALA ANSALDO WORKSHOPS

34, Via Bergognone
• Open Tuesday and Thursday, 9am–12 noon and 2pm–4pm
• Guided tours only, reservation necessary: tel. 02 88795650
or e-mail servizi@civita.it
• Public transport: MM2 Porta Genova; bus 68

> **Behind
> the scenes
> at La Scala**

Housed within the old Ansaldo Steel Works, the workshops of the Teatro della Scala let you go behind the scenes of this famous Milanese opera house, discovering not only how the scenery and accessories are made but also various other aspects of stage machinery and costume-making.

The workshops occupy a vast structure: a total floor space of 20,000 square metres divided into three separate buildings, named respectively after film director Luchino Visconti, set designer Nicola Benois and costume designer Luigi Sapelli (whose stage name was *Caramba*). Most of the production design activity is concentrated here. But the place also serves as a wardrobe for more than 60,000 costumes, as well as having rehearsal rooms for the chorus and a space (the same size as the Scala stage) for trying out set designs.

The theatre's vast heritage of costumes and sets exists thanks to the daily work of more than 150 craftsmen and women: carpenters, locksmiths, joiners, decorators, sculptors, seamstresses and wardrobe mistresses, each of whom generally works from just a simple sketch. It was with the precise intention of sharing this microcosm of craft activity with the wider public that the Teatro della Scala decided to throw open the doors of the Scala Ansaldo workshops, beginning with a programme of guided tours that lets you see the backstage work that goes into the creation of a production. The tour, led by specialist personnel working in collaboration with the heads of the various workshops, takes you through the various buildings and sections, ending at pavilion number 36, which is sometimes used for concerts, public conferences and exhibitions.

PLAQUES BY THE VIARENNA LOCK

Via Conca del Naviglio
• Public transport: tram 3, 9, 29/30

A gift from Ludovico Sforza transformed into a fishpond

When the Navigli canals were still in use* the Viarenna Lock gave access from the Naviglio Grande into the outer ring (*cerchia*) of the Navigli. It was constructed by the Venerable Fabric of the Duomo of Milan in the years 1551–1558 to replace a previous lock which dated back to 1438 and was demolished to make room for city fortifications. A wooden bulkhead recently discovered set within the dock bears witness to its existence.

Designed by the engineers Filppo da Modena and Aristotele Fioravanti, that earlier lock had, by the end of the century, already been raised by Leonardo da Vinci, as can be seen from a drawing in his famous *Atlantic Codex* (f. 148r) now in the Biblioteca Ambrosiana.

When the Cerchia dei Navigli and the Naviglio canal in Via Vallone were filled in (1933), the Viarenna Lock was at first left connected to the dock but then became an isolated, unused structure. Nowadays it is enclosed and its gates have been removed. However, a small kiosk has been built facing towards the narrow water basin, which today contains freshwater fish.

Within the kiosk are two plaques dating from the fifteenth century. The most important of these concerns Ludovico Sforza, known as Ludovico il Moro: "Under the aegis of the Protecting Virgin, a lock – built upon a gentle gradient due to differences in ground level – was offered to the Fabric of the Duomo by Ludovico, Duke of Milan, the year in which his wife, Beatrice d'Este, died: 1497. It allows vessels to circulate easily from one end of the city to the other upon payment of duties and customs."

The other plaque is located higher up on the side of the kiosk and depicts the symbol of the Venerable Fabric of the Duomo – the Virgin of Mercy – who envelops the façade of the cathedral within her outstretched mantle.

Originally, these two plaques were fixed to the façade of a building which stood on the Naviglio, borne out by early-twentieth-century photographs. Earlier they had been located alongside the Fabric Lock, near the Naviglio landing-stage in the dock.

ORIGIN OF THE ITALIAN EXPRESSION *A UFO*

The vessels bearing the marble for use in the construction of the Duomo were marked A.U.F. (*ad usum Fabricae*: "for use in the fabric [of the cathedral]") and were exempt from duties and customs. It appears that the Italian expression *a ufo*, which means "on expenses" or "to be charged to the public purse" derives from this abbreviation.

---

*Man-made canals constructed between 1179 (Naviglio Grande) and the sixteenth century (Naviglio Martesana) to link Milan to the Ticino area and to the River Adda for transporting merchandise.

HAUT-RELIEF DEPICTING THE TRANSPORT OF THE MORTAL REMAINS OF THE MAGI ⑰

Basilica of Sant'Eustorgio
1, Piazza Sant'Eustorgio
• Open 7.30am–12.30pm and 2pm–6.30pm
• Public transport: tram 3, 9, 15, 29, 30; bus 59

What are the Three Magi doing in Milan?

Although difficult to see clearly, the haut-relief on the capital of the fifth column to the right of the nave in this basilica depicts the transport of the bodies of the Three Magi to Milan. Dating from the eleventh century, it shows Eustorgio leading oxen drawing a wagon on which stands a marble sarcophagus containing their mortal remains. Tradition has it that, thirty-three years after taking part in the Nativity, the Three Kings returned to Jerusalem to be present at the Crucifixion, and that they died there, one after the other, as martyrs. Collected together, their three bodies were later taken to Constantinople, where Queen Helena, mother of Constantine the Great, was gathering together the first collection of Christian relics. It was Constantine's son, Emperor Constans I, who gave the relics to Eustorgio during the latter's visit to Constantinople prior to becoming Bishop of Milan. The future saint then had a marble sarcophagus or ark sculpted, placed on a wagon drawn by two oxen and set off in 344 for Milan. This is the scene depicted on the capital in the basilica. When he arrived at Porta Ticinese, not far from the city's first baptismal fonts, the wagon became bogged down in the mud and was impossible to move. Eustorgio took this as a sign from God and ordered that the Basilica of the Magi – now known as the Basilica of Sant'Eustorgio – should be built on that very spot. Eight centuries later, the forces of Frederick I Barbarossa sacked the city and seized these precious relics, which the emperor gave to the archbishop of Cologne, Rainald von Dassel, in 1164. All attempts to bring the remains back to Milan failed. Then, in 1904, Cardinal Ferrari, archbishop of Milan, was finally able to restore to Sant'Eustorgio the bones of the Magi (two fibulas, a tibia and a vertebra), which

had been presented to the city by the archbishop of Cologne, Mgr Fischer. A procession held on the Feast of the Epiphany still celebrates this event. The crypt and small chapel containing the relics are in the south transept of the basilica. At the top of the bell-tower – the highest in Milan and, in 1306, the first in the city to have a clock that told the time rather than a mechanism that simply rang the hours – the spire does not end in the usual cross but in an eight-point star, recalling the star the Magi followed to Bethlehem.

THE FORGOTTEN SYMBOLISM OF THE MAGI

The wise men or Magi are referred to in the Gospel According to St Matthew (2:1–12) but without any mention of their names, their number or the fact that they are kings. It was an apocryphal Armenian gospel of the fifth or sixth centuries – the so-called Gospel of the Infancy – that gave the names of Melchior (or Belchior), Balthazar and Gaspar, and identify them as the kings of the Persians, Hindus and Arabs respectively. The three gifts they brought – gold, frankincense and myrrh – symbolised recognition that the new-born Christ was both a king (gold) and the priest (frankincense) and prophet (myrrh) of God.

The Roman Catholic Church honours the Magi on 6 January, the Feast of the Epiphany, originally the sole Christian feast intended to celebrate the manifestation of Christ in the world. In fact, it was only in 354 that Pope Liberius, struggling against pagan worship and the spread of Mithraism in particular (see our *Secret Rome*), instituted the feast day of Christ's birth on 25 December. This was the date of the birth of the Eastern god, Mithras (in conjunction with the winter solstice and the beginning of the return of light to the world) and was chosen so as to absorb within the Christian faith the worshippers of that god. 6 January, on the other hand, was a feast day of the epiphanic Greek gods (the Greek word *epiphanos* means "manifestation" or "revelation"), celebrating the appearance of (Greek) deities to humanity. It falls twelve days after 25 December, the first day of the new solar year.

Tradition has it that Melchior represented the races of Europe and was descended from Japhet, son of Noah; Balthazar represented the races of Africa and was descended from another son of Noah's, Ham or Cham; and Gaspar represented the races of Asia and was descended from another in the line of Noah, Sem. The three initials of Japhet, Ham and Sem – JHS – obviously form a reference to Jesus Christ, whose name was often abbreviated to *JHS* (*Jesus, Hominum Salvator* – Jesus, Saviour of Mankind). Certain sources argue that in following the "Star of Bethlehem" to Christ's birthplace, the three kings were actually following a conjunction of the planets Jupiter, Mercury and Saturn, which form a triangle with the Sun at the centre. Here again the initials JHS (Jupiter, Hermes [the Greek name for Mercury] and Saturn) occur, indicating that the Light of Jesus, Saviour of Mankind, had taken corporeal form on Earth.

Tradition has it that the three gifts borne by the Magi are now in the Monastery of Saint Paul on Mount Athos (Greece).

THE VIRTUES IN THE PORTINARI CHAPEL ⑱

Museo di Sant'Eustorgio
3, Piazza Sant'Eustorgio
• Open 10am–6pm (closed Mondays)
• Public transport: tram 3, 9, 15, 29, 30; bus 59

Symbols of the theological and cardinal virtues

The famous monumental tomb of St Peter Martyr in the sublime Portinari Chapel within the Basilica of Sant'Eustorgio is borne up by eight female figures. It is not often noticed that each of these rests on an animal, some of them mythological. Both the female figures and the animals depict the virtues that the soul should cultivate for its own spiritual health.

Justice is shown with a sword and a pair of scales (broken at some point) and rests on dogs that symbolise "Watchdogs of the Faith" and refer to the phrase *domini cani* (Hounds of the Lord) which was often given as the meaning of the name of the Dominican Order to which St Peter Martyr belonged.

Temperance is shown pouring water from one jar to another and rests on a figure that is half-human, half-animal; a sort of sphinx, this creature symbolises the point of moral separation between the human and the bestial.

Strength or Courage (Fortitude) does not have her usual symbol of a tower but holds a rose-window-like disc against her chest with her hands crossed; this symbolises heavenly virtue. The lions on which she stands represent the spiritual power that has been established upon the world.

Prudence (Sapientia) has two faces, one in front and one behind. She is holding a book and observing a small object which is undoubtedly a mirror, reflecting wisdom and prudence.

Charity (Caritas) suckles two infants at her breast. This symbolises unconditional Love nourishing Humanity without reserve. The figure rests on two dogs that symbolise tenderness and affection.

Faith (Fides) holds a cup in her left hand and a cross in her right, thus expressing faith in the spiritual and bodily salvation to be found within the bosom of the Church thanks to its sacrament of the Eucharist, represented by the cup/chalice. She stands on two dogs that defend her.

Hope (Spes) does not have her usual anchor but rather holds a bunch of flowers. These symbolise the openness to the influence of God which generates a perfume of hope, the ultimate virtue for humanity as it passes through this world of pain and suffering. She is borne up by two gryphons, which in medieval iconography symbolised the dual, human and divine, nature of Christ.

Obedience holds the closed book of The Rule and the cord associated with monastic orders. She is borne up by two lions that symbolise how the obedience of the Just is rewarded in Heaven; the Lion was an earthly symbol of the spiritual sun of celestial Paradise.

The virtues are usually divided into two groups: the theological, which originate in and draw upon the Holy Spirit as revealed through Faith, Hope and Charity, and the cardinal. These latter are the main virtues implicit within humanity itself: Justice, Prudence, Strength (or Courage), Temperance and Obedience (either to the monastic Rule or to social order).

The Portinari Chapel was built in the years 1462–1468 for the Florentine banker Pigello Portinari, the Milan agent of the Medici Bank. It is considered to be a masterpiece of the Lombard Renaissance and its frescoes, by Vincenzo Foppa, recount the life of the Dominican St Peter Martyr (1205–1252), also known as Peter of Verona. The tomb dates from 1336 and was the work of the master sculptor Giovanni di Balduccio. Originally it was located to the left of the nave of Sant'Eustorgio church, only being moved here in 1737.

SCULPTURE COMMEMORATING GIAN GIACOMO MORA

Junction of Corso di Porta Ticinese and Via Gian Giacomo Mora
• Public transport: tram 3; MM3 Missori

> *A barber unjustly accused of spreading the plague*

The name of the poor barber who was unjustly accused of being an *untore* (spreader of the plague) and then brutally executed was not cleared until several centuries after his death (see "Column of Infamy", p. 89). In 1868, however, the street where his barber's shop had stood, at the corner of Corso di Porta Ticinese, was named after him. The present building on the site of that shop now bears a sculpture and plaque in his honour. Hidden away beneath a corner porch, they are easy to overlook.

The sculpture by Ruggero Menegon, installed in 2005, uses the interplay of solid masses and open spaces to suggest the area formerly occupied by the inglorious "column of infamy". The plaque directly opposite bears this quotation from Manzoni: "Here there once stood the home of Giangiacomo Mora, unjustly tortured and put to death as an *untore* during the great plague of 1630. There is some comfort in thinking that if the executioners knew not what they did, it was because they did not want to know. It was as a result of this ignorance that man [could] take it upon himself to destroy as he saw fit; such [ignorance] is not an excuse but a fault."

PIAZZA VETRA, THE EXECUTION GROUND

This vast green area – also known as "Parco delle Basiliche" because it extends between the basilicas of San Lorenzo and Sant'Eustorgio – was until 1840 one of the places in Milan where executions were carried out.

In Roman times there were barracks nearby for soldiers guarding the imperial palace, hence the Latin name *Castra Vetera* ("Old Forts", *castrum* being a fortification). The name "Vetera" was then used for the Canale della Vetera, a water channel that once ran along the north side of the area. This was where commoners condemned to death were executed; aristocrats were put to death in front of the Broletto. Piazza Vetra was also used for executions ordered by the court of the Inquisition, which sat in Corso di Porta Ticinese. Here, witches and heretics were burnt alive at the stake. The last "witches" to suffer this terrible fate in this square were Anna Maria Pamolea and her maid Margarita Martignona, condemned by the Inquisition on 12 November 1641.

COURTYARDS OF PALAZZO ARCHINTO   ⓴

6, Via Olmetto

• This palazzo can be visited either during the days of the "Open Courtyards" (*Cortili Aperti*) initiative in late May, or by application to Luoghi Pii Elemosinieri, a charitable foundation housed here for over a century: www.golgiredaelli.it

• Public transport: MM1 Duomo; tram 2, 3, 14

> *A "medieval" tower, blazons and old patrician crests*

Palazzo Archinto was built in the fifteenth century, restructured in the eighteenth and then extensively restored after damage caused by the 1943 bombing. Its courtyards are usually closed to the public, but when they are accessible you'll find a Romantic-style garden complete with a massive wisteria plant and tower that appears to be medieval but is in fact neo-Gothic, built in 1830 when a taste for such medieval architecture was common among the patrician classes in the city.

Despite the wartime bomb damage, the palazzo is still one of those luxurious Milanese residences which has best maintained its original charm and layout. In the first courtyard are arcades of Tuscan columns, while in the second (the one with the tower) is a gallery surmounted by a terrace with a Baroque stone balustrade. There is also an iron gate designed in 1910 by Giuseppe Bagatti Valsecchi, and fixed to the walls are two crests of the Visconti Aicardi family (from their fiefdom of Riozzo) as well as a plaque designed in 1923 by Adolfo Wildt to commemorate the war dead who had been employees of Luoghi Pii Elemosinieri – the palazzo has belonged to this charitable foundation, one of the oldest in Milan, for over 150 years. Unfortunately, the frescoes by Gian Battista Tiepolo and Vittorio Maria Bigari which once graced the reception rooms were destroyed during the war.

CASA ISIMBARDI POZZOBONELLI

4, Via dei Piatti
- Open during the "Open Courtyards" (Cortili Aperti) days; a polite request to the porter may also gain you admission
- Public transport: MM1, MM3 Duomo; tram 2, 3, 14

> *A Bramante courtyard within a characterless modern building*

When you first turn into Via dei Piatti, it is difficult to believe that one of these rather characterless post-war buildings actually contains a real gem of Renaissance architecture, which has been attributed to Donato Bramante (1444–1514).

Although modified over the centuries, this fine courtyard has preserved all its original features; it is, indeed, one of the few structures to still bear witness to the elegant harmony that was characteristic of so many buildings in fifteenth/sixteenth-century Milan.

The four sides of the building, enclosing a quadrangle, have a ground-floor arcade of rounded arches. Surmounted by Corinthian capitals, the granite columns themselves bear plaques with blazons and crests. The elegant decoration of the structure is completed with small consoles

and traces of fresco comprising: grotesques, vertical bands of colour, cartouches and a series of medallions depicting the busts of Roman emperors in profile.

The original palazzo renovated in the eighteenth century prior to becoming the residence of Cardinal Giuseppe Pozzobonelli, Archbishop of Milan, later passed from the Pozzobonelli to the Isimbardi, another important Milanese family. That restructuring and modification survived right up to 1943; however, when restoring the bomb-damaged palazzo it was decided to return to a less elaborate style, while still preserving the full magnificence of its internal courtyard.

FONDAZIONE ALESSANDRO DURINI ❷❷

2, Via Santa Maria Valle
- Open during exhibitions and conferences
- www.fondazionedurini.com
- Public transport: MM1 and MM3 Duomo

"A place for the arts in a historic palazzo"

Dating from the Middle Ages, this palazzo once belonged to the Visconti family and has since 1939 housed the Alessandro Durini Foundation, a centre that aims not only to assist painters, sculptors, art historians and critics but also to organise exhibitions, conferences and other cultural events. The palazzo, listed as a structure "of historic and artistic interest" by the Regional Government of Lombardy, has in fact been associated with the arts throughout its history. In the eighteenth century, for example, it housed the studio of the sculptor Antonio Canova, who gathered here a collection of plaster casts and ancient works of sculpture that is in the Accademia di Brera. From 1809 to 1815 the building was home to Giuseppe Bossi, painter, art theoretician and collector. Furthermore, the palazzo collection included sheets of Leonardo drawings (now in the Venice Accademia and the Biblioteca Ambrosiana), coins, medals and such famous paintings as Andrea Mantegna's *Dead Christ* (now in the Brera).

Used for cultural events, the ground-floor rooms are decorated with sixteenth- and seventeenth-century paintings as well as various pieces of period furniture, including the famous Durini Table, which the sculptor Giuseppe Rusanti made in the mid-seventeenth century for Gian Giacomo Durini.

NEARBY

COURTYARD OF PALAZZO STAMPA DI SONCINO ❷❸

At 2 Via Soncino stands one of the most characteristic buildings in the city: Palazzo Stampa di Soncino. This was built in the sixteenth century for Massimiliano Stampa, the commander of Castello Sforzesco who was ultimately raised to a marquisate by Emperor Charles V. Open to visitors during the "Open Courtyard" days, the courtyard contains nineteenth-century stable buildings and arcades within which are displayed various marble and stone fragments. There is also a sixteenth-century well-head decorated with the blazon of the Marchese Stampa.

HOUSE OF THE "MONSTER OF MILAN" IN VIA BAGNERA

24

Access from Via Torino
• Public transport: tram 2, 3, 14

> *The narrowest and most sinister street in Milan*

Via Bagnera, one of the most characteristic remnants of nineteenth-century Milan, is perhaps the only small street to have survived either demolition or conversion into a private route. Although central, this short and narrow street is far from easy to find, tucked away as it is between Via Santa Marta and Via Nerino. It is, in fact, the shortest street in Milan, being a simple L-shape just wide enough for a single vehicle to pass. Unsurprisingly it used to be known as Via Stretta (Narrow Street) – the name Bagnera derives from the fact that the baths (*bagni*) of Roman Milan were located nearby.

A small building in this street served as both office and home for Antonio Boggia, the infamous "Monster of Milan" in the first half of the nineteenth century: acquaintances who had the misfortune to visit him here ended up murdered, hacked to pieces with an axe. The motive behind these crimes was basically money: when Boggia found out that someone he knew owned property or other wealth, he dispatched them and then, with the help of a calligrapher, forged letters in which the deceased announced they were travelling abroad and granted Boggia power of attorney during their absence. His choice of Via Bagnera as the place to conceal both murders and bodies was no accident: its shape and size meant that carriages could not get through and therefore passers-by were very rare. The chance of being disturbed by

unwanted witnesses or the night-watch was minimum. Furthermore, Boggia's house had a cellar which could be reached only by an inside stairway, and so provided the perfect place to bury his victims. Finally caught, the "Monster of Milan" was hanged at Porta Ludovica and his head given to the Anatomy Cabinet of the Ospedale Maggiore. All trace of it has since been lost, although the axe used in committing the crimes mysteriously reappeared on the collectors' market in October 2009.

CARROBBIO TOWER

Largo Carrobbio, at the junction with Via Medici
• Public transport: tram 2, 3, 14

*The tower
of horrors*

Carrobbio was the location of the Roman city gateway on the road to Pavia. Now little remains of those ancient fortifications, even if a tower with a very sinister reputation has survived.

In Roman days, *carrobbi* (there were several of them) were places where the ritual liberation that turned slaves into freemen was performed. Subsequently, they became places of trade and excise officers set up their counters here to collect duty on goods entering the city. The *carrobbio* of Porta Ticinese was also the seat of the Holy Inquisition and the place where it put its victims "to the question" – in other words tortured them.

The gateway, giving onto the road toward Pavia (*Ticinum* in Latin), was flanked by two towers. One of these still survives and is known by various names: the Archers Tower, the Evil Tower (*Torraccia*) and the Disease Tower (the leprosarium of San Materno – later demolished during the building of Ospedale Maggiore – stood nearby). Nowadays, the tower is partially enclosed within a number of private buildings, but it can be reached through the restaurant at 4 Largo Carrobbio: the back room leads into a small garden that gives onto the ruins. The tower can also be seen from the small courtyard used as a car park by a hotel at the beginning of Via Medici.

Standing just 6 metres high, the tower has a single small window and one slit opening for use by archers. In the nineteenth century the Milanese used to say that the Inquisition had tortured its victims here, but also that the moaning of leprosy victims could still be heard. It was even claimed to have been used for human sacrifice. In fact, not far away (in Via Torino), a building destroyed during a bombing raid in 1943 was said to have revealed the remains of a Mithraic temple. Animals were sacrificed to Mithras, a deity of eastern origin. That was all it took for the fertile imagination of the local residents to transform the 2,000-year history of this structure into a catalogue of horrors.

It seems that the name of the district, Carrobbio, derives from the Latin term *quadruvium*, a crossroads of four or more roads leading towards a city gateway, or else from the word *carrivium* (a road that could be used by carts). In his novel *I Promessi Sposi*, Manzoni describes this area as "one of the most desolate in Milan"; in fact, being a "frontier zone", it was the haunt of criminals, brigands, prostitutes and cheats.

CLOISTER OF THE HUMILIATE SISTERS

7, Via Cappuccio
• Public transport: MM1–2 Cadorna
• Visits upon polite request to the porter, or else during "Open Courtyard" days

> *A delightful glimpse of medieval poetry*

Built towards the end of the fifteenth century, the convent of the Humiliate Sisters of Santa Maria Maddalena al Cerchio owes its name to the fact that it stands on the ruins of the old Roman Circus, in the area of the imperial *podium* (*cerchio* in Italian comes from the Latin *ad circulum*). The name of the street onto which the cloister itself gives seems to derive from that of the wimple worn by the nuns (*cappuccio* = hood).

The convent, suppressed by Napoleon, was sold in 1811 to the Società dei Classici Italiani. The church itself was demolished, the upper gallery of the cloister walled in and the windows altered, then the structure was annexed to the adjacent Palazzo Lita Biumi, which dates from the eighteenth century.

Bought in 1915 by the engineer Guido Ucelli, the cloister was finally restored and declared a national monument in 1923. Access today is via the arcades within the courtyard of Casa Ucelli, with permission from the porter; also open to the public on "Open Courtyard" days (*Giornate dei Cortili Aperti*).

The sight that meets your eyes here is among the most harmonious and poetic in Milan, as the cloister has kept all the austere sobriety typical of the medieval architecture commissioned by the Humiliate Sisters.

If you look carefully you can see how the building developed: the arches in the medieval arcades reveal the influence of Bramante (1444–1514), while in the upper gallery there are clear traces of the sixteenth century.

Along the walls are set eight columns in *serizzo* (grey Italian granite) from the now-demolished convent of Vettabia (near Piazza Vetra). However, the provenance of certain other remains – including a radiant Roman head in marble – are unknown. Note also a massive ship's anchor and the pintle for a rudder, copies of those found in 1930 at the bottom of Lago di Nemi in the wrecks of two imperial Roman ships.

NEARBY

CHURCH OF SAN BERNARDINO ALLE MONACHE

At 13 Via Lanzone you can see the remains of the monastery of the Order of Santa Maria di Cantalupo (fourteenth century). The small brick-built church dates from 1450 and in recent years has been reopened for worship. Note the decoration of the façade, with what looks like faience bowls, and the magnificent cornice of small arcades directly under the roof.

GARDEN OF THE VIRGINS

Università Cattolica del Sacro Cuore
1, Largo A. Gemelli
• Open Monday to Friday, 8.30am–5pm
• Public transport: MM2 Sant'Ambrogio; bus 50, 58

While the Milanese are perfectly familiar with the Università Cattolica del Sacro Cuore, the place does contain some spots that are less well-known, even if on weekdays they are perfectly accessible if you pass through the building.

> *A garden to which men are not admitted*

One feature particularly worthy of note is to the right of the Aula Magna (Main Lecture Hall): at the end of a central arcade that separates the two quadrangles/cloisters is a large glass window that overlooks the Giardino delle Vergini (Garden of the Virgins), so called because it is reserved exclusively for female students and men are not allowed to enter. This garden with its lush vegetation is dedicated to St Catherine of Alexandria and contains some sarcophagi from the ancient Roman cemetery (first to third centuries AD) that was discovered on this site during extension work in the 1980s. Be warned, this garden *really* is reserved for women: the university guards are prompt to impose respect for the regulation on any male visitor who tries to enter.

The Aula Magna itself was originally the refectory of the old Cistercian monastery of Sant'Ambrogio and contains a few hidden gems: a vaulted ceiling frescoed with geometric motifs and some gigantic pictures of *The Marriage Feast of Cana*. Painted by Callisto Piazza in 1545, these works are considered to be this particular artist's masterpiece. During his stay in Milan, Callisto, the main figure in a sixteenth-century dynasty of painters, also painted the *Eight Angels, Friezes and Garlands* to be seen in the Saletta Negra of Castello Sforzesco (see p. 101).

In the "Refectory Crypt" beneath the Aula Magna are other traces of the ancient history of the structure, including some tomb inscriptions in Ancient Greek dating from the second to fourth centuries AD. However, the main treasures of the Università Cattolica, of which only the students themselves seem to take advantage, are the two light and airy cloisters. The first, the one you pass through on entering, is the most recent (1620–1630) and is known as the Doric Cloister because of the Doric capitals. The older cloister is more beautiful, with a fine upper cornice much more sophisticated in design than the one in the later cloister. It was built in 1497 to designs by Bramante and is known as the Ionic Cloister.

SECRETS OF SANT'AMBROGIO

Basilica of Sant'Ambrogio
15, Piazza Sant'Ambrogio
• Open daily, 7am–12 noon and 2.30pm–7pm
• Public transport: MM2 Sant'Ambrogio

> **Long-forgotten symbols and stories, unsolved riddles …**

As well as being one of the oldest churches in Milan and a building of fundamental significance to the history of the city, the Basilica of Sant'Ambrogio is also a rich source of legend and arcane fact.

Outside is an immediately noticeable feature that was very unusual in Italy but common to the north of the Alps: two bell towers. The one on the right is the oldest, dating from the eighth century. Known as the "Monks' Tower", it is built in the austere style of the defensive towers of the day. The "Canons' Tower" on the left dates from 1124. This division between canons and monks reflects the constant rivalry between the two groups over custody of the basilica and responsibility for the various offices associated with worship.

The original plan for the Canons' Tower – designed by the architect Gaetano Landriani – envisaged that it should be two storeys higher than its neighbour, with the space being used to house the bells. For a long time it was believed that those two additional floors were demolished in 1552 by order of Don Ferante Gonzaga, Governor of Milan, who did not want there to be any towers or bell towers tall enough to overlook the inside of the castle. However, documents later came to light revealing that those two floors had never actually been built – until, that is, 1891, when it was decided to complete the original design.

Enclosed by a portico on all four sides, the medieval-style atrium contains a unique collection of antique remains: plaques, bas-reliefs, sarcophagi and Latin inscriptions. The capitals atop the eighteen columns are particularly worthy of note: each is adorned with both domestic animals and such fantastic creatures as winged horses, chimeras, gryphons, dragons, mermaids

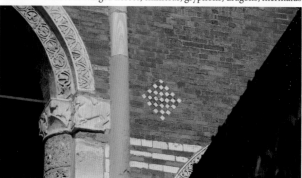

and centaurs. Long believed to be merely an expression of the exuberant imagination of the craftsmen who carved them, these capitals actually have a more profound allegorical significance. The entire outside of the church depicts the world and the temptations and dangers of earthly life, hence these are images of the forces of evil – diabolical monsters and embodiments of vices and sins – that threatened the Church and kept Christians from attaining the Heavenly Jerusalem. However, throughout these images there is the repeated presence of a cross, symbolising the possibility of salvation and protection against evil. The lamb, an animal that is often associated with the cross, also appears as a symbol of good, while the goats and cattle represent the Lord's flock. In short, the entire iconography is an allegory of the struggle between Good and Evil that comes before entrance into the church, itself a symbol of Paradise and the abode of the Elect.

The façade of the basilica poses an enigma that is yet to be resolved. To the right of the entrance – beneath the Monks' Tower – is a chessboard pattern motif. Some argue that this is a biblical reference, a magical symbol intended to ward off evil spirits, while others claim it symbolises Milan itself. However, the most intriguing suggestion is that this records the passage through the city of the Knights Templar. Returning from the Crusades in 1135, the Knights actually lodged in the cloister of Sant'Ambrogio, and given that chess is probably of Indian origin it is often thought that the game may have been introduced into Europe from the Holy Land by the Templars themselves. Indeed, the Knights' standard – half white and half black – is a sort of simplified chessboard motif. Although the suggestion may seem a little strange, there is other evidence in Milan of the Templars' passage through the city. Furthermore, this basilica also has two more "chessboards" – inside, just to the left of the entrance.

AN ACTUAL PORTRAIT OF ST AMBROSE

The sacellum of San Vittore in Ciel d'Oro is a small crypt that dates from the fourth century and was built by Bishop Materno to house the body of Vittore, a martyr. Later it was incorporated within the basilica and its walls and ceiling decorated with precious gold mosaics. The curious feature of these mosaics is that they contain what is probably an actual portrait of St Ambrose himself. Whereas later painted images depict the saint as an imposing old man with a white beard, here he is shown rather skinny and  unprepossessing, with one eye lower than the other (and closed), thinning curly hair, a short beard and protruding ears. Scientific analysis of the saint's skeleton, which is preserved in the crypt of the basilica, has confirmed that the saint was far from imposing (being about 1.63 metres tall) and was rather stiff in his movements because he suffered from severe arthritis.

ORDER OF THE KNIGHTS TEMPLAR IN MILAN

The Order of the Temple (1118–1312) left its mark on Milan. Various writers record that the knights arrived in the city between 1132 and 1135, with traces of their presence here to be seen in various places, from the Basilica di Sant'Ambrogio (to which they were said to have brought the actual Cross from Jerusalem) to the Cistercian Abbey at Chiaravalle, founded 22 January 1135. The ground-plan and lines of this religious foundation still reflect this era, when religious architecture was the work of monks who enjoyed the protection of the Templars. The temporal and spiritual association with the monks who built the abbey can be seen in the cloister, where a group of four slim columns intertwine in a sculpted knot from which emerge splay-winged eagles facing the four points of the compass: the reference is to the supreme spirituality to be found in the work of St John the Evangelist, of whom the eagle was the iconographical symbol.

The first Milanese document attributed to the Knights Templar bears the date 29 April 1142. It concerns the donation by Ugo and Guglielmo Girindelli, citizens of Milan, of a piece of land near Chiaravalle to Bacone, a Cistercian monk, for the construction of an extension to the monastery. The parchment dates this gift as having been made in October 1135 and bears the Cross of the Knights Templar; it is authenticated by the judge and notary Martino, a Templar, and bears the signatures of various witnesses and the donors.

Another letter, written in 25 May 1148 by the Master Templar Bonifacio, talks about the "church and house of the Templars built *extra muros* of the city of Milan". This commandery was thus located outside the old Porta Romana city gateway, near to the (no longer extant) church and convent of Santa Maria Latina and the hospital of St John the Baptist run by the Order of the Knights Hospitaller (who also had their city commandery there). This document says that the Templars lived at the "orchard of St Ambrose", which is referred to as a *brolium* (a brolio being a sort of garden enclosed by trees); this *brolio* or *brolo* is the site of the modern-day Piazza Mercato di Porta Ticinese. Within the city itself, the Templars had also received donations of small areas of land referred to as *broletum* – for example, the *Broletum Vecchio* (near the site of Palazzo Reale), the *Broletto Nuovo* (the site of Piazza Mercato) and the *Broletto Nuovissimo* (Via Rovello, Via San Tommaso and Via Broletto). The city still has a Via Brolo and a Piazzetta di San Nazaro in Brolo (with a nearby church of that name).

Said to date from around 1289, the *Liber Notitiae Sanctorum Mediolani* – a manuscript now in Milan's Biblioteca Capitolare (Capitulary Library) – is the work of Goffredo da Bussero, who was certainly a Templar. It was republished in 1917 by Marco Magistretti and Ugo Monneret de Villard. The work tells us that the first building raised by the Templars in Milan was a modest house, which was subsequently added to and enriched to the point of becoming a veritable palazzo and a fitting commandery for the military Order. It included a chapel known as Santa Maria al Tempio between the modern-day Via Santa Barnaba and Via Commenda. The construction of the commandery outside the city walls, between Porta Romana and Porta Tosa, was primarily due to the strategic importance of the site: on the main route into the city, it offered the knights wide freedom of action.

According to Goffredo da Bussero, the Milan commandery took for its distinguishing mark the "double Patriarchal Cross" – that is, a cross with two horizontal crossbars which was associated with the Patriarchs of Jerusalem. In the second half of the twelfth century this would become the more familiar cross pattée associated with the Templars (comprising four converging triangles). This dating seems to be borne out by the recent discovery in the church of San Giovanni Battista in Cesano (to the west of Milan) of a twelfth-century tomb adorned with the red cross pattée of the Templars.

The Order also rented various tracts of farmland around the city, and held a market or fair on regular feast days. According to some sources, this fair was held in the present-day Via Larga, which was then called Contrada del Brolio. The Milan commandery housed a force which comprised a Master Knight and various brother knights, all of noble lineage. Dalmazio de Verzario, who belonged to this commandery, donated his property to the deacon Adelardo Comino. The entire zone of Verziere is named after his powerful family. Apart from the master and the priest, whom even the former recognised as the spiritual superior of the commandery, the hierarchy included knights, squires and lay brothers or servants. Having been raised within the Order of the Templars, Frederick Barbarossa, during his first invasion of 1154, undoubtedly spared the city of Milan as a result of the intercession of the knights. Chronicles state that during the second invasion – on 6 August 1158 – he installed his headquarters in the "Brolo Castle of the Templars", which proves that the commandery was still active at the time.

Towards the end of the thirteenth century the Templars became the object of spiritual and material persecution by the French king Philippe IV and Pope Clement V. As a result, their activities in Milan gradually declined. And as all traces of the Order were quickly erased, its presence here passed from a vague memory to totally forgotten.

HOLES IN THE DEVIL'S COLUMN

15, Piazza Sant'Ambrogio
• Public transport: MM2 Sant'Ambrogio

> *Two holes made by Satan's horns?*

Outside the basilica, in the piazza to the left of the church, stands a Roman column known as "The Devil's Column", which seems to have been brought here from elsewhere.

Popular legend has it that the two holes on the side of the column were made by the devil himself when, frustrated at his failure to lead St Ambrose into temptation, Satan tried to run him through with his horns. However, he missed and ended up stuck in the column, disappearing in a cloud of sulphur after a frantic struggle to free himself. Tradition also has it that, if you lean close, you can still get a whiff of sulphur; and if you put your ear to the hole, you hear not the sea but the roaring of the Styx, the river of the Underworld.

The truth is that the column was used during the coronation of Holy Roman Emperors, who embraced the column itself as a symbol of embracing Christianity and the Roman Church. These gestures were obviously inspired by political pacts which were unknown to the superstitious populace of the day, hence the birth of the legend which linked the column with the Devil.

Having sworn upon a missal, the emperor received the iron crown and then embraced the column. This is how Galvano Fiamma (1283–1344), a Dominican chronicler of medieval Milan, describes the ritual: "When the King of the Romans wishes to receive the crown of the Kingdom of Italy within the basilica of Sant'Ambrogio, the emperor has to go first to the marble column that stands in the basilica of Sant'Ambrogio itself, and one of the counts of Angera must present him with a missal. The emperor then swears that he will obey the pope and the Roman Church in all things temporal and spiritual. The archbishop or the abbot of Sant'Ambrogio must crown him with the iron crown as King of Italy. This having been done, the emperor must embrace the upright column of marble to signify that he will be upright in the administration of justice."

SERPENT COLUMN

Basilica of Sant'Ambrogio
15, Piazza Sant'Ambrogio
• Open daily, 7am–12 noon and 2.30pm–7pm
• Public transport: MM2 Sant'Ambrogio

A serpent cast in metal by Moses himself?

On the left side of the nave stands a Roman granite column whose capital is surmounted by a curious serpent in black bronze. Tradition has it that this was a serpent made by Moses himself. The Book of Exodus tells how the prophet cast such a figure, the mere sight of which was enough to cure the Hebrews who had been bitten by a plague of poisonous snakes. Later, King Hezekiah, angered at what had become a veritable cult of worship, had all statues of snakes destroyed; however, the one that had actually been made by Moses was said to have survived this iconoclasm and ultimately came into the hands of the Byzantine Emperor Basil II. He then presented it to Archbishop Arnolfus so that, on his return from Constantinople, he could donate it to the city of Milan in 1007. Until fairly recently, the Milanese believed prayers to the serpent were beneficial against certain illnesses – especially intestinal worms and other stomach complaints. Another legend has it that on the Day of Judgment the serpent will whistle and descend from the column to return to the valley of Jehoshaphat in Jerusalem, where it was first made.

NEARBY

SECRET COURTYARD

If you go right to the end of the left side aisle of the basilica you come to a small door that leads through into the presbytery courtyard, which once served as a cemetery. The presbytery, rebuilt after the war over the ruins of Bramante's unfinished structure, now enjoys this calm and silent space. Note, under the portico, the tree-trunk columns of the main central arch. From here you can make your way to the Basilica Museum, which contains various precious artefacts relating to the church's history. The small Romanesque-style church at the centre of the courtyard is the Oratory of San Sigismondo. This was perhaps built around the eleventh century, but there is very little historical information about it, although the arches in the narthex rest on columns that may have come from the fourth-century Basilica of Sant'Ambrogio. The oratory, severely damaged during wartime bombing, was rebuilt in the 1960s.

CIO CHE SIETE VOI NOI SIAMO ADESSO
CHI SI SI CRDA DI NOI SCORDA SI STESSO

THE SMALL CAPPELLA DEL FOPPONINO

Piazzale Aquileia/Viale San Michele del Carso
• Open at the same time as the parish church: 7.30am–12 noon
and 3.30 pm–7pm
• Public transport: tram 29, 30

*A reminder
of the plague*

The now-forgotten cemetery at Perta Vercellina, known locally as Il Fopponino (*foppa* in Milanese dialect means "grave") is a macabre reminder of the terrible plague epidemics that tore through seventeenth-century Milan.

Surmounted by three time-ravaged death's heads, the stone gateway bears a still legible inscription which reads: *Ciò che sarete voi noi siamo adesso / Chi si scorda di noi scorda se stesso* (What we are, you will be / He who forgets us, forgets himself). Through the iron gate a small altar can be glimpsed and, beneath a glass plaque in the floor, some of the bones and skulls of those once buried here.

This cemetery was established in 1576, during the first great plague. At the time there were so many victims that numerous lazarettos had to be built outside the city walls, each with its own cemetery. When the epidemics came to an end, all of these were closed down, with the exception of this one at Porta Vercellina, which remained "active" – if such an expression might be used of a burial ground – up to 1895. Then, in 1912, the site of the cemetery was redeveloped completely.

Nowadays, the large gateway surmounted by copies of statues of the saints John the Baptist and Carlo Borromeo (the originals are now in the nearby church of St Francis of Assisi, designed by Giò Ponti) is concealed behind a thick door covered with graffiti. However, when the parish church is open (7.30am–12 noon and 3.30pm–7pm) you can gain access to the garden, which is the sole surviving remnant of the cemetery and still contains a few tombstones. Among those who were buried here were the patriot Amatore Sciesa, the theatre designer Alessandro Sanquirico and such figures as Melchiorre Gioia, Carlo Salerio, Barnaba Oriani and Gaetano Monti.

One plaque, raised by the Fondazione Giuseppe Verdi, commemorates Margherita Barezzi, the famous composer's first wife, who died at the age of 36 of encephalitis. If you wish you can apply to the parish offices for permission to visit the small chapel dating from 1663, which is nowadays used as a place of worship by the Ethiopian Orthodox community in Milan.

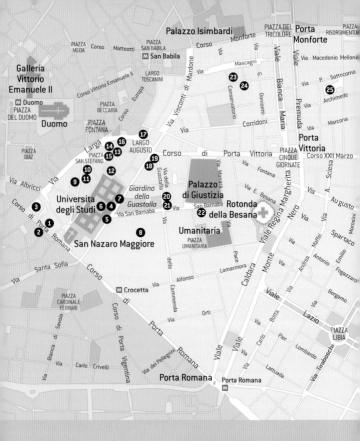

SOUTH-EAST

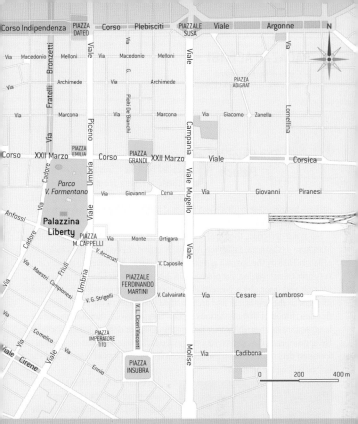

PALAZZO ACERBI

3, Corso di Porta Romana
• Public transport: MM3 Missori

The Devil's Palace

On the old Corso di Porta Romana – so-called because it was the gateway that those arriving from Rome entered – there are various houses with a long and curious history. One with a most unusual history is the early-seventeenth-century Palazzo Acerbi: it was actually said to belong to the Devil!

To avoid detection, the Devil was said to have taken on the identity of the Marchese di Cisterna, Ludovico Acerbi. A native of Ferrari, he was called to Milan in 1615 by the Spanish government. However, he arrived in the city at a very unfortunate period: the place was in the ravages of a plague which carried off rich and poor alike. Nevertheless, there was one person who seemed immune to the contagion, and an unnamed chronicler of the period gives us this description of that mysterious figure: "fifty years old, thereabouts, with a long, square-cut beard; neither fat nor thin, neither dark- nor fair-skinned. He appears each day, driven in a magnificent carriage with sixteen glabrous footmen dressed in gold-trimmed green livery and lots of jewels, and six horses pulling his carriage."

This was the Marchese Acerbi. Totally unaffected by the plague, he had decided to stay in the city while others of his rank had fled. From Pietro Maria Rossi, Count of San Secondo, he took the opportunity to buy the palazzo at 3 Corso di Porta Romana, and used his enormous wealth to have it entirely refurbished. The large rooms were decorated in a Baroque style, with marble statues and the finest paintings of the day, whilst the façade was adorned with three monstrous and demonic-looking heads.

Totally unperturbed by the plague, Acerbi continually held magnificent balls and parties – and, legend has it, that none of his guests fell ill either. And who was it who could remain indifferent to the plague if not the Devil himself?

CASA DEI BERSAGLIERI

A few metres away, at 20 Corso di Porta Romana, two *bersaglieri* have been standing guard since 1865, the statues of these two soldiers giving Casa Bettoni its nickname. The façade, by Giuseppe Palazzo, has twin-light windows within mixtilinear arches and is decorated with bas-reliefs which depict various incidents from the Risorgimento and bear witness to the enthusiasm of the city's bourgeoisie for the Unification of Italy.

CRYPT OF SAN GIOVANNI IN CONCA ❸

Piazza Missori, corner of Via Albricci
• Open (admission free) in spring/summer Tuesday to Friday,
9am–12 noon; Saturday, 2.30pm–5.30pm • Winter months, booking
required (tel. 02 20404175) • Public transport: MM3 Missori

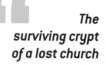

The surviving crypt of a lost church

I n the area of the traffic island at the centre of Piazza Missori are the remains of a Romanesque church. These comprise part of the apse of the Church of San Giovanni in Conca, founded in the fourth century and then rebuilt in the eleventh. In 1162 the church was destroyed by the forces of Frederick Barbarossa and again rebuilt in the thirteenth century by Bernabò Visconti, who wanted a private chapel alongside the palazzo he had built here. Bernabò also had an imposing tomb built for himself alongside the altar of the church – a work that is now in the Museo d'Arte Antico at Castello Sforzesco.

In 1531, Francesco II Sforza gave the church to the Carmelite Order, with the building being deconsecrated by the Austrians in the nineteenth century and then used by the French as a warehouse. In 1879, it was truncated to make way for Via Mazzini and the façade was sold to the Waldenses, who transferred it to Via Francesco Sforza to incorporate in their own church (where it still stands).

In 1949 it was decided to demolish the church entirely, to make way for

a road link between Piazza Missori and Via Albicci, but the Superintendent of Historical Heritage stopped the work before completion. This decision saved the apse (with a Romanesque single-light window bound by columns with capitals, and blank arching along the external coping) and, more importantly, the crypt, access to which is via the steps leading down from the side of the ruins. This is one of the few Romanesque crypts to survive over the centuries, and admission is free thanks to the assistance of the Italian Touring Club.

The space contains the original capitals and the remains of a basin, ledge and Roman sarcophagi; there is also a series of photographs showing the church before demolition and the various parts of it that have been transferred elsewhere. Some artefacts from the church – not only the tombs of Barnabò Visconti and his wife, Regina della Scala, but also an Early Christian fresco, a Lombard inscription and fragments of a beautiful third-century mosaic floor discovered beneath the church – are now to be seen in the Museo Archeologico at Castello Sforzesco. Two panels depicting *The Annunciation* are in the Castello's Picture Gallery, while beneath the Portico dell'Elefante in the Ducal Courtyard of the same building is a work of sculpture from the church; some say it depicts Eve, others St John in the vat of boiling oil used in an attempt to kill him.

CEREMONIAL STANDARD

4

Ospedale Maggiore
28, Via Francesco Sforza
• Open Monday to Friday, 8am–5.30pm
• Public transport: tram 12, 23, 27

A masterpiece of embroidery in gold and silk

Entering the administrative offices of the Ospedale Maggiore, you immediately notice a glass display case containing the hospital's superb *gonfalone* (ceremonial standard).

Designed by the architect Giò Ponti in 1935, this is one of the most precious artefacts in the hospital's collection, undoubtedly a masterpiece of twentieth-century Italian art.

The front depicts *The Annunciation*, from which the hospital takes its name, while on the back is the embroidered figure of a dove. The symbol of the

organisation, the dove is surrounded by heraldic devices representing the main benefactors and the work carried out.

This highly refined work of embroidery in gold and silver thread was produced by the Fratelli Bertarelli. The metal and jewellery work on the standard are by the goldsmith Alfredo Ravasco, who donated all the precious stones used therein: topazes, garnets, rubies, rock crystals and river pearls.

The standard was blessed in the city's Duomo on 25 March 1935 during an official ceremony celebrated by cardinal Ildefonso Schuster.

NEARBY

SCULPTURE DEPICTING GOOD HOSPITAL MANAGEMENT

5

In the garden that runs along Via Sforza in front of the hospital, there is a large sculpture made by Angelo Biancini in 1964. This depicts various aspects of the institution: the duties that the hospital must perform, its good administration, and its work in providing aid and assistance to the sick. Envisaged as a narrative continuum, it comprises a sequence of five images. Along the outer walls of the hospital you can also see some archaeological remains of the old Cà Granda.

CHAPTER ROOMS
OF THE OSPEDALE MAGGIORE

❻

28, Via Francesco Sforza
• Open Monday to Friday, 9am–1pm and 2pm–6pm
• Ask the porter if you can take a quick look inside
• Public transport: bus 77, 94

The Old Hospital Archives

On the Via Francesco Sforza side of the Cà Granda are the Archives of the Ospedale Maggiore. They contain over 10,000 dossiers and registers and even 16,000 parchments, including an Egyptian papyrus from 1700 BC. All the material comes from the archives of the various city hospitals that were incorporated within this complex.

At the entrance to the building you pass through corridors lined with display cases containing medical equipment from various periods in history. These include some gynaecological equipment that will strike the more faint-hearted visitor as indistinguishable from instruments of torture. One bust commemorates Luigi Mangiagelli, the first chancellor of Milan University and head of the Gynaecological Department at the Ospedale Maggiore. One of the best-known obstetrics clinics in the modern city, this now bears his name.

Beyond a small courtyard you come to the Chapter Rooms, once occupied by the hospital's Board of Administrators. Built in 1637, these magnificent rooms – which are well worth a visit – are only open to the public during the special days sponsored by the FAI (Fondo per l'Ambiente Italiano), which are held at the beginning of April.

With a vault frescoed by Volpino, the Summer Chapter Room was one of the largest secular spaces in seventeenth-century Milan. The bookcases date from 1808, and were installed when the amount of documents required the room to be fitted out as it is today. The neighbouring Winter Chapter Room – also called the Walnut Room – is surrounded by precious veneers created in 1767. Both rooms were damaged by bombing in 1943, but survived. However, the old seventeenth-century pharmacy – which was meant to have been

converted into a Museum of Health Care – was entirely destroyed.

Whereas these two rooms are generally closed to the public, in the antechamber you can see a massive and rather mysterious studded cabinet, which may once have been used as a strongbox.

CRYPT OF THE CHURCH OF THE BEATA VERGINE ANNUNCIATA AT OSPEDALE MAGGIORE

❓

32, Via Francesco Sforza
• Open Monday to Thursday 9am–5pm
• Public transport: MM3 Crocetta; bus 77, 94

" *Mausoleum to the patriots who fell during the "Five Days"*

Entering the Ospedale Maggiore from Via Sforza or the courtyard of the Università Statale, you come across a small door that opens onto a flight of steps leading to the crypt under the Church of the Annunciation (Beata Vergine Annunciata), built in 1637. The structure rests on pillars and is supported by lowered barrel vaults and large intersecting rib vaults.

The Ospedale Maggiore burial ground was below the crypt, and it is thought that between 1473, when the hospital began its care work, and

1695, when burials were no longer authorised within the city walls, some 500,000 Milanese were laid to rest here. However in more recent times the burial chambers have been restored. Indeed in 1848, during the Five Days of Milan* (see also page 131), with the city besieged by Austrian troops, it was impossible to reach the cemeteries. Thus 141 victims of the fighting were buried in this crypt. Their names can still be seen on the walls, along with commemorative inscriptions dictated by Andrea Verga, clinical professor of psychiatry at the hospital. There are also traces of frescoes by Paolo Antonio de Maestri, known as Il Volpino (the Little Fox), dating back to 1638 (the best of them are on the back wall near the courtyard).

The crypt subsequently became a site of celebration for Milanese patriots, to the extent that in 1860 it was turned into the city mausoleum. But when in 1895 the remains of the victims were transferred to the charnel house beneath the monument in Piazza Cinque Giornate, the crypt was abandoned.

A visit to the crypt – now restored and overseen by volunteers of Touring Club Italiano's Aperto per Voi (Open for You) initiative – includes a lapidary museum with epigraphs and fragments of funerary monuments, such as the particularly striking statue of a little girl. A museum of old surgical instruments is also being set up.

*The Cinque Giornate (18–22 March 1848), a popular uprising of Milanese citizens against the Austrian occupation, is remembered as one of the most glorious episodes of the Italian nationalist movement known as the Risorgimento.

REPRODUCTION OF LOURDES GROTTO

Ospedale Maggiore Policlinico
Mangiagalli neonatology department
12, Via della Commenda
• Hospital open 24/7
• Public transport: MM3 Crocetta; bus 60, 73, 77, 94; tram 12, 23, 27

*Lourdes
in miniature*

I n addition to the reproduction of the Lourdes grotto at the Basilica of Santa Maria (see p. 289), Milan has another reproduction of the sacred site, albeit smaller, in the Mangiagalli neonatal hospital.

The grotto can be reached through the corridor that leads from the hospital entrance to the neo-Romanesque church of San Giuseppe. Once at the church,

take the little door on the right to find an open space surrounded by hospital buildings and the social club café. In the centre is the small reconstruction of the grotto with its Madonna statue, another of a female figure in prayer (perhaps one of the Watchers) and many ex-votos from mothers grateful for a successful childbirth.

An ancient proclamation by Archbishop Schuster, engraved on a stone, announces that reciting three Hail Marys will earn you two hundred days of indulgences.

THE GATE LEADING TO THE CEMETERY

If you leave the hospital by the Via Sforza exit and cross the street to number 34, you can see the ruins of a stone gateway in Baroque style. Built towards the end of the seventeenth century, it marked the access to a metal bridge that crossed the Naviglio. What is now Via Sforza was part of the section known as the Fossa Interna (Inner Ditch). This bridge gave onto Via San Barnaba and from there it was no distance to the former cemetery, known as Foppone dui San Michele, now built over by the Besana roundabout. So the bridge and gateway were built as a shortcut by which people who died in the old Ospedale Maggiore could be carried from the sanatorium directly to the cemetery. Hence the bleak reputation (now forgotten) of the bridge which was demolished at the beginning of the twentieth century after the canals were filled in, and of the gateway that is still in place although no longer for any reason.

PALAZZO GREPPI'S *SALA NAPOLEONICA* 　❾

Palazzo Greppi
12, Via Sant'Antonio
• The main staircase is open to the public during normal office hours;
the rooms can only be seen during conferences, lectures and lessons
organised by the Università Statale (State University)
• Public transport: MM1 Duomo, MM3 Missori

> *A little-known corner of eighteenth-century Milan*

Just a short walk away from the main university buildings, the little-known main rooms of Palazzo Greppi offer a charming glimpse into eighteenth-century Milan.

The palazzo, built in 1772–1778 when the city was under Austrian rule, was the work of Giuseppe Piermarini, the most fashionable architect in Milan at the time. Among his other designs are the Teatro de la Scala, the Palazzo Reale and the gardens in Corso Venezia.

After the doorway, turn right and go up the main staircase, whose walls are entirely covered in frescoes. On the first floor are rooms which now serve as lecture and conference halls for the Università Statale. Immediately after the entrance come two small reception rooms, the vaulted ceiling of the longer one decorated with a fresco of *Jupiter and Ganymede* by Andrea Appiani. A little further on is another small frescoed room and then the

"Ballroom" (also known as the Sala Napoleonica), again designed by Piermarini. The stucco-work is by Giocondo Albertolli and Giuseppe Levati, with the frescoes by Martin Knoller.

It was Count Antonio Greppi, "tax-farmer general" in Austrian-ruled Lombardy, who commissioned this palazzo from Piermarini. Of Venetian origin, he had been appointed in 1751 by Luca Pallavicini, Governor of Milan, to the highly profitable position of collector of indirect taxes on such goods as salt and tobacco. Within just twenty years, this skilful entrepreneur had made a fortune, enough to build for himself this patrician palazzo in the very heart of Milan.

CHIOSTRO TRIVULZIANO

5, Via Sant'Antonio
• Open during public events
(information at www.indialogo.it/siti/chiesa_s_antonio.htm)
• Public transport: MM3 Missori

The cloister of a medieval hospital run by friars

The present-day Church of Sant'Antonio Abate stands on the site of the old cloister of the monastery of the Antonine friars, who had established themselves here some time before 1272. This was the location of a hospice and small hospital that cared for persons afflicted with what is known in Italy as "St Anthony's fire" (shingles). At the time of Barnabò Visconti, the structure was enlarged under the patronage of Gian Galeazzo Visconti. Then, in 1442, Filippo Maria Visconti granted the monks a number of privileges. However, the health reforms introduced by Francesco Sforza led to the construction nearby of the Cà Granda and the resultant closure of the earlier hospital. The building itself was partly demolished and converted.

The only surviving structure dating from 1456 is the square bell tower. The cloister itself was renovated in the sixteenth century. Within the frieze decorating the entablature of the cloister note a series of winged gryphons and heraldic blasons. On the east and west walls, the gryphons are shown with the heads of bearded old men, whereas on the north wall the heads are those of young people. Once the residence of Cardinal Ildefonso Schuster, the building now houses all the lay associations active within the diocese and is also used by the University of Milan.

ORGAN IN THE CHURCH
OF SANT'ANTONIO ABATE

⓫

5, Via Sant'Antonio
- Open Monday to Saturday, 10am–6pm
- Public transport: MM3 Missori

> *The last
> surviving organ
> in the city
> played
> by Mozart*

The Church of Sant'Antonio Abate not only houses a proper art gallery, with works by some of seventeenth-century Lombardy's finest artists (Bernardino Campi, Camillo and Giulio Cesare Procaccini, Ludovico Carracci, Tanzio da Varallo and Cerano), it also contains an organ that is both a remarkable masterpiece of craftsmanship and a piece of great historical value.

The instrument, probably built in the eighteenth century by the Brunelli family of organ builders, was enlarged in 1864 by Livio Tornaghi, a famous organ-maker from Monza. The drawings for this project, still in the church's archives, are very interesting because they show that the new organ incorporated all those parts of the old that were still in good working order. Note the ebony keyboard, in which the usual colours are reversed: the diatonic keys are black and the chromatic keys are white.

However, what makes this organ truly special is the fact that during his last visit to Milan, in winter 1772, the young Wolfgang Amadeus Mozart composed for this small church his joyful *Exsultate, Jubilate* for soprano and orchestra (K. 165), a work dedicated to Venanzio Rauzzini. The virtuoso Rauzzini had already performed the lead role in Mozart's *Lucio Silla* (premiered in December 1772 in Milan's Teatro Regio Ducale, on what is now the site of the Palazzo Reale) and it was he who, on 17 January 1773, gave the very first performance of *Exsultate, Jubilate* in the church of Sant'Antonio.

Unused for more than fifty years and buried under a thick layer of dust, the organ was restored in 2006 for the 250th anniversary of Mozart's birth.

In his short lifetime, the composer spent a total of almost a year in Milan, performing on various organs in the city's churches; this in Sant'Antonio is the only one to have survived, at least in part, down to the present day.

The City Museum of Musical Instruments in Castello Sforzesco also contains the harpsichord that Mozart played when guest of the Austrian governor Charles Joseph, Count of Firmian, at Palazzo Melzi.

THE COAL PORTERS' EX-VOTO

Cà di Tencitt
2, Via Laghetto
• Public transport: MM3 Missori

> *The witch's house in Verziere*

In the seventeenth century the populous area of Verziere was one of the most disreputable and sinister in Milan. And contemporary legends said that the house at 2 Via Larghetto was inhabited by a powerful witch, who was the head of all the fortune-tellers and sorceresses of the area. The reason for this belief in the concentration of witchcraft here was simple: the area had been spared in the last outbreak of the plague, hence it must be watched over by some witch or other. In fact, the explanation for the area's good fortune was more prosaic: the presence of a port used by the boats bringing materials for the building work on the Duomo. (The existence of that man-made water basin is commemorated in the name of the present-day Via Laghetto.) Among the materials shipped through the port was coal, which meant that the whole area was covered in black coal dust, which being remarkably absorbent probably prevented the propagation of the germs which spread the disease.

The coal porters were known as *tencitt* (literally, "dirty"') and many lived with their families at number 2, which thus became known as *Cà di tencitt* – a name that has stuck, even if the *tencitt* are long gone and the place is now rather elegant.

On one wall of the house is a painting almost 2 metres high that has been there for nearly four hundred years. This is the *Madonna de'Tencitt*, patron saint of the coal porters. The actual image was raised as an ex-voto by Bernardo Cottone, chaplain to the Guild of Coal Porters, in thanks for having spared them during the plague. Together with the Virgin of the Assumption are St Roch (with dog), St Sebastian and St Carlo Borromeo; at their feet you can just make out the ground plan of the old lazaretto.

Until 1989 the canvas stood neglected behind two wooden doors that protected it from the elements; it was only on public display on 15 August, the Feast of the Assumption. Then, having survived a serious car accident, a Milanese lawyer who lives nearby decided to pay for the full restoration of the painting as his own ex-voto to the Madonna. So, since 1993, the canvas – although badly damaged – is permanently on show behind a sheet of glass.

NEL LUOGO CHE TU VEDI E GIA APPELLATO DEGLI INNOCENTI
CHIUSO DA GRATA DI BRONZO
SI CONSERVA LA PIETRA CHE GIA SERVI DI DEPOSITO
DI QUATTRO DISTINTI CRISTIANI AULICI
DALL' IMPERATORE VALENTINIANO I.
INGIUSTAMENTE TRUCIDATI
NELL'ANNO 367

STONE OF THE INNOCENTS

Basilica of Santo Stefano Maggiore
Piazza Santo Stefano
• Open Monday to Friday, 7.30am–12 noon and 1pm–6pm; Saturday and Sunday, 9am–12 noon
• Public transport: MM 1-3 Duomo; tram 12, 23, 27; bus 54, 60, 65

> *A stone that bears witness to martyrdom and murder*

Just beyond the threshold of Santo Stefano Maggiore basilica the floor contains an iron grille placed over what is known as the "Stone of the Innocents", upon which – legend has it – the emperor Valentinian I had four Christians martyred in 367. It was also near this stone that, almost a thousand years later (on 26 December 1476), the Duke of Milan, Galeazzo Maria Sforza, was stabbed to death by three patrician conspirators as he made his way to the church on the saint's feast day.

Orfeo Cenni da Ricavo, adviser and friend of the duke, was present that morning and later described the assassination. A traitor by the name of Giovanni Andrea Lampugnani was in the middle of the church when Galeazzo arrived, kneeling to greet him and then drawing a dagger which he thrust into his groin and chest. The duke cried out *Sono morto* ("I am dying") before

the assassin stabbed him a third time. Two other conspirators then stabbed their victim in the throat, head, wrist and thigh. It all took place in an instant, with Galeazzo then stumbling backwards and almost collapsing on top of his friend, who tried in vain to hold him up. The duke sank to the floor, and while he lay there prone, two of the assassins made sure he was dead before making their escape.

A few metres from the "Stone of Innocents", a plaque commemorates the murder of the Duke of Milan.

CHURCH WHERE CARAVAGGIO WAS BAPTISED

On 30 September 1571, the painter Michelangelo Merisi, better known as Caravaggio, was baptised in the church of Santa Stefano Maggiore. The 2007 discovery of his certificate of baptism, found in the basilica archives that are now housed in the Diocesan Museum, put an end to the long-running debate among scholars as to his actual birthplace: some had argued that he had actually been born in the small town of Caravaggio, near Bergamo.

OSSUARY OF THE CHURCH OF SAN BERNARDINO ALLE OSSA

(14)

2, Via Verziere (access from Piazza Santo Stefano)
• Open daily, 7.30am–1pm (until 12 noon on Sunday)
• Public transport: MM1–3 Duomo; tram 12, 23, 27; bus 54, 60, 65

> ### The most macabre place in the city

Just to the right on entering the medieval church of San Bernardino alle Ossa is a narrow passageway, dating from 1705, which leads through to the small ossuary chapel. Originally raised in 1210 but then entirely rebuilt in 1695, the walls of this chapel are entirely covered with human bones and skulls. A number of them are arranged to form enormous crosses and the letter "M", for Mary.

Some legends say that these are the bones of the Christians who, led by St Ambrose, died in a battle against the Arian heretics; others that they are the mortal remains of the Milanese who perished during the sixth-century Goth invasions, while still others claim the deceased were victims of the plague.

The truth is that this church stands on the site of a medieval cemetery, where the dead from the nearby Ospedale del Brolo were buried. By the thirteenth century that cemetery had become too small, so bodies were exhumed and the bones stored in the church, which was then dedicated to the Passion of the Virgin Mary. The present-day Church of San Bernardino, which dates from the fifteenth century, was built for the *Disciplini*, a twelfth-century lay order which venerated the dead and expiated sin through self-flagellation.

In sharp contrast to the austerity of the walls and the faint light that makes its way through the high windows is the frescoed vault painted by Sebastiano Ricci, which depicts *The Souls of the Dead in Triumph amidst the Angels* and is a riot of colour.

NEARBY

SOLE SURVIVOR OF A FIRE

The pillar standing in the churchyard of the Basilica of Santo Stefano Maggiore – alongside the church of San Bernardino – is the sole remnant of a *quadriportico* (monumental cloister) that stood opposite the original basilica. Built in the Middle Ages, it was destroyed by fire in 1070.

STATUE OF CARLO PORTA

In Via Verziere, which runs behind the ossuary and was the site of a street market in the days of classical antiquity, there is a statue by Ivo Soli. Raised in 1966, it depicts the poet Carlo Porta, who celebrated this area in a number of his vernacular poems.

FORGOTTEN ORIGINS OF THE COLONNA DEL VERZIERE

Largo Augusto
• Public transport: bus 54, 60; tram 12, 23, 27

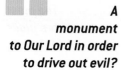

A monument to Our Lord in order to drive out evil?

Nowadays, Verziere is one of the busiest central districts in Milan. It takes its name from the fruit and vegetable market that was held here up until 1783 (*verza* means cabbage), and for a long time the entire district was a place of ill-repute. Inhabited by labourers, street porters, prostitutes and those skilled in invoking good (or bad) luck, it was even said to be a place where witches gathered. For all decent folk, it was definitely somewhere to be avoided.

Now commemorated by a statue in the nearby garden, Carlo Porta captured the local colour of the place in a number of his dialect poems. However, seeing the area as appalling rather than poetic, the Confraternity of Porta Tosa decided to raise a monument here to Our Lord, the idea being that if the local authorities did nothing to root out evil from the district, then the Most High would have to do so. The original project was for a tall column surmounted by a statue of Christ the Redeemer, but work came to a halt shortly after it began in 1583: in its reforming zeal, the Confraternity had forgotten to apply to the local council for permission to use public land. Twenty years then passed before the column in Bavena granite was finished; and then another seventy years before the statue was finally raised, in 1674.

Some say, however, that this column is actually an ex-voto to mark the end of the plague in 1577. What is true is that during that plague, the ledges of the column's base served as an altar for outdoor masses that could also be attended by the sick and weak.

In 1860, this – one of the very few surviving votive columns and "crosses" that had been so common in Counter-Reformation Milan – was converted into the first monument commemorating the famous "Five Days". It was renamed the *Colonna della Vittoria*, and on its base you can still read the names of the 354 Milanese who died during the course of that uprising.

WHY IS CHRIST LOOKING TOWARDS VIA DURINI?

Legend has it that the statue of Christ used to face towards the Church of San Bernardino alle Ossa and not Via Durini. The story goes that an attractive girl, Barbarinetta, who lived in a building giving onto the piazza, was attacked one night as she was coming home with her father. He was killed and she was kidnapped, only to be saved by a nobleman who at the time was in disgrace and himself a fugitive from the law. The girl fell in love with her saviour, but then the handsome bandit was arrested and condemned to death. Heartbroken and totally alone, Barbarinetta threw herself to her death from her window. Having witnessed the suicide, the statue turned its eyes away out of pity.

SALA DEL GRECHETTO

Palazzo Sormani
7, Via Francesco Sforza
• Open during cultural events; see www.comune.milano.it
• Public transport: MM1 San Babila, MM3 Missori; tram 12, 23, 27;
bus 54, 60, 73, 84, 94

A hidden gem

Open to the public only when it is hosting cultural events, the Sala del Grechetto is a real hidden gem, tucked away within the palazzo that houses the Sormani library. The walls of this conference room are entirely covered with a cycle of twenty-three large canvases depicting the myth of Orpheus, whose music was said to have charmed even wild beasts. One picture is missing, however, as it is on display as part of the City Art Collections in Castello Sforzesco.

These remarkable paintings were long attributed to Giovan Benedetto Castiglione, known as *Il Grechetto* (The Little Greek), a court painter to the Gonzagas who was famous for pictures teeming with various animals. However, art critics now recognise that they are the work of a northern European artist known simply as the *Pittore dei Lonati-Verri* (Painter of the Lonati-Verri). This name itself derives from the fact that these paintings originally hung in the home of the Verri brothers, champions of reform in Enlightenment Milan. Purchased around 1880, they have been hung in Palazzo Sormani since the early twentieth century, just as they were in their original location. This was possible thanks to a painting by Francesco Colombi Borde, now in the library offices, which shows the room in Palazzo Verri for which the cycle was first conceived.

NEARBY

SHELL FROM MILAN'S "FIVE DAYS"

Palazzo Sormani also contains a memento of the famous "Five Days" of popular rebellion in Milan in 1848 (18–22 March). A small ground-floor room to the right of the main doorway – now used as library storage space

– contains a window frame in which is embedded what looks like a metal sphere but is in fact a cannonball fired during an episode remembered as one of the most glorious events of the Risorgimento, the popular uprising against Austrian rule in 1848. The projectile can also be seen from the outside of the palazzo: the window is the second on the right from the main doorway, and the cannonball is embedded in the upper-right inner side of the frame.

FAUNS AT VIA DELLA GUASTALLA

15, Via della Guastalla
• Public transport: tram 12, 23, 27, 73; bus 60, 77, 84, 94

A nymphaeum turned into a doorway

The modern building at 15 Via della Guastalla has a striking entrance: complete with two fauns shown supporting the architrave, the doorway comprises the figures of a man and woman (Adam and Eve?) covering their nakedness with fig leaves, plus two children riding rather strange-looking creatures. Atop the architrave itself are two semi-reclining *putti* holding cornucopias. The Latin inscriptions refer to the theme of water, so this doorway may have originally come from a grotto/nymphaeum that was part of a fountain which, judging from the style, must have been seventeenth-century.

In ancient Greece and Rome, nymphaea (sanctuaries dedicated to water nymphs) comprised fountains and other water features, complete with statues, mosaics and plants. With the addition of falls and other water features, they became fashionable "aquatic theatres" in the period from the Renaissance to the eighteenth century. One of the finest nymphaea in the Milan area – and one particularly appreciated by Stendhal – was in the garden of Villa Borromeo Visconti Litta in the Lainate district.

NEARBY

VISIT THE SYNAGOGUE ON VIA DELLA GUASTALLA

On the first Sunday in September – the date of the annual European Day of Jewish Culture – the doors of the synagogue at 19 Via della Guastalla are open to the general public. The original Jewish temple here, a basilica with central nave and two side aisles, was designed by Luca Beltrami in 1892. However, that structure was flattened by the bombs of 1943, with the sole exception of its façade, adorned with precious mosaics in blue and gold. The temple, rebuilt in 1953, became a major reference point for the city's Jewish community. The interior is now a prism-like structure surmounted by a cupola and lit by twenty-three stained-glass windows. The work of American artist Roger Seldon, these polychromatic compositions are a collage of Jewish symbols and Hebrew letters.

MONTHLY VISIT TO THE CHURCH OF SANTA MARIA DELLA PACE

40, Via San Barnaba
• Open first Thursday of the month, 10am–12 noon
• Public transport: MM3 Crocetta, Porta Romana

Premises of the Crusaders' descendants

The Church of Santa Maria della Pace is one of the most inaccessible in all Milan. Until quite recently, a written application to visit had to be made to the secretary of the Equestrian Order of the Holy Sepulchre of Jerusalem, whose premises are alongside the church. Now, fortunately, it is regularly open to the public on the first Thursday of every month, although only for two hours. Founded in the fifteenth century, thanks to a donation from Bianca Maria Sforza and her son Galeazzo, the church was built in Gothic-Renaissance style and linked with the adjacent monastery of the *Amadeisti* (a community founded by Blessed Amadeo Menez de Silva, a Portuguese nobleman who had taken vows as a Franciscan monk). The church was suppressed and deconsecrated in 1805, with its walls stripped of frescoes and the space used for various purposes: as a military warehouse, a hospital, a stable and riding school. Purchased by the

Bagatti Valsecchi family in 1900, it was restored and fitted out as a concert hall, known as Salone Perosi. Then, in 1906, the owners were forced to sell for tax reasons, and the church became the property of the Sisters of Santa Maria Riparatrice, who undertook the restoration and had the site reconsecrated. Finally, in 1967, the church was acquired by the Equestrian Order of the Holy Sepulchre of Jerusalem, which still uses it for religious functions. Both the circular window (visible from outside) and various other parts of the interior are decorated with the Order's symbol: a red cross potent surrounded by four smaller crosses.

ORDER OF THE HOLY SEPULCHRE AND SYMBOL OF THE CROSS

The emblem of the Order is a red cross potent surrounded by four smaller crosses. The five crosses symbolise the five wounds of the crucified Christ, even if the original meaning of the symbol was that the Cross of Christ is spread throughout the world. The wounds are also honoured in the choice of the colour red, a symbol of life, strength and blood. In the East, the cross potent is in gold, symbolising the incommensurable value of Christ's Passion.

WHAT IS THE EQUESTRIAN ORDER OF THE HOLY SEPULCHRE?

Contrary to what is sometimes said, the Equestrian Order has no links with the old order of the Knights Templar. It is a Roman Catholic order and a lay association of the Catholic faithful set up by the Holy See.

It takes its origins from the Order of the Canons of the Holy Sepulchre, the church built on what was said to be the site of Christ's tomb and resurrection. The Order is thought to have been founded by Goffredo di Buglione after the conquest of Jerusalem during the First Crusade (1099), and historians consider it to be the oldest surviving Christian equestrian order dedicated to the provision of charity and assistance to the needy.

The Order's headquarters are in Rome – at Sant'Onofrio al Gianicolo – and it has fifty-two branches throughout the world.

Totalling around 10,000, the Knights and Ladies of the Holy Sepulchre work under papal authority towards their main objective: the propagation of the Christian faith in the Holy Land.

Today the Order runs forty-four Catholic schools in the Jerusalem area, teaching some 15,000 Christian and Muslim students. In France, the Order is the guardian of the reliquary of Christ's Crown of Thorns (see *Secret Paris* in this series of guides).

FONDAZIONE VICO MAGISTRETTI

20, Via Conservatorio
• Visits on request
• Tel: 02 76002964 • fondazione@vicomagistretti.it
• Public transport: MM1 San Babila; tram 12, 23, 27; bus 54, 60, 61, 73

> *A great designer's studio now a museum*

" **I** like the concept of 'design', a modern, functional aesthetic that is so straightforward it does not even have to be given in drawings. I myself have communicated a number of my designs over the phone." This comment by the great designer Vico Magistretti provides the guiding theme for this foundation-museum, which is dedicated to his work and sited in what was his architectural studio from 1946 to the year of his death (2006). It was here that he created most of his great designs, not only buildings but also household objects and furniture, a number of which have come to epitomise Italian design – for example, the *Eclisse* bedside lamp, the *Maralunga* settee, the *Selene* chair and the *Vidun* table – and here you can see how they gradually took shape through sketches, drawings and original prototypes.

In 2010 Susanna Magistretti decided to open her father's studio to the public, converting it into a museum and venue for temporary exhibitions. The conference room has remained as it was, with models of entire buildings hanging against the walls; the only change has been the addition of a few chairs. Magistretti's workspace has also been maintained intact, with all its original atmosphere.

A large touch screen lets you flick through a chronological presentation of Magistretti's vast output, with a wide selection of material from his photographs, dossiers and designs.

OPEN-AIR MUSEUM

As well as visiting the museum, the best way to understand Magistretti's work is to follow a special itinerary prepared by the Foundation. This guide covers fourteen buildings designed by the architect through which you can appreciate the breadth of his achievement. Examples include the Gallaratese tower blocks, the church of Santa Maria Nascente, the Biology Faculty Building at the Università Statale, the metro train depot at Famagosta and various office and residential buildings. One of the criteria for the selection of these fourteen buildings was that each should be close to a metro station, thus easy to get to.

CHAPTER ROOM OF SANTA MARIA DELLA PASSIONE BASILICA

14, Via Conservatorio
- Open Monday to Saturday, 7am–12 noon; Sunday, 9am–12 noon and 3.13pm–6.15 pm
- Public transport: MM1 San Babila

> *Like attending a symposium of saints and Apostles*

Walking along the nave of this sixteenth-century church – the second largest in Milan, after the Duomo – past the niche housing the organ, you come to the crypt entrance. Although this is not open to visitors, a polite application to the church administration will gain you admission to the Chapter Room, one of the best-kept secrets in the city.

The room, of a rectangular floor-plan typical of the fifteenth century, was part of the old monastery and where the canons met. It is particularly noteworthy for its splendid decoration, with a monumental cycle of paintings around walls and ceiling by Ambrogio di Stefano da Fossano, known as Il Bergognone.

All the perspective lines of the composition converge on the figure of Christ, which dominates the wall opposite the entrance. These convergences, to be found in the compositions on each wall, create a real impression of attending a symposium of Apostles, popes, saints and doctors of the Church.

Nine pictures, painted around 1514, show Christ surrounded by his Apostles. On the opposite wall are frescoes of the saints and doctors of the Latin Church, while the wall on the left has frescoes of St Augustine and the Archangel Michael. These paintings and frescoes are surmounted by twenty-four lunettes containing half-figure images of saints and canons of St John Lateran. Finally, the vault is decorated with a star-spangled sky, while the vault segments depict grotesques with angel musicians (in accordance with a style that was common in fifteenth- and sixteenth-century Lombardy). This magical place is worthy of the splendid church that houses it, a church which is distinguished by another feature that is unique in Milan and almost throughout Lombardy: the presence of two organs. Set up facing each other, these were necessary for the dazzling two-voice concerts that were held here, playing upon the possibilities offered by echoes and stereophonic sound.

In a church rich in paintings, frescoes and sculpture, note also the two Baroque-style holy-water stoups in marble. Located near the entrance, these are decorated with threatening images of serpents, symbols of the struggle between Good and Evil, between the blessing brought by the holy water and the curse associated with the serpent.

VIA LINCOLN

- Public transport: tram 9, 23, 29, 30

L ocated near Piazza Cinque Giornate, Via Lincoln is unusual in being lined with small semi-detached houses painted blue, green, yellow or red, each with a private garden rich in plants and shrubs. These houses, built in 1886 for workers, artisans and public employees, give the short street something of the air of a seaside resort.

An authentic "workers' housing estate"

The original project envisaged a proper "garden city" which was to extend throughout the entire Porta Vittoria district. Ultimately, the buildings comprised not only workshop space but also two hotels, reserved for working-class clientele, which have since been demolished. Difficulties in financing – and the problems resulting from two world wars – all disrupted the project, and finally the only houses built were these in Via Lincoln. Originally, they were made over to tenants on lifetime leases, but later were sold to them outright. Understandably, the present-day owners seem disinclined to sell up and move away from this little urban paradise.

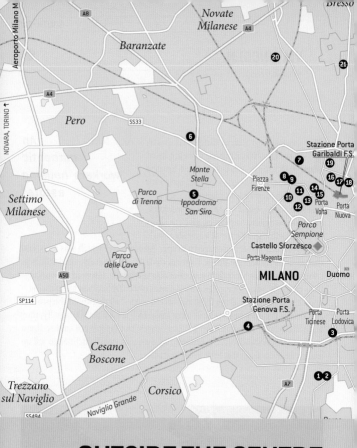

OUTSIDE THE CENTRE

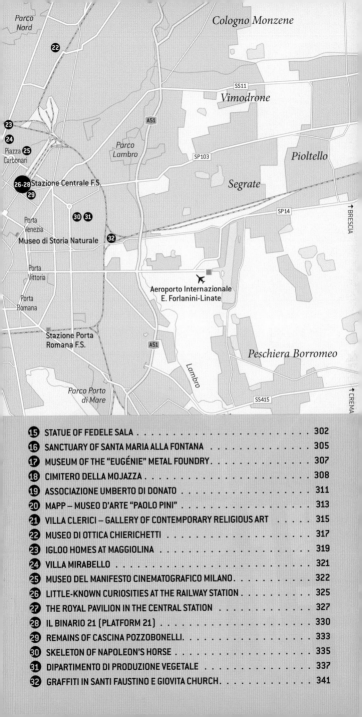

Parco
Nord

22

Cologno Monzene

SS11

Vimodrone

A51

23
24
Piazza
Carbonari
25

Parco
Lambro

SP103

Pioltello

Segrate

26-28 Stazione Centrale F.S.
29

SP14

↑BRESCIA

Porta
Venezia

30 **31**

Museo di Storia Naturale

32

Porta
Vittoria

Aeroporto Internazionale
E. Forlanini-Linate

Porta
Romana

Stazione Porta
Romana F.S.

A51

Peschiera Borromeo

Lambro

↑CREMA

Parco Porto
di Mare

SS415

NEON CHURCH OF SANTA MARIA ANNUNCIATA IN CHIESA ROSSA

❶

24, Via Neera
• Open daily, 8.30am–12 noon and 4pm–7pm
• www.smacr.com
• Public transport: MM2 Abbiategrasso; tram 3, 15 ; bus 79

> *A church bathed in coloured fluorescent light*

A twentieth-century church, Santa Maria Annunciata in Chiesa Rossa is unusual in that its interior is bathed in the coloured light cast by a curious lighting installation. The work of the American artist Dan Flavin, this permanent installation – "Untitled" – was a gift to the parish from the Prada Foundation in 1997. The large neon tubes of red, blue, yellow, pink and green cast an ultraviolet light that gives the church a distinctive and comforting atmosphere, especially if you visit it after nightfall.

NEARBY

COLLA BROTHERS PUPPET WORKSHOP

❷

Alongside the church, at 35/1 Via Montegani, a small doorway leads through to the workshop of Carlo Colla & Sons, a family business of

craftsmen who have been creating puppet shows for more than two hundred years. Colla puppets are to be seen, for example, in the 1936 film *The Four Musketeers*, Italy's first and only full-length feature with an entire cast of puppets: all in all there were 3,573 of them, operated by thirty puppeteers, and the work was considered "the Austrian answer to American cartoons". Sometimes it is possible to visit the workshop and see the preparation of a puppet show from behind the scenes, everything from the creation of the sets to the making of the puppets themselves. For information, call 02 89531301 or consult the site www.marionettecolla.org.

SMALL TUDOR HOUSES

Corner of Via Ottolini and 5, Via Caimi
• Public transport: tram 15; bus 90, 91

> *A corner that is forever England in Bocconi district*

Lining Via Giambologna are timber-framed houses that seem to have come straight out of the English countryside. With their sloping roofs, tall chimney stacks and, above all, their exposed beams and plaster-faced walls, these town villas appear to be in perfect Tudor style. They seem to have been built by two importers of German or English pianos – the area they chose for their curious Tudor cottages contains various period villas with gardens.

ENGLISH ARCHITECTURE IN MILAN

There are other examples of British-style architecture in Milan, in particular the work of the priest-architect Spirito Maria Chiapetta (1868–1948), who was a learned enthusiast of Gothic architecture. Among his other works in Milan, two in particular are inspired by Northern Gothic: the Istituto Vittoria Colonna (Via Conservatorio), a private school whose crenellation and large windows would not be out of place in an Oxbridge college, and the church of San Camillo De Lellis (at the corner of Via Boscovich and Via Lepetit). The dark-brick Litta Building at the clinic in Via della Commenda was built in 1895, again in keeping with the Northern Gothic style.

"HIS FAMILY NAME WILL GET A TANNING"

In ecclesiastical circles an amusing anecdote used to be told about Monsignor Spirito Maria Chiapetta. At one time he lived above Cardinal Domenico Tardini, the Vatican Secretary of State, who was increasingly annoyed by the Monsignor's curious habit of moving furniture around in the middle of the night. At the end of his tether, Tardini one day whispered to a nun: "Please go and tell him that if he keeps this up, his family name will get a tanning" (*chiappetta* is Italian for "little buttocks"). The blushing nun passed on the message and thereafter the night-time shifting of furniture stopped. Even Pope Pius XII heard the anecdote and one day, repressing a smile, took the cardinal aside to ask: "So, his family name got a tanning?" To which Tardini replied. "How could I take it out on his forenames? He's called Spirito Maria!"

CHURCH OF SAN CRISTOFORO

④

Towpath (*alzaia*) of the Naviglio Grande
- Open daily, 9am–12 noon and 3pm–6.30pm
- Public transport: tram 2; bus 90-91

A generally overlooked small gem, rich in legendary associations

Even if usually ignored by tourists because of its non-central location, this fourteenth-century "double" church contains artworks of great value. The first peculiarity of the structure is that it is actually two small churches knocked together. In Roman days a church was built here on the site of a pagan temple to Hercules, this was then replaced by a medieval church to which Gian Galeazzo Visconti had a small ducal chapel added in 1398, in the hope of invoking St Christopher's protection against an outbreak of the plague. Even though the duke actually died in that outbreak, the chapel was finished by his son.

Note the superb Romanesque porch in brick; the Gothic rose window with its twelve interlaced rays; the blazons of the Visconti family, of the City of Milan and of cardinal Pietro Phylargis of Candia, archbishop of Milan and the future Pope Alexander V.

On the left in the interior there are rich frescoes depicting *The Virgin with Saints Sebastian, Anthony and Roch and a Bishop*. These are by the school of Ambrogio Borgognone, while the frescoes of *God the Father with Angels and Saints John the Evangelist, John the Baptist and Christine* are by the school of Bernardino Luini. Note also, on a wall to the right, a fourteenth-century wooden statue of St Christopher with the Christ Child. The ducal chapel is decorated with numerous works of fifteenth-century painting, practically piled on top of each other.

The church has many legendary associations. It was, for example, by this church that passed the marriage procession of Ludovico il Moro and Beatrice d'Este, and the building also saw the Naviglio canal flood numerous times (so often that the Milanese finally decided to raise the embankment). Then there is the legend that, with the battle-cry *Ultreia!**, a large group of Lombards left from here for the First Crusade. It is also said that messengers who had travelled down the River Olona landed here with news of the victory of the Lombard League over Frederick Barbarossa at Legnano on 29 May 1176. What is definitely true is that in 1192 there was a hospice alongside the church known as the Ospizio della Porta Genovese, which offered shelter to the sick and homeless.

*This interjection in Low Latin is a compound of *ultra* ("beyond") and the suffix *eia* indicating movement; it might therefore be translated as "Forward!". Common in the Middle Ages, it was above all associated with pilgrimages to Compostela.

LEONARDO'S HORSE ❺

Ippodromo di San Siro
6, Piazzale dello Sport
• Open daily: 9am–7.30pm
• Public transport: MM1 Lotto Fiera; bus 49; tram 16

> **Leonardo's lost horse lives again at San Siro**

Although the huge bronze horse (7.20 metres high, 8 metres long and weighing 15 tonnes) at San Siro racecourse was designed by Leonardo Da Vinci, it has taken exactly 500 years to materialise.

The story began in 1482, when Ludovico Il Moro instructed Leonardo build "the largest equestrian statue in the world" to pay tribute to his father, Francesco Sforza. Leonardo devoted himself to the project, making studies of living animals and drawing up preliminary designs. Although at first he wanted the horse to be rearing as if trampling the enemy, the colossal size and complexity of the project would have required several years, so he changed his mind.

The final design for the sculpture was with the horse stepping out. In 1491, Leonardo completed a clay model that was 7 metres high. Everything was ready for casting the metal, but the required 100 tonnes of bronze were no longer available – used to make the cannons for defence against the invading French troops under Louis XII. When the troops eventually entered Milan, the soldiers even used the horse as target practice and destroyed it.

When he was back in the city in 1506, Leonardo agreed to create a new equestrian statue for the monumental tomb of Giacomo Trivulzio, who had commanded the French troops at the city gates, but this one would never see the light of day either.

Five hundred years later, in 1977, Charles Dent, a former American pilot and art lover, was seized with enthusiasm when he heard this story and vowed to fulfil Leonardo's dream. It took him fifteen years to raise the money for the enterprise (around US$2.5 million), but he died before it was completed. In 1999, the bronze horse was finally erected thanks to the sculptress Nina Akamu. The statue, donated to the city of Milan as Leonardo had wished and Dent had planned, was placed at the entrance to the racecourse, considered to be the most suitable place (despite no lack of controversy).

Although this is certainly not "Leonardo's horse", it is similar to his designs and, therefore, beyond its artistic value, should be seen as a tribute to the great genius of the Renaissance.

CHARTERHOUSE OF GAREGNANO ⑥

28, Via Garegnano
• Open daily, 7.30am–6pm (for guided tours, visitors are asked to make a contribution) • Public transport: MM1 Uruguay; tram 14; bus 80; rail link (station: Milano Certosa)

Milan's little known "Sistine Chapel"

Perhaps it is because it is located on the outskirts of the city that most Milanese have never heard of – and almost certainly never visited – the old Charterhouse which Bishop Giovanni Visconti had built in 1349. This is a shame, as the interior is remarkably reminiscent of the masterpiece that Michelangelo painted for the ceiling of the Sistine Chapel. Here, the frescoes mark the highest achievement of Daniele Crespi, a Mannerist master. Depicting the history of the Carthusians, these paintings,

in which shades of white and purple predominate, reflect that Order's main principles: purity and humility (white) and penitence (purple).

Also noteworthy is the painting of *The Crucifixion* in the apse. This is by Simone Peterzano, Caravaggio's teacher, who also painted for the Charterhouse a *Nativity* and an *Adoration of the Magi*. The Chapter Room is also worth a visit, if only for the frescoes by the monk Biagio Bellotti. Recent restoration work has revealed a vault fresco of the Archangel Michael which has been attributed to Bernardo Zenale.

PETRARCH AT GAREGNANO: "HERE I AM IN PARADISE"

Petrarch visited this Carthusian monastery a number of times in 1357, his presence enhancing the aura of sanctity enjoyed by the monastic community. "So, I have already visited Heaven," the Tuscan poet later wrote. "I have seen the angels of the Lord on earth; I have seen those whose abode is Heaven living amongst us in earthly bodies." Lord Byron also visited the monastery at the beginning of the nineteenth century. His letters contain a description of the frescoes, which made a deep impression on him.

CHARTERHOUSES AND THE CARTHUSIANS

The contemplative order of the Carthusians was founded by St Bruno in 1084, in the Dauphine region to the north of Grenoble. In fact, it was the Chartreuse *massif* that gave the order its name, and it was there that La Grande Charteuse was built, soon becoming the main monastery of the Carthusians. The rules imposed by St Bruno were severe: a diet of bread and water, a simple robe of white homespun fabric and regular use of hair shirts and penitential flagellation.

One of the most famous Charterhouses in Italy is near Pavia. Built at the behest of another Visconti, Gian Galeazzo, it became the family mausoleum of the Dukes of Milan.

BRIGANDS' HIGHWAY

The Milanese were always wary of the Strada Comasina, which led from Milan to Como and then on towards Switzerland and Germany; nowadays it is a state highway known as Strada dei Giovi.

The problem lay in the fact that this route, the only way down from the Alps, passed through a thick forest (Bosco della Merlata) which extended from the gates of Milan as far as Novara, Varese, Como and beyond. And such a forest was a perfect hiding-place for ill-doers.

An inn associated with the danger these brigands long posed to Milanese travellers survived until quite recently – until, that is, it was demolished in the 1960s to make way for a garage. Called the Cascina Malgasciada, it stood in the old Musocco district (now Via Mantegazza) and was said by some to have been the headquarters of the Legorino gang, led by two famous brigands who terrorised all those in the area of Bosco della Merlata. Having been first a post inn (*locanda*), this business became a normal inn (*osteria*) and finally a *trattoria*.

The façade of the building was decorated with a seventeenth-century fresco depicting the two bandits taking their oath of allegiance; alongside them was a mule, which they used to transport their booty, and this inscription: "The mule heads ('mugs') of the two famous brigands Giacomo Legorino and Battista Scorlino, executed in May 1566, have thus been walled up in this inn."

Another *cascina* of ill-repute has survived, even if long abandoned. Cascina Merlata (Crenellated Farmhouse) owes its name to the fact that the façade was once topped with *merli* (crenellations). This place, too, was a refuge for brigands and bandits.

It is no coincidence that the last band of "old-school" gangsters to plague Milan – the Renato Vallanzasca gang active in the 1970s – was nicknamed the *Banda della Comasina*, even if no member of the gang came from this area.

BRANCA COLLECTION

7

2, Via Resegone
- Visits on request, Monday, Wednesday and Friday, 10am–3pm
- To book, write to collezione@branca.it or call 02 8513970
- Public transport: MM3 Maciachini; tram 3; bus 90, 91, 92

A great distillery reveals its secrets to the public

The Fratelli Branca distillery – famous for its bitter-herb liqueur, Fernet-Branca – is still housed in its original early twentieth-century building. Within the heart of the complex is the Branca Collection, which offers a glimpse into the natural herbs and spices that made up the world of the company's founder, Bernardino Branca, who dealt in such products.

This museum, occupying over 1,000 square metres, covers the history not only of a company but of a period of history. Its numerous exhibits include a number of works of graphic art, with a rich and curious collection of material reflecting period merchandising: ashtrays, "shot" glasses, miniature suitcases that served as presentation boxes for individual bottles, and printed material such as calendars, posters and other advertising. Other wonders worth seeing in the Via Resegone distillery include equipment dating from the founding of the company, plus more than 500 large casks used for ageing Fernet-Branca bitters and Stravecchio cognac. Almost incongruously, these are stored beneath one of the busiest city streets in Italy.

Overall you can follow 150 years of a company that established a worldwide reputation on the strength of a single product: Fernet-Branca. The famous label of the drink, showing an eagle flying above a terrestrial globe as it grips a bottle in its talons, was created in 1893 by Leopoldo Metlicovitz, one of the period's greatest graphic designers and poster artists.

The Branca family has always been particularly interested in the promotion and communications side of their business, participating in a number of great twentieth-century exhibitions. The family has also been associated with various other cultural initiatives – for example, saving the tower in Parco Sempione (which has since been renamed Torre Branca), converting the company's factory in Saint-Louis (France) into an exhibition venue for modern art, and setting up the Museo Carpano in Turin.

SALTIMBANCHI DOC FESTIVAL ⑧

Piccola Scuola di Circo
48, Via Messina
• Daily, May and June • Free
• Public transport: MM2 Garibaldi; tram 29/30

> *A school for tumblers and acrobats*

This "Small Circus School" is a permanent charitable association entirely devoted to sporting, recreational and cultural activities. Set up in 1994, it is unique of its kind in Italy and has trained hundreds of young people over the years. Each year in May–June, the school holds a festival of *Saltimbanchi DOC* ("genuine, old-style acrobats"), which is open free of charge to the public. Held under canvas in the courtyard, this is a veritable "happening" during which the school pupils put on shows of street theatre, acrobatics, music, dance and clown performances, with the participation of other companies from France and Peru as well as elsewhere in Italy.

For the rest of the year, the school offers courses of circus-linked activities in accordance with pupils' age, level of training and years of attendance. Circus skills had previously never been the object of specific programmes of professional training, but from time immemorial were either handed down within families already working in the circus or acquired by those with a particular personal interest in such skills. The Piccola Scuola di Circo is the first attempt in Italy at cooperation between physical education instructors and circus professionals

NEARBY

HOUSE WITH 56 ECHOES ⑨

Villa Simonetta
36, Via Stillicone

A little further on, right at the end of Via Messina, stands Villa Simonetta (36, Via Stillicone), which was built at the end of the fifteenth century as "La Gualtiera" and in the sixteenth century became a sort of pleasure resort for the Spanish governor, Ferrante Gonzaga, and his court. Now, it is the only surviving example of a suburban patrician villa in Lombardy. Until a few decades ago, the building also enjoyed a certain fame for the extraordinary echo effect within the colonnade on the ground floor. It was also said that this colonnade was where Clelia Simonetta, after whose family the villa is named, had her lovers strangled. As for the echo itself, it was claimed that if you shouted (in the Milanese dialect): "*Ma come se fa a avegh inscì tanta bella ròbba?*" ("But how do you manage to have so much fine stuff?"), the echo came back with the answer: "*Ròbba, ròbba, ròbba*" ("Steal, steal, steal!"). However, the acoustics are not the same since the 1962 restoration to make good the damage caused by bombing in the Second World War. Still, music continues to play a part here: since 1973 the villa has been home to Milan's City Music School.

BASILICA OF SANTA MARIA DI LOURDES

12, Via Induno
- Open daily, 7am–7pm
- 11 February: Special Blessing for the Sick and Ill
- Public transport: tram 12, 14, 29, 30, 33; bus 43, 57, 78

The Grotto of Lourdes reproduced in Milan

When it was first created in 1894, this grotto dedicated to the Virgin stood in the middle of fields on the outer edge of Milan. It was a votive chapel built by two priests who were also brothers – Antonio and Giuseppe Videmari – in thanks for the latter's recovery from a serious illness. The two priests spent years gathering funds, collecting a ten-cent "sponsorship" for each brick; the future Pope Paul VI paid for one such brick when he was a boy. When, in 1894, the two brothers managed to buy a plot of land in the present-day area of Sempione, building work could begin.

The grotto is modelled on that in Lourdes where, in 1858, a young peasant girl called Bernadette Soubirous said that the Virgin had appeared to her on a number of occasions. Today, millions of the faithful travel every year to Lourdes; but, in its own small way, this Milan replica – built in just two years and flanked by the small Church of Sant'Anna and a Convalescent Centre – has become a centre for pilgrims, who come here to lay wreaths of flowers, say the Rosary and listen to the sermons.

The architect, Chiappetta, originally intended that the grotto should form a single whole with the façade of a new sanctuary and serve as the base of a bell tower. However, this plan was then changed, creating the present layout.

The church built by the faithful as a sanctuary in honour of the Madonna of Lourdes was designed by the architect Campanini and opened for worship in 1902. It is in Byzantine style with bare brickwork and a nave, side aisles, transepts and apse; the frescoes are by Lazzaro Pasini. As the city continued to expand, the sanctuary was converted into a parish church.

In 1958, the centenary of Bernadette's visions, Pope Pius XII declared this church a Minor Roman Basilica.

Each year, on 11 February, the anniversary of the appearance of the Virgin at Lourdes is marked by a special blessing for the sick.

MUSEUM OF MILAN FIRE BRIGADE

Fire station of 35/37, Via Messina
• Visits by appointment: tel. 02 3190261 or museovvf-mi@libero.it; also open every 4 December, feast of St Barbara, patron saint of firefighters
• http://www.museovvfmilano.it
• Public transport: MM2 Garibaldi; tram 29, 33

> *History of Milan's brave firefighters*

This museum dedicated to the city's firefighters, located within the provincial headquarters of Milan Fire Brigade, gives a fascinating account of the development of Milan's 52nd Fire Brigade Corps, which began life as the "Sapper Firefighters" founded in 1812 on orders from Napoleon.

The museum itself was established in 1910 to mark the centenary of the brigade and was originally housed in one of the rooms of Castello Sforzesco. With its photographs of the most serious fires, documents relating to their causes and objects recovered from the blaze, the museum was inspired by a desire to make people more aware of the need for fire prevention. From the castle, it was transferred to the barracks in Via Ansperto, the headquarters of the city fire brigade; some of the historic equipment contained there – including steam-powered pumps on horse-drawn carriages – was actually used during the 1945 bombing raids because of the shortage of modern motorised fire engines.

Relocation to Via Messina was completed in 1960. Today, the museum – in a basement of the barracks – has one of the largest collections of this type of material in Italy. The exhibits include old wine kegs filled with water and sand; early hand pumps, stream pumps and hand-powered smoke extractors; early twentieth-century "Isotta Fraschini" fire engines and other engines dating from just after the First World War. There are even bicycles equipped with water pumps, which were used by cyclist firemen who arrived on the scene before the stream-driven pumps and rescue vehicles.

Other equipment on display includes helmets of all shapes and sizes, various kinds of fire extinguishers, a collection of period uniforms and even the material used by fire-brigade divers (from an old-fashioned diving-suit to the most modern wetsuits).

One of the centrepieces of the collection is a reconstruction of the telephone exchange that used to be in the fire brigade premises in Via Beato Marcello: the telephonist would receive calls from the various "fire phones" located throughout the city and then promptly dispatch the brigade to the blaze.

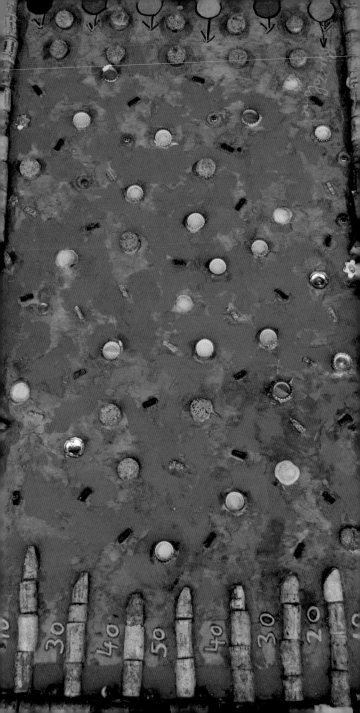

ACCADEMIA DEL GIOCO DIMENTICATO

4, Via Procaccini
- Open Tuesday, Thursday and Saturday, 3pm–7pm
- Visits only by phone appointment: 328 9065684
- www.giocodimenticato.it
- Public transport: MM2 Garibaldi; tram 1, 12, 14, 29, 30

> **Space to rediscover the games of yesteryear**

Since 2008 the former Fabbrica del Vapore (Steam Machine Factory), whose floor space has been divided up between various associations and workshops, has housed the Accademia del Gioco Dimenticato (Academy of Forgotten Games), whose aim is to collect, study, protect and bring new life to traditional games and toys now recreated using recycled materials.

Open by appointment only, this establishment, which was the brainchild of Giorgio Reali, is a veritable "academy", its shelves laden with toys and games made using all sorts of materials and objects: corks (table football, billiards), wood (stilts, diabolos, spinning tops, skittles, reels), elastic (toy rifles and catapults), paper (kites, planes, dolls and puppets), rope (skipping ropes and tug-of-war ropes), metal (hoops, rings), balls and marbles (flipper games, peashooters, ball-maze games). Other materials used include pebbles, coins, shells, beans, rags, strands of wool, pasta, plastic bottles, spools, paper cups, etc.

The range covers all those toys and games which our parents and grandparents used to make in the street or out in the courtyard – simple games that are part of a folk tradition now being forgotten.

To be admitted to the Academy, toys and games have to satisfy two conditions: be low cost (perhaps even zero cost; sometimes a game just requires a group of children) and have a sizeable creative component. Imagination – the raw material of any game worth its salt and a resource of which children seem to have an endless supply – plus the participation of the parents in the creation of the toy/game, these, according to the philosophy that inspires the Academy, are enough to satisfy a basic human need: enjoyment and amusement.

Not only does the association make its premises available for play three afternoons a week, it also organises events and private parties at various public places in Milan: schools, libraries, parks, rest homes, shopping centres and – most amazing of all – the Idroscalo, Milan's former hydroplane station and now a water leisure park.

ATM GARAGE

14, Via Messina
• Can be visited on the "open day" which the public transport authority holds once a year (usually in October, see www.atm-mi.it for details)
• Public transport: MM2 Garibaldi; tram 29, 33

> *A gem of industrial architecture*

New and old trams, vintage trains and the newest ecological models, buses and trolley buses – once a year, the public has the chance to see all these within their "natural habitat": for two days in autumn, the ATM (Azienda Trasporti Milanesi), which runs the city's public transport system, usually opens up four of its garages: those at 14 Via Messina; 89 Via Teodosio; 60 Via Molise and 27 Via Impastato.

The garage in Via Messina is a real gem of 1930s industrial architecture with vast glass walls and a central iron structure of pillars and truss beams supporting a tiled roof pierced by large skylights. The pillars mark out various bays, the widest being nearest the centre of the structure. Here you can not only see trams of recent design but also such special vehicles as the *sabbiera*: still in use, this is an old tram that was modified in 1946–47 to carry out the important job of sanding (*sabbiare*) the tram tracks when they are made too slippery by rain or snow.

The Via Teodosio General Repair Shop dates from 1929 and contains some of the vehicles which have become veritable symbols of Milan – from the historic *Carrelli* trams to the modern hi-tech *Sirietto*. During the visit it is generally possible to board the vehicles and even have your photo taken in a tram driver's uniform. Around 200 people work in this repair shop on the maintenance of about 400 trams and 700 metro cars.

At Via Molise there is a display of buses and trolley buses of all sizes, from vintage vehicles to hi-tech ecological vehicles that meet today's environmental standards.

Finally, there is the Via Impastato garage, the most modern of the four. Here you can find out more about Milan's metro trains, with a variety of carriages on display. The star of the show is undoubtedly the ultra-sophisticated *Meneghino*.

BERNOCCHI FAMILY TOMB

Cimitero Monumentale di Milano

> ## *Hidden message in the Bernocchi Via Crucis*

The Bernocchi family monument in Milan's Cimitero Monumentale stands out both because of the height of its spiral and the figures that adorn it. The work of the architect Alessandro Milani and the sculptor Giannino Castiglioni, the structure was built in stages between 1931 and 1936 to serve as the tomb of Antonio Bernocchi (Castellanza, 17 January 1859 – Milan, 8 December 1930), a textile entrepreneur who had since his death lain in a rather more modest tomb.

In accordance with the wishes of the profoundly religious Antonio Bernocchi, the sculptural decoration of the tomb is a *Via Crucis* rising in a spiral – an iconography that was traditional among the Franciscans and in some ways echoes the Tower of Babel. Drawing an analogy between the Old and New Testament stories, both clearly have a parallel tragic meaning: the *Via Crucis* recounts the death of Christ at the hands of men who "know not what they do", while the Tower of Babel story tells of God's curse upon men who had dared to defy him and to match their human pride against divine grandeur.

In a less obvious sense, this tomb also reflects the *Scala Coeli* (Ladder of Heaven) in that it portrays the progression from an unsanctified state (represented by the figure at the base of a man prostrate beneath the weight of the entire sculptural ensemble) to the state of initiation in which the individual finally casts off the old vestments of his profane existence (represented at the top by the winged horseman preventing the man on the ground from proceeding any further). Ending abruptly, the spiral also creates the impression that it continues invisibly up into the sky, thus further exemplifying the purpose of the monument as a whole: a place of burial for mortal remains, this is surmounted by a spiral of eternal souls in search of spiritual resurrection, having followed the Way of the Cross through the mortal afflictions that we all must face here on Earth.

Just like the Tower of Babel (see double page overleaf), the *Via Crucis* embodies the stages of spiritual initiation for humanity, which has one sole hope: ascension to the Heavenly Jerusalem. There, we will finally speak the language of the angels who inhabit the Celestial City, welcoming those who – like Antonio Bernocchi – are judged to have been true and faithful to both Man and God.

FROM ZIGGURATS TO THE TOWER OF BABEL AND PENTECOST

Babel is a Phoenician word which comes from the name *Baal*, meaning "Lord" or "God". According to both mystical and historical tradition, the Tower of Babel is associated with the worship of Baal, the main god of the peoples of Asia Minor. In effect, his worshippers would raise to him ziggurats (stepped towers) that clearly reflected man's progressive initiation as he drew closer to God. When monotheistic worship of Baal was replaced by the veneration of a multiplicity of gods – a polytheism tantamount to the sort of challenge to God on which the Bible story hinges – the deity's anger was such that he cast down the ziggurat, the Tower of Babel, whose name might also be linked with the Phoenician word *bil*, meaning "to confound" or "confusion". Thus, more than being a simple punishment of human pride, the destruction of the Tower of Babel is a condemnation of humanity which, though spiritually immature, was presumptuous enough to raise itself ever higher towards God, forgetting that it is impossible for man to move beyond his human condition. Confusing the terrestrial and spiritual, men thought solely of themselves, and this egoism meant that they could no

longer understand each other; that they no longer spoke the same language. Consensus had ceased to exist. The biblical account of the Tower of Babel comes at the end of the chapters that deal with the origins of humanity and before the account of the patriarchs, which is more chronological in organisation and less mythological in content. Thus it could be said to mark the conclusion of the first phase in the history of humanity, which had been characterised by the gradual formation of large empires and the foundation of great cities. It is noteworthy that the end of this period should be associated with a great social catastrophe such as the collapse of the Tower of Babel (Genesis 11:1–9). In effect, the confusion of Babel is also the punishment of a society which, by oppressing the individual, leads to the emergence of various groups that are hostile to each other – a fact symbolised by the diversity of languages that God imposed upon humanity, thus making it impossible for groups to understand one another.

The message is clear: human society without soul and understanding is condemned to dispersal and frustration, and union can only come about through spiritual renewal and a new understanding. According to the *Acts of the Apostles* (2: 5–12), that new union would be established by Christ. It is, therefore, particularly appropriate that the gift bestowed upon the Apostles at Pentecost is "the gift of tongues", the very antithesis of the confusion of languages generated at Babel.

STATUE OF FEDELE SALA ⑮

Crematorium
Cimitero Monumentale di Milano

Masonic crematorium

The crematorium at Milan's Cimitero Monumentale is a remarkable testimony to nineteenth-century Positivism and faith in science. Making Milan the first city in the whole of Europe to adopt the practice of cremation, it was built at the behest of Alberto Keller (Rome, 1800 – Milan, 23 January 1874), a businessman, industrialist, Freemason and philanthropist of Protestant origin.

At the time, cremation marked clear opposition to the Roman Catholic dogma of the "resurrection of the body"; in fact, right up to 1963 the Catholic Church condemned the practice. However, cremation also marked a return to Classical Greek rituals, to the ancient notion of corporeal purification through the reduction of the body of the deceased to ashes. By preventing the corruption of the body, this was said to preserve its dignity, leaving the memory of the deceased untouched and intact. The first body to be cremated here was that of Alberto Keller himself, who had died two years prior to its completion in 1876.

Given its inspiration, the crematorium was naturally built in the Doric style of Classical Greece, although it was later modified. The original part

of the structure (1875) was by the architect Carlo Maciachini (1818–1899) and the engineer Celeste Clericetti, the cremation apparatus itself being developed and perfected by the physician and scientist Paolo Gorini. The facility was then donated to the City of Milan by the Cremation Society, whose Chairman in 1876 was Malachia De Cristoforis (Milan, 9 November 1832 – Milan, 1915), a physician and Grand Master of the Grand Orient of Italy.

It is thought to have been De Cristoforis himself who ordered

a monument to Fedele Sala (a symbolic or perhaps imaginary character of whom nothing is known) to be set up within the crematorium to the right of the central square-shaped "temple". Rich in explicit Masonic symbolism, this monument was intended to highlight the contrast between the liberal Masonic Order and the conservative notions of the ecclesiastical authorities.

The life-size statue of Fedele Sala depicts a man with his right hand resting on his chest and his left holding a parchment. It stands within a Doric-style niche (identical to the typical form of a Masonic Lodge), flanked by the traditional columns of *Jakin* and *Boaz* (Strength and Rigour) that were said to have stood in the Temple of Solomon in Jerusalem and adopted by Masonic iconography.

The tympanum of the niche is decorated with the eye of the Great Architect of the Universe, shown at the centre of a delta of light. And beneath the architrave of the arch is an open compass intertwined with a set square, the symbol of the second grade of Masonic fellowship. The respective positions of compass and set square refer to the three basic levels of such fellowship: the set square placed on the compass indicates an Entered Apprentice, the two intertwined a Fellow mason, and the set square placed beneath the compass a Master Mason.

On the column to the left of the niche, the caduceus emerging from the leaves represents the soul rising upwards to the Eternal. The ship's wheel set within the leaves on the right-hand column symbolises movement and progression.

At the foot of the statue is an anchor engraved with the word *Rosario*, together with a length of rope. In both Freemasonry and Christianity, the anchor symbolises hope of salvation for the soul, while the rope symbolises the path to be followed to enlightenment. As for the word *Rosario*, it may be the name of the unknown sculptor but could be a reference to the *Rosario Philosophorum*, the name given to the hermetic alchemical treatises of the old "Philosophers of Fire" who strove to turn lead into gold and the unsanctified condition of mortal men into a state of initiation into immortality.

The base of the Fedele Sala statue is a square, which may also be an allusion to the Cubic Stone of Perfection, said in Freemasonry to be the basis for the construction of the Human and Spiritual Temple.

SANCTUARY OF SANTA MARIA ALLA FONTANA⑯

11, Piazza Santa Maria alla Fontana
• Open Monday to Saturday, 9.30am–12 noon and 2.30pm–5.30pm;
Sunday, 9.30am–12 noon and 2.30pm–5.30pm
• Public transport: MM3 Zara

> *A miraculous well within a pretty cloister*

Long attributed to Leonardo da Vinci, the Renaissance sanctuary of Santa Maria alla Fontana is one of the most secret and poetic places in the city.

The site was originally in the middle of the countryside, beyond the Porta Comasina city gateway, and the sanctuary was founded in 1507 by Charles II d'Amboise, governor of Milan, on behalf of Louis XII of France. According to tradition, Charles II, who suffered from eye disease, used the waters of a spring on this site and vowed that should they cure him he would build a sanctuary in honour of the Virgin Mary. He is then said to have commissioned Leonardo to build it. However, recently discovered documents show that the architect was actually Giovanni Antonio Amado. Initially entrusted to the Benedictine monks of San Simpliciano, this sanctuary – together with the Cà Granda and Il Lazzaretto – became one of the three lynchpins of the city's health service.

Inside you can still see the old frescoes attributed to Luini's workshop. There is also a plaque commemorating the foundation of the sanctuary on 29 September 1507.

Within the sacellum, initially open on three sides so that the sick could hear Mass from outside, an altar stands just opposite the hole from which

the water flows endlessly through eleven different taps. The ceiling is striking as it consists of a coloured spherical vault divided by twelve ribs, unique in Italy. At the centre of that vault the figure of God blessing those below is not only painted on the surface, it is carved into the wood and modelled in the plaster. The figures between the ribs are the twelve Apostles – or rather, eleven plus St Paul after his conversion. Attributed to the sixteenth-century Campi brothers, the large painting behind the altar depicts the Virgin and Child with cherubs and archangels; at her feet is a solitary man, shown first stricken with sickness then cured.

MUSEUM OF THE "EUGÉNIE" METAL FOUNDRY ⑰

21, Via Thaon Di Revel
• Visits on request; write to museo@fonderianapoleonica.it
• Public transport: MM3 Zara; tram 7, 31; bus 82, 86, 90/91, 92

*A one-off
collection*

These buildings are two hundred years old but have recently been restored to their original state. At their core was the old Eugènie Metal Foundry dating from Napoleonic times, which has now been converted into a series of offices and spaces for exhibitions, concerts and other cultural events.

The presence of the foundry here is marked not only by the preservation of its original space but also by a small museum housing documents, photographs and tools relating to the art of metal foundry practised here for more than a century by the Barigozzi company. Specialising in the casting of bells and works of art, this bronze foundry became one of the most renowned of its day.

The museum collection includes a vast number of the plaster and terracotta moulds used when casting the saints and other pious figures that decorated bells. This unique collection gives a good idea of the complex iconography that was used in decorating such pieces. Along with an inscription commemorating the donor or community that had commissioned it, each bell might bear a dedication and a figurative composition, generally a Crucifix flanked by the particular saints that the community intended to celebrate. Note also a less extensive, but no less significant, collection of plaster sculptures within the museum.

Seeing the original foundry furnace and inspecting the photographs and illustrations on display lets you understand the various phases involved in creating a bell – from modelling its form to its final casting. The collection contains more than 1,500 period photographs in all, depicting the interior of the foundry, the different phases in the manufacturing process, the casting of the finished form and the celebrations that accompanied the transport, blessing and installation of the bells in the churches for which they were commissioned.

When originally set up in 1806, the foundry was given the name "Eugénie" in honour of the then Viceroy of the Kingdom of Italy, Eugène de Beauharnais. Right up to its final closure in 1975, it produced not only bells but also bronze sculptures. Among these sculptures still on public display are the six-horse chariot atop the Paris Arc de la Paix, the equestrian monument to Vittorio Emanuele II in Piazza del Duomo, the monument to Alessandro Manzoni in Piazza San Fedele and even the statue of Dante Alighieri in New York's Dante Park.

CIMITERO DELLA MOJAZZA

1, Piazzale Lagosta
• Public transport: MM3 Zara; tram 7

> ## *Where is Giuseppe Parini's tomb?*

Although most Milanese know very well where Manzoni lies – in the Cimitero Monumentale – not many have asked themselves where Parini's tomb is. The answer is easy: nobody knows. When the Italian satirist and poet died in August 1799, his funeral was very simple. Moreover, he had left written instructions: "I want, I order and command that my funeral expenses shall be limited to what is strictly necessary, as is customary for the lowliest of citizens." His remains were interred in the cemetery of Porta Comacina,

called "Mojazza" after a nearby farm. The cemetery had been constructed in 1686 in the district known as "Isola" near what is now Via Borsieri. In 1787 Parini's remains were moved a short distance to the site that is now Piazzale Lagosta. Other illustrious Milanese such as Cesare Beccaria and Melchiorre Gioia were buried alongside Parini.

The practice of the time was not to set headstones at the grave, but on the inside wall of the cemetery near the burial plot. This was only for the most important occupants, of course, as the others only merited a simple and anonymous wooden cross. The Mojazza cemetery was closed in 1895, when the Monumentale and Maggiore cemeteries were opened. The exact location of Parini's remains, like those of his illustrious compatriots, had probably already been forgotten by then.

The poet Ugo Foscolo, who had known Parini in later life, was indignant at this disrespectful treatment: his remains lay alongside common mortals and perhaps the worst of criminals, as Foscolo noted in a passage from his *Dei Sepolcri* (Of the Sepulchres).

From the twenties, the massive building programme in that part of town also affected the old cemetery. Today there is little or nothing left, except two columns at the junction of Via Lario and Via Arese, which had marked one of the entrances. But the gravestone of Parini, whose body many people think still lies beneath Piazzale Lagosta, was not lost. It is still in place, in the second courtyard of a large building dating from 1925, at number 1 of this same square. The wall that surrounds the courtyard is also the boundary wall of the cemetery – Parini's tombstone has never been moved from where it was placed over two centuries ago in 1799.

ASSOCIAZIONE UMBERTO DI DONATO

Museo della Macchina da Scrivere
10, Via G.F. Menabrea
• Admission free, Tuesday, Friday and Saturday 3pm–7pm
• Guided tours by appointment • Tel: 347 8845560
• Public transport: MM3 Maciachini, Zara; tram 2; bus 90, 91, 92
• www.umbertodidonato.org

> *A museum dedicated to the typewriter*

This unique typewriter museum, open since 2007 in a private building, is the brainchild of its owner, Umberto Di Donato. A former financier and bank manager, he is above all a great typewriter enthusiast, to the point of having collected and displayed almost 1,400 of them here.

They come in all shapes and sizes: portable or fixed, for office work or home, sturdy or lightweight, glossy or matt, rare or common. Among the rarest pieces collected by Di Donato since 1952 are an 1898 Underwood that had belonged to the Austro-Hungarian Emperor Franz Joseph made on the occasion of his Jubilee, an Olympia owned by the Neapolitan journalist and novelist Matilde Serao, an Odell from 1887, a William I Curved of 1891, the 1885 Blickensderfer, the Optima model with Arabic keyboard and the classic and legendary Olivetti M40, the lovely Tippa-B portable, and the famous Lettera 22, made famous by Indro Montanelli and so many other journalists who used it before the invention of the laptop.

Also on display are some mechanical calculators dating from the first half of the twentieth century, cumbersome to operate but very accurate.

The museum, which has been lovingly set up, piece by piece, is testament to Di Donato's passion for the world of writing. Each of these machines has a story to tell, all fascinating anecdotes, so we recommend a guided tour.

THE NEGUS TYPEWRITER

At the headquarters of the Associazione Lombarda Giornalisti (7 Viale Monte Santo), a glass case in the first-floor offices holds the original model that belonged to the Ethiopian Emperor Haile Selassie, found by Italian soldiers in the sovereign's cave during the Battle of Mai Ceu (Maychew) of 31 March 1936.

MAPP – MUSEO D'ARTE "PAOLO PINI"

45, Via Ippocrate
• Open Monday to Friday, 10am–4pm (visitors are requested to make a donation) • www.mapp-arca.it
• Public transport: MM3 Affori FNM

> *A museum of art therapy from the old psychiatric hospital*

The art section of the Regional Museum of Psychiatry in Niguarda Hospital offers a vast collection of works, produced in part by psychiatric patients themselves, in part by established contemporary artists such as Emilio Tadini and Enrico Baj. The collection, already containing the works of some 140 artists, has grown each year since 1993 with new installations, murals and sculptures. Furthermore, the museum exhibits a number of works in rotation that are the fruit of collaboration between artists and patients in art-therapy sessions or during the special art workshops organised by the MAPP and dedicated to specific themes.

The thinking behind the "four-handers" is that patient and artist should work on the same canvas, or else be involved in a show of some kind (performance art, music, theatre, etc.). The final result is not merely the sum of individual contributions but also the expression of a shared journey,

the synthesis of various languages. On the one hand are the artists themselves, who can share their own experience and skills; on the other, the patients, who through this exercise discover a new means of communication. Both thus contribute to a fruitful and regenerative exchange. Everything produced within these workshops and sessions (paintings, videos, performances, plays, music, dance) is then given the opportunity to engage with the world through special exhibitions, discussions, shows, publications and other forms of cultural exchange.

Until a few years ago, the first floor of the Istituto Paolo Pini housed a collection of mummified human remains that had been amassed by Dr Giuseppe Parravicino in the early twentieth century. This included two entire female bodies, six heads, a head and torso, and various other smaller body parts (each head complete with its original hair, beard or moustache). However, the collection is no longer to be seen in the Museo Paolo Pini and nobody knows what became of it. Those curious about such things can see a similar collection in the Museo Paolo Gorini at the General Hospital in Lodi.

VILLA CLERICI – GALLERY OF CONTEMPORARY RELIGIOUS ART

㉑

14, Via Terruggia
• Open Tuesday to Friday, 9.30am–12.30pm and 2pm–4.30pm
• Public transport: tram 4–5; bus 40, 42, 51

A collection of religious works of art in an eighteenth-century villa

The gallery of Villa Clerici is little known, although it has been open since 1955, because it is some way from the city centre. Few in fact know that it has recently reopened after being long closed for maintenance work. This museum is one of the first in the world – and the first in Italy – to bring together works of solely religious art. Two hundred pieces are on display (the collection storerooms contain around 3,300 other pieces, comprising drawings, paintings, bronzes and plaster casts) and the whole enterprise was the result of the passion of one man, Dandolo Bellini. Covering religious art produced in the twentieth century, the collection contains noteworthy examples of the work of Bellotti, Bodini, Carena, Carpi, Hernandez, Manfrini, Manzù, Minguzzi, Soldi, Usellini and Zigaina – to name but a few. An entire room is devoted to some fifty sculptures by Francesco Messina alone.

Villa Clerici itself was built for the family of that name in the first half of the eighteenth century, to designs by Francesco Croce. The building was later purchased by Count Melzi, who stripped it of its decorations and used the premises as workshops and spinning mills. In 1927 the villa became a halfway-house for the social reintegration of ex-convicts; then, after the Second World War the institution focused primarily on ill-adjusted teenagers. When this service was rehoused in a modem building next door, the villa was free for other use. The idea to convert it into a gallery of religious art came from Dandolo Bellini, a friend and assistant to Giovanni Battista Montini, the future Pope Paul VI.

Along with the collection itself, the lower-floor rooms in the villa still have their late eighteenth-century frescoes, while the upper floor – reached by a monumental staircase ornamented with statues of Atlas – contains *trompe-l'œil* work representing The Arts.

Don't miss the two gardens, at front and back. The one behind the villa is the larger and has fountains, statues and two open-air theatres. One of these statues, depicting St John Nepomucen, used to stand alongside the Naviglio but was broken during a 1943 bombing raid and subsequently brought here after restoration.

MUSEO DI OTTICA CHIERICHETTI

Faculty of Mathematics, Physics and Natural Sciences
Università di Milano – Bicocca
3, Piazza della Scienza; Building U2
• Open Monday to Friday, 9am–6.30pm
• Public transport: MM1 Precotto; bus 40, 86; tram 7, 11

> *A collection of optical instruments from a local legend*

Located on the walkway linking buildings U1 and U2 of the Università Bicocca are four large steel-and-glass showcases, two pyramidal in form. These contain the collection of equipment and instruments that Arnaldo Chierichetti used in his optician's shop, a local legend, at Porta Romana.

Set up in 1994 by Elda Chierichetti, the optician's daughter, this Optometry Museum is a veritable history of all types of spectacles, binoculars, field-glasses, bellow-lens cameras, projectors, microscopes and telescopes – to say nothing of the equipment and instruments that opticians use to measure eyesight (for example, the Hess-Lancaster test or the dichromatic test).

Among the more unusual objects note the stereoscope, which – as early as the eighteenth century – was used to view specially made slides that created the illusion of three-dimensional images. The museum collection also contains a number of stereographic plates dating from the early twentieth century, and a magic lantern. This instrument, the forebear of the slide projector, was in use as early as 1665 as a sort of sideshow attraction to impress the curious with unusual or amusing images. Only later, from around 1830 onwards, did it become a teaching instrument for professors and lecturers. The museum also has a wide assortment of coloured slides on glass.

Listed by the Milan Chamber of Commerce as one of the city's historic shops, the original Chierichetti premises (74 Corso di Porta Romana) have kept the appearance they had in 1914. Inside are further period objects and artefacts, including a collection of seventeenth- and eighteenth-century spectacles and a table stereoscope.

IGLOO HOMES AT MAGGIOLINA

Via Lepanto
• Public transport: MM5 Istria

I n the north-eastern district of Maggiolina are some bizarre little igloo-shaped houses, dating from 1946. The work of the engineer Mario Cavallè, these domed homes of around 45 square metres each are still inhabited. They are on two levels: outside, above the road level, and a basement.

> **The ancient Via degli "Gnomi"**

Only eight of the original twelve houses remain. There were once two other houses in the form of a mushroom (pictured), designed by the same Cavallè, demolished in 1965 to make way for a construction without planning consent. These little houses were one of the reasons why Via Lepanto was known as Via degli "Gnomi" (Street of the "Gnomes"). Three very similar mushroom houses can still be seen today in the commune of Novate Milanese (Via Puccini).

NEARBY

REINFORCED CONCRETE STILTS

A short distance from the igloo houses in Via Perrone di San Martino is the so-called "stilts" villa, designed in 1934 by architect Luigi Figini for his own home. The rectangular building, resting on the series of reinforced concrete pillars after which it is named, is a model of rationalist architecture reminiscent of the Le Corbusier school.

JOURNALISTS' VILLAGE

The Maggiolina district, perhaps so called because it was the site of Maggiolina farm until its demolition in 1920, dates back to the sixteenth century. It was in the twenties that the so-called Journalists' Village grew up here, characterised by small villas nestling in the greenery. The early residents gave the place a good write-up and clearly enhanced its reputation. Despite being one of Milan's most exclusive districts, it has historically been surrounded by mainly working-class apartment blocks.

VILLA MIRABELLO

6, Via Villa Mirabello
• Visible in part from outside; interior to be seen only during exhibitions
or public events (see website: www.salvis.it)
• Public transport: MM3 Zara; tram 5, 7, 11; bus 90/91, 92

> *A Tuscan villa in the heart of fifteenth-century Milan*

Partially tucked away within the heart of the so-called Villagio dei Giornalisti (Journalists' Village), a delightful property development of detached houses built in 1912, Villa Mirabello is – together with Villa Bicocca degli Arcimboldo – one of the best-preserved examples in the city of a fifteenth-century suburban *villa-cascina* (villa farmhouse). The bare brick villa, with ogive windows enclosed within terracotta frames surrounded by strips of incised roughcast, stands alongside a small church. Dedicated to the *Mater Amabilis*, this contains a fifteenth-century fresco of a saint raising the Cross. At the centre of the courtyard stands a bristling dragon fountain; nicknamed the *Mangia Bagaj* (Child Devourer), this is a perfect replica of the original which is now within Castello Sforzesco (see p. 99). Inside, the walls are decorated with the armorial bearings of the Landriani and Brivio families – successive owners of the villa – along with decorative frescoes of heraldic motifs, flowers and pomegranate trees. Immediately beneath the roof timbers is a fresco of a courtly scene with a mandolin player and a lady with a tambourine.

Built for the Mirabello family, the villa became the property of Pigello Portinari in 1445. A Florentine nobleman – descended from Dante's Beatrice herself – he was in Milan to oversee the affairs of the Medici bank and commissioned the Portinari chapel while here (see p. 212). It was he who appointed the Tuscan architect Michellozzo to restore and transform this *cascina* into a villa fully in keeping with the style of the Tuscan-Lombard Renaissance. Ludovico il Moro then stayed in this villa during his brief return to Milan.

Since 1916 Villa Mirabello has been the Lombard headquarters of the association for those who have lost their sight in wartime.

MUSEO DEL MANIFESTO CINEMATOGRAFICO 25
MILANO

Fermo Immagine45, Via Cristoforo Gluck
- Open Tuesday to Sunday 2pm–7pm, closed Monday
- Tel: 02 36505760
- www.museofermoimmagine.it

> *Discover the beauty of movies on paper memorabilia*

As an addition to the Museo della Cineteca di Milano, in 2013 a new museum space was inaugurated dedicated to anything featuring the cinema "on paper": posters, stills, storyboards, brochures and advertising flyers – over 150,000 exhibits in all.

The museum is housed in a renovated factory, in historic Via Gluck, made famous by Adriano Celentano in his song about the street where he was born.

Visitors are immersed in a world of colourful images, sometimes even more evocative than the films they represent.

The imaginary journey begins in the street where an imposing mural, by artist FabioAcme107, sums up the history of famous movie posters. Inside is a large space divided into two sections: one room for conferences and another for temporary exhibitions. The first has an extensive library with hundreds of books and monographs on the cinema and is open to researchers; its walls are entirely covered with posters, from the oldest (*I misteri di Parigi* of 1924) to more recent blockbusters. The second room, which is even more striking, hosts exhibitions on great cinematic themes: Liz Taylor, Dracula and the vampires, Star Wars, and so on. There are exhibitions not only of posters relating to the theme, but also props, models, reconstructions, and memorabilia often from private collections never before on public view.

You can complete the tour with a visit to the bookshop and café, the "Caffè degli Ignoranti", aptly dedicated to Adriano Celentano, with posters of his films, posters, original discs, videos of his television appearances and lyrics from his best-known songs inscribed on the tables and walls.

LITTLE-KNOWN CURIOSITIES
AT THE RAILWAY STATION

Piazzale Duca d'Aosta
• Open daily, 5.50am–0.20am
• Public transport: MM2, 3 Stazione Centrale

> *Mussolini*
> *at the Central*
> *Station ...*

Recent restoration work at the Central Station has brought to light a number of previously overlooked aspects of this remarkable building, as well as uncovering some that had been deliberately concealed.

First there is the former waiting-room, which is now incorporated within the third floor of the Feltrinelli bookshop. Between the bookshelves you can get some idea of what this long-closed space must have been like, its walls painted with 1930s depictions of aerial views of a number of Italian cities: Assisi, Padua, Pisa, Naples and Bologna. These views might be said to complement those of other major cities which decorate the central hall of the station; those faïence mosaics, too, have now regained their original splendour thanks to careful cleaning. Within the waiting-room, also note a superb period drinking fountain in marble.

In the concourse leading to the platforms, the polychrome mosaics produced by the Padoan workshop in Venice – long hidden behind newspaper kiosks – have also been revealed once more. In 1940s Art Deco style, they are allegorical depictions of technological advances – from the discovery of fire to the harnessing of radio waves.

Don't miss the allegorical paintings by Basilio Cascella (the artist of the views of Italian cities) that dominate the three entrances to the Royal Pavilion in the station (see p. 325); the choice of painted faïenceware here, rather than mosaics, was because the work had to be rushed in order to finish before the official opening of the station. The images depict three episodes from the history of the Royal House of Savoy, one of them containing a detail of some historical significance. This is the image which, with some certain poetic licence, shows the meeting between Mussolini and King Vittorio Emanuele III after the famous "March on Rome": if you look closely, you'll see that Mussolini's face has been erased. The story goes that on 25 April 1945, the date of the Liberation, Italian partisans pelted the painting with stones until they had obliterated Mussolini's face. However, it seems more likely that it was one man up a ladder who hammered away at a likeness that nobody wanted to see any more. Curiously, some of the Roman *fasces,* together with the inscription "IX Year of the Fascist Era" (that is, 1931 – the year the station was opened), have survived, clearly visible on the building's façade.

THE ROYAL PAVILION IN THE CENTRAL STATION

Stazione Centrale
Piazzale Duca d'Aosta
Open during public events (announced on the Facebook page "Milano
Centrale è un vero spettacolo")
Public transport: MM2, 3 Stazione Centrale

Although one of the most luxurious and best-preserved traces in Milan of the Kingdom of Italy, the Royal Pavilion in the Central Station is surprisingly little known.

About halfway down the last platform (it can also be entered directly from Piazza Luigi di Savoia), this pavilion, sometimes open to the public, is regularly used for films and photo-shoots.

> *One of the most luxurious and best-preserved traces in Milan of the Kingdom of Italy*

Designed by Ulisse Stacchini and opened at the same time as the Central Station (in 1931), the two-storey pavilion was intended for use by members of the royal family when travelling by train. On the ground floor is the hall and the Guards Room. From here a large marble staircase leads up to the single space of the *Sala Reale* (Royal Hall). Recently restored, this has maintained its charm because the materials – parquet, columns, marble friezes, splendid crystal glass chandeliers, bas-reliefs and coffered ceiling – are all original.

Almost all the fascist symbols here have been removed – for example, the *fasces* on the ground-floor ceiling (their outlines are still visible) and the bust of Mussolini in the Guards Room (now covered by a block of marble). However, various other symbols dating from that period have survived: the

Roman she-wolf that suckled Romulus and Remus, an imperial eagle, the blazon of the House of Savoy and, above all, a series of small swastikas carved into the wood within the *Sala Reale* (probably added for a planned visit by Hitler). The toilets at the back of the *Sala Reale* contain another curious detail: behind a wall mirror is the opening to a secret passageway and small staircase which, in case of emergency, allowed the king to leave the station undisturbed. This escape route seems never to have been used.

THE SPIRITUAL SYMBOLISM OF MILAN CENTRAL STATION

Opened in 1931, the Central Station was designed in 1912 by the Italian architect Ulysses Stace (1871–1947), who took Union Station in Washington D.C. as his model. Various decorative elements in the Milan station are inspired by Greek and Roman mythology: winged horses, lions, eagles, chimeras and signs of the zodiac, all rendered with a sense of movement, of passage from one space to another, which is perfectly suited to this place of transit. It is less well-known that all these symbols also serve to convey a spiritual message that is in keeping with the message on the commemorative plaque dedicated to St Francesca Cabrini, patron saint of emigrants, which was unveiled on 13 November 2010 by the President of Milan City Council, Letizia Moratti, accompanied by various ecclesiastical dignitaries. Part of the inscription reads: "From this place, Francesca Cabrini (1850–1917) often ventured out along the highways of the world, a saint of the Catholic faith and an apostle of solidarity with all travellers".

Above the ticket offices within the station a large panel depicts the twelve signs of the zodiac. Just as the Sun symbolically travels through the different signs, so the traveller passes through various stations before reaching his final destination. His journey allows him to discover an inner world and the different facets of his personality (again symbolised by the different signs of the zodiac), until ultimately he arrives at Divine Light and the Sacred Fire, represented by an allegorical mosaic that shows the "Discovery of Fire", wherein Prometheus is seen over a tunnel that symbolises the subterranean realm of the soul and of this world. The figure is shown raising a burning stake from which emerge flames and smoke, symbols of the initial confusion afflicting those who undertake the most mysterious and sublime of journeys – that of self-discovery. It is also a confusion which is reflected in the agitation of the thousands of people who hurry through the station every day.

The mosaic that depicts a section of winged rail track further highlights the transcendental aspect of travel. In the vestibule to the station there is also an image of the winged horse Pegasus; straining to depart, he is held back by a horseman, probably Bellerophon, who will then mount this horse and ride off to kill the Chimera, whose image is sculpted in various parts of the station. According to Greek mythology, Pegasus was born of the blood of the

gorgon Medusa, an underground deity; but he was also said to be the son of Poseidon, god of the seas. He would subsequently be tamed by Bellerophon, with the help of the goddess Athena; this took place near the Pirenian spring, where the horse used to drink. Such a spring is present on the façade of the station building, its waters tumbling into

the basin beneath through the open mouth of Jupiter, the god of prudence and wisdom who, according to the same legend, was the one who sanctified the Pirenian spring. Part lion, part ram and part serpent, the Chimera symbolises materialist desires (the lion), sexual perversity (the ram) and deceit (the serpent). Bellerophon's receipt of Pegasus from Athena, goddess of war, signifies that man can overcome these different failings if he engages in a combat that teaches him to master the spiritual energy symbolised by Pegasus. Therein lies the symbolic message of Milan Central Station: each and every journey is ultimately a voyage of inner discovery and spiritual enhancement.

IL BINARIO 21 (PLATFORM 21)

28

Shoah Memorial in Milan
1, Piazza Edmond J. Safra (Central Station)
• For individual visitors, the site is open for bookings the first and third
Thursday (3pm–6.30pm) and the last Sunday (9.30am–12.30pm) of
each month, always as part of a guided tour
• Tel: 02 2820975• presidenza@memorialeshoah.it

Departure of the deportees

Four old cattle wagons dating from the Second World War. A platform to road level on Via Ferrante Aporti, along the east side of the Central Station. This is "Platform 21", from which Jewish deportees left Milan for unknown destinations. They were sent to the Italian transit camps of Fossoli or Bolzano or, more often, directly to the now infamous camps of Auschwitz, Mauthausen or Bergen-Belsen. The platform was the one the mail wagons used for loading and unloading, and the Nazis and fascists had not chosen it at random. Its location, at the same level as the street, made it almost invisible to anybody passing through the station, boarding or alighting from other trains: nobody was to be aware of what was happening. The Jewish citizens, men, women and children, who often arrived directly

from San Vittore prison, were crammed into the wagons. These were then tightly sealed and hoisted to the level of the other platforms to be attached to the locomotive. Thus began their dramatic journey, which lasted many days.

At least twenty trains departed from this platform, each of which carried hundreds of people.

This is probably the only intact site among the many in Europe that witnessed the departure of the deportation trains. To return Platform 21 to its original appearance, post-war additions have been removed, leaving the bare concrete and those scarred walls that were the last thing thousands of deported Italians were to see.

Today this is the home of the Shoah Memorial of Milan, which is not only a museum but a place of confrontation, study and research. The space is divided into three main sections. The first is the "Hall of Witnesses", in which you can listen to the voices of the few survivors. Next is the "Platform of the Unknown Destination", where the wagons were loaded, two of which can be visited, and where plaques are affixed with the dates and destinations of each journey. Finally there is the "Wall of Names", listing all the names of those who left from this platform: those underlined are the few survivors who made it back to Italy.

REMAINS OF CASCINA POZZOBONELLI

4, Via Andrea Doria
• Public transport: MM2, 3 Centrale F.S.; tram 1, 5; bus 60, 92

A forgotten beauty

Just a short walk from the central railway station, a Renaissance chapel has miraculously survived. Its arched portico, squeezed in between the large buildings, is reminiscent of the Ponticella del Bramante at Castello Sforzesco (see p. 101). Long neglected – and thus a victim of vandals, the elements and repeated cleaning with heavy detergents that erased a large part of the decoration – the chapel underwent a number of restoration projects during the twentieth century. In spite of this chequered past, it does still maintain some of the refined *graffito* decoration typical of the late fifteenth century (the effigies of saints and prophets in the cupola are, however, only partly recognisable). This feature confirms that the chapel dates from the same period as the Ponticella. A small three-apsed oratory surmounted by an octagonal drum and a slender lantern, the chapel stands on ground purchased in 1498 by Gian Giacomo Pozzobonelli, a nobleman close to the Sforza family, in order to extend his estates. The following year he commissioned a ten-bay portico to link this small building to a complex of three other structures and two courtyards. Given its location in what was then open countryside, this must have been a rural residence (*cascina*), perhaps based on a previous structure that had belonged to a monastery. There is debate among historians as to who actually built the chapel and portico. True, some features – such as the shell motifs, the fake pilasters in the portico and the *tondi* used to emphasise geometrical shapes – are typical of Donato Bramante, but this is probably the work of one of his followers. The urban development regulations approved in 1898 led to the demolition of the *cascina* and part of the porticoed arcade. However, when around this time Luca Beltrami was carrying out restoration work at Castello Sforzesco, he based part of his reconstruction on one of the graffito scenes decorating the portico, which depicted the Filarete Tower before its demolition in 1521. That original graffito work has since been lost, but there is a reproduction of it under the Ponticella at the Castello.

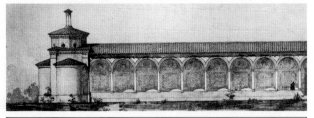

A curious fact: a 1930's graffito showing the remains of Cascina Pozzobonelli can be seen in the entrance hall of the building at 44 Via Soperga.

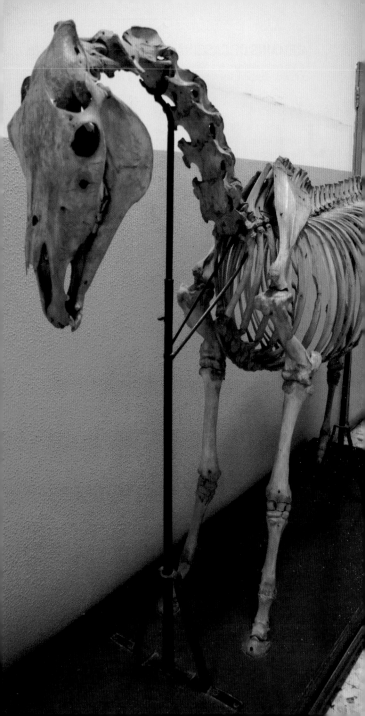

SKELETON OF NAPOLEON'S HORSE

Collezione Anatomica della Facoltà di Medicina Veterinaria
Università degli Studi di Milano
10, Via Celoria
• Opening hours: temporarily closed
• To visit, contact Sig. Antino Carnevali (02 50317983)
• Public transport: MM2 Piola

> *The horse from Napoleon's Egyptian campaign*

I n the corridors of the Faculty of Veterinary Medicine are some samples and preparations that were previously part of the nineteenth-century Cabinet of Anatomy. Among them is the skeleton of an Arab horse which Napoleon Bonaparte rode during his Egyptian campaign. This horse was later presented to the Viceroy of Italy, Prince Eugène de Beauharnais, the son of the emperor's wife Josephine. When the animal died, aged 30, in Monza, its body was given to the Scuola de Mascalcia, then housed in the old lazaretto. Its skeleton was prepared by the anatomist Luigi Leroy and the pupils of his school in the years 1810–1812. Although there is no documentary proof that this is the self-same animal, all the evidence suggests that this really is Napoleon's horse; we know, for example, that Leroy never worked on any other equine skeleton.

Awaiting relocation to a more suitable site, the anatomic collection contains more than 1,500 exhibits, including a spectacular ox (complete with exposed musculature), a dog, a horse, a ram, a monkey and a man. The cadaver, complete with part of its vascular system, was probably from the city hospital.

STOPPOLONI COLLECTION

The Anatomical Museum also possesses exhibits, the work of Giuseppe Stoppoloni, a highly-skilled anatomist and dissector, which were once part of the Museum of Veterinary Anatomy at the University of Camerino. When he died in 1965, they were bequeathed to the Milan Museum. Stoppoloni was capable of producing samples that were so clear that they could serve as the basis for exhaustive morphological descriptions. The collection includes a series of placentas from domestic animals as well as foetuses at various stages of development, plus a certain number of deformed animals and those with more than the usual number of limbs. There are also mummies of lambs of various ages and some very fine myological (revealing the muscle structure) statues of different animals. Note, in particular, that of a dromedary in which you can still see the innards.

Cologno rosso di Lombardia

Settembre

DIPARTIMENTO DI PRODUZIONE VEGETALE ③①

Università di Milano
2, Via Celoria
• Visits on request, check info at 02 50316536 (any public exhibitions listed on the site www.diprove.unimi.it)
• Public transport: MM2 Piola; tram 23, 33; bus 62, 90, 91

Francesco Garnier Valletti's Garden of Pomona

The University of Milan contains man-made reproductions of a total of 792 different fruits. These are by one of the nineteenth century's best-known masters of ceroplastics, Francesco Garnier Valletti, one of the last exponents of the art to work on the scientific and documentary reproduction of fruits and flowers.

Having worked at the courts of Vienna and St Petersburg, and also been head of the Museo Pomologico at the Royal Academy of Agriculture in Turin, Garnier Valletti developed a "secret" technique based on a mix of vegetable resins and alabaster dust (the alabaster subsequently replaced

with a compound of chalk dust and ash). This could be poured molten into moulds and had the advantage over the usual wax models that the end results survived better over time.

The reproductions in the Dipartimento di Produzione Vegetale are one of the five Italian collections making up what is known as Garnier Valletti's "Pomona Artificiale" (Man-Made Garden of Pomona); the most famous of these is undoubtedly the Museo della Frutta in Turin, but the collections are generally unknown. These painstakingly modelled works, painted to catch the striations and nuances of colour typical of each variety of fruit or flower, reveal the great skill of this master of ceroplastics, whose attention to detail is further borne out by the thousands of preparatory drawings discovered in the Turin Accademia di Agricultura in 1996.

OTHER TEACHING MUSEUMS WITHIN THE UNIVERSITY OF MILAN
Largely unknown and struggling to survive in the face of financial cuts, the museums of the various faculties of the University of Milan contain a number of surprises.

The Dipartimento di Biologia (26 Via Caloria) houses the **Museo didattico di Zoologia** (http://users.unimi.it/ffmuseozoo; 02 50314736. Open Monday to Friday, 10am–12 noon and 2pm–4pm). This contains almost 800 wall panels covering zoological and botanical subjects, together with around 100 boxes of insects dating from the early years of the twentieth century. Some of the material is in the form of small dioramas, and the historical value of the museum also rests on its collection of teaching books and anatomical models.

The Dipartimento di Scienze della Terra (34 Via Mangiagalli) houses the **Museo di Paleontologia** (02 50315493) which was set up to house the materials found by the explorer and geologist Ardito Desio; the collection has since been further enriched thanks to material discovered by his pupils and successors. The most important collections here include thousands of small palaeontological samples: ammonites dating from the Triassic and Jurassic Periods, brachiopod fossils dating from the Permian Period and molluscs from the Plio-Pleistocene Period, all material from Italy. There is also a Mineralogy Collection with over 10,000 mineral samples and 30,000 rock samples, as well as scientific equipment and instruments of great historical interest.

The Dipartimento di Scienze dell'Antichità (7 Via Festa del Perdono) houses the **Archivi e la Biblioteca Egizia,** whose collections comprise documents, letters, diaries and more than 40,000 photographs that belonged to six of the most important egyptologists of the nineteenth and twentieth centuries: Auguste Mariette, Heinrich Brugsch, Victor Loret, Alexandre Varille, Elmar Edel and William Kelly Simpson. In the same road, at number 3, is the **Centro di Papirologia "Achille Vogliano"** (centro.papirologia@unimi.it), one of the few collections in the world of printed editions of all the various Latin and Greek papyri and *ostraca* (pottery used in the ancient world as a writing surface). Among the curiosities here are twenty writing tablets of wood and wax, a bundle of Arab paper and a very rare inscribed bone.

Within the Dipartimento di Biologia, the Sezione Botanica Sistematica (26 Via Celoria) houses an **Erbarium** (02 50314852; herbarium@unimi.it) set up in 1925. The department is also linked with the **Orto Botanico "Cascina Rosa"** (7 Via Valvassori Peroni. Booking required: 02 50320886). This large botanical garden contains some of the most classic types of ornamental plant as well as boasting three state-of-the-art greenhouses. Some of the plants are very young, but there are also huge trees that survive from the grounds of the fifteenth-century Cascina Rosa, of which only the ruins remain.

The Dipartimento di Matematica (50 Via C. Saldini) houses an interactive mathematics exhibition entitled **"Simmetria, giochi di specchi"** (bookings online: http://specchi.mat.unimi.it or tel. 02 50316110). Designed for visitors of all ages, this aims to illustrate the problems involved in the classification of plane and three-dimensional figures in relation to the type of symmetry they exemplify.

A list of other university museums and collections can be found on the website of the Università Statale di Milano: www.unimi.it/ENG/heritage/29536.htm. Online (www.tesorostatale.unimi.it) you can also pay a virtual visit to the "Tesori della Statale", a site set up as the result of a 2004 exhibition celebrating the eightieth anniversary of the founding of the Università Statale.

COLLECTION RÉMY PERRIER & CÉPÈDE

·MIMÉTISME·

1. *Cyphocrania gigas.* 2. *Phyllium bioculatum.* 3. *Carausius (Dixippus) morosus.*

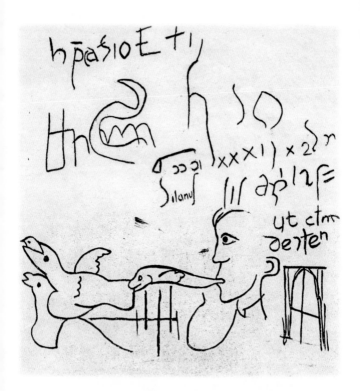

There is a legend that in the past the church had a secret underground passageway, which ran southwards to the farmhouse (now 60 Via Cavriana) and the Oratory of Sant'Ambrogio. It was known as *El passagg scappapret* (The Priests' Escape Tunnel), although no one knows what the clerics were escaping from. Nowadays, there is no trace of this underground passage – perhaps because restoration work and road maintenance has caused the ground to subside.

GRAFFITI IN SANTI FAUSTINO E GIOVITA CHURCH

㉜

90, Via Amadeo
- Opening hours: contact the sacristy (02 215856)
- Public transport: tram 5; bus 54; MM2 Lambrate

Mysterious graffiti

In the Ortica district of the city stands the small church of Santi Faustino e Giovita, a single-nave structure measuring just 20 by 8 metres. However small, the church does have a secret – a sort of historical mystery. When the old fresco of the Madonna della Grazie was removed in 1979 for restoration, a mysterious work of graffiti came to light. It looked like a treasure map; the text proved to be in Caroline script – introduced during the time of Charlemagne and here full of abbreviations – and when it was deciphered, it turned out to be a prayer. The Latin reads: *Haec praecatio est † anno MCL XXXII x2 mensis aprilis ut clementiam dei teneamus,* which translates as: "This prayer is of the 12th day of the month of April of the year 1182, in appeal for divine clemency to succour us." The prayer is signed "Silanus", the name of the monk-scribe (who, some claim, also painted the fresco).

This supplication for divine succour was on behalf of the inhabitants of the Porta Renza district, who had been exiled here by Emperor Frederick Barbarossa when he razed Milan to the ground in 1162. The graffiti also depicts the abundance of fish in the River Lambro (the eel emerging from the man's mouth) and the area's rich supplies of game (the wild ducks) and agriculture (the river in the upper left, running down from the Valassina hills to then flow through the fields of Brianza). The city gateway shown lower right is Porta Renza itself, and symbolises the hope of a speedy return to the city. In fact, after the Peace of Costanza in 1183, Barbarossa was forced to recognise Milan's independence and thus the Milanese could return to their city. This is why the Church of Santi Faustino e Giovita was also known as the "Madonna delle Grazie".

ALPHABETICAL INDEX

ALPHABETICAL INDEX

ALPHABETICAL INDEX

Acknowledgements

Maria Abbatescianni, Viviana Ambrosi, Mami Azuma, Enrico Banfi, Giorgio Bardelli, Luigi Bavagnoli, Elena Bottaro, Fiamma Bozzolo, Alice Calcaterra, Marta Campostano, Maria Teresa Candalese, Daniela Candia, Antino Carnevali, Mario Carpino, Alfredo Castelli, Elda Chierichetti, Valeria Conigliaro, Francesco Corni, Patrizia Delbiondo, Claudio Di Francesco, Matteo Dones, Grazia Facchinetti, Simona Franco, Elena Fumagalli, Mauro Gaffo, Marco Garzonio, Franca Guidali, Roberto Labanti, Pierluigi Ledda, Monica Leonardi, Anna Rita Longo, Lele Manzani, Marco Maradini, Alberto Montali, Lorenzo Montali, Valentina Murgia, Daniela Nencini, Maria Cristina Osnaghi, Erminio Pasut, Aurelio Paviato, Matelda Pellini, Margherita Pellino, Lara Perego, Luigi Petrazzoli, Elisa Polidoro, Daniele Quartieri, Giorgio Reali, Giovanni Rubin de Cervin, Claudio Salandini, Guido Salsili, Stefano Sandrelli, Riccardo Santi, Tiziano Sclavi, Cristina Sclavi, Cristian Scotti, Claudia Taddei, Ivan Toschi, Valeria Zanoni, Paolo Ziggiotti.

Photography credits:

All photos were taken by Massimo Polidoro with the exception of:
18-19: Museo Mangini Bonomi
22-23, 33, 36, 39, 48-49, 114, 151, 201, 209, 229, 264, 295, 296, 297, 298, 299 318-319: VMA
140-141: Museo astronomico di Brera
204-205: Laboratori Scala Ansaldo
282-283: Collezione Branca
304-305: MAPP – Museo d'arte Paolo Pini
308: Museo della cineteca di Milano
309: Fondazione Pirelli

Maps **Cyrille Suss** - Layout design: **Roland Deloi** - Layout: **Stéphanie Benoit** - Translation: **Jeremy Scott** – Proofreading: **Caroline Lawrence** and **Kimberly Bess**

© **JONGLEZ 2015**

Registration of copyright: May 2015 – Edition: 02

ISBN: 978-2-36195-125-2

Printed in Bulgaria by Multiprint